THE ART & CRAFT OF OLD LACE

THE ART HANDICRAFTS
ENCYCLOPAEDIA SERIES

THE ART & CRAFT
OF OLD LACE

By

FREIHERR ALFRED VON HENNEBERG

With an Introduction by

WILHELM PINDER

LONDON
B · T · BATSFORD · LTD
15, NORTH AUDLEY STREET W. 1.

FIRST PUBLISHED IN 1931

PRINTED IN GERMANY. ALL RIGHTS RESERVED
COPYRIGHT 1931 BY ERNST WASMUTH A.-G., BERLIN W8
PRINTED BY SPAMERSCHE BUCHDRUCKEREI, LEIPZIG

CONTENTS

7

INTRODUCTORY NOTE BY WILHELM PINDER

This introduction is written by one who has not the smallest right to consider himself an expert in the province dealt with in these pages. He has been encouraged by the qualities of the book itself. The author, a so-called layman, whose sphere of life was originally far removed from any such thing as art and its history, was not led from scientific study to his subject, but from his subject to scientific study; that is, indeed, the right connecting link between the two. An amateur in the best sense of the word, his distinguished association with the subject he has studied so devotedly, and his absorption in it, have enabled him to raise it to the plane of intellectual survey. The historical importance of old lace has at last been made evident. But, in the first place, it is shown as a concrete entity. What Freiherr von Henneberg calls the character of lace-ornament, texture, technique — has, after years of observation, become so real to him that the most delicate photographic processes would not suffice to portray what he has here achieved. The special distinction of this book is that in a large range of plates, hitherto unavailable, by the exact representation of the threads in different colours, the painful eyesight destroying work of these masterpieces of feminine industry has been displayed in fullsized illustrations. These illustrations show both the old processes and the results of subsequent observation and study. The theme is expounded in a sound, artistic and lively manner. Feminine work is portrayed by a masculine mind with absolute accuracy, and composition, instrumentation, rhythm and variation are clearly shown.

Creative invention, having been made manifest with a lucidity hitherto unknown, has proved itself to be a part of history. Hence, we have in the history of lace a history of formal composition coinciding with the phases of the higher forms of art, although, as a feminine product, standing somewhat apart from them; an art which is at the same time independent and yet related to history as a whole. An entire lost world of polyphonic elegance is here made accessible as an art and as the history of that art. The pleasure to be derived from such an achievement, in which nuance is proved to be the essential, is so great that even one ignorant of the subject may be justified in expressing it and in wishing the author the full measure of success his honest, thoughtful work deserves.

Munich, May 1931.

AUTHOR'S FOREWORD

The author's interest in old lace was awakened many years ago by the pieces in the possession of his family. He satisfied it at first by reading all available books, by studying collections and by endeavouring to make a small collection of samples for himself. As his mind became stored with memories of the examples seen and studied, his interest impelled him to give the many different forms a scientific order, guided by the history of art. Wölfflin's *Kunstgeschichtliche Grundbegriffe* showed that lace should be classified as either classical or baroque. When examples of lace of identical or similar styles were assembled, some of the groups were either purely classical, or purely baroque. There remained, however, a number of distinct groups not capable of classification either as classical or baroque. The essential properties of these groups and their seqence has been explained by Pinder in *Das Problem der Generation in der Kunstgeschichte Europas.* The author owes Herr Pinder a deep debt of gratitude for the insight thus afforded him and for encouraging him to formulate his ideas on lace. The arguments set forth in Strzygowski's book *Die Krisis der Geisteswissenschaften* also helped in this search for a formular. The author is especially grateful to Professor Berliner for his assistance in the examination of the exhibits in the National Museum of Bavaria and for his valuable instruction on the characteristics of different styles.

Any detailed study of lace must necessarily reveal that other domain, technique, and the author has made it his special task to examine and expound it. Quite apart from manual skill, the technique of lace-making plays an important part in the evolution of style, so that the peculiarities of any lace cannot be fully appreciated without a realisation of the finer distinctions in its production.

I have to thank Mme. Paulis of the Royal Art and Historical Museum of Brussels for her courtesy in answering fully various enquiries, thus enabling me to avail myself of her extensive knowledge. Herr Fritz Iklé of St. Gallen placed his collection at my disposal with unfailing kindness. I have to thank him, too, for my good fortune in being able to visit Frau Marie Andree-Eysn at Berchtesgaden shortly before her eightieth birthday and draw on the rich store of her experience. I must also thank M. L. Metman, of the Museum of Decorative Art at the Louvre, Paris, for his ever-ready assistance. Finally, I should like to mention here Dr. Graf Karlfried v. Dürckheim, lecturer in Philosophy at the University of Leipzig; my numerous interviews with him have assisted me greatly in the theoretical presentation of my data.

Steingaden, Upper Bavaria, May 1931.

FREIHERR ALFRED VON HENNEBERG.

AIM AND METHOD

This work has for its object the identification of the technical and artistic qualities of old lace by detailed dissection, the grouping of the types according to their characteristics, and the defining of periods. An endeavour has also been made to associate the chronological sequence of the different style groups with similar productions in the pictorial arts.

It opens with a few notes on the general history of lace and on the essential characteristics of each kind, a knowledge of which is indispensable to investigation.

The second section is devoted to a study of the different laces. From an analysis of individual pieces emerge certain features which on comparison lead to an arrangement based on style.

Generally it is impossible to make a detailed examination of lace in public collections, owing to the manner in which it is preserved. Illustrations in books on lace do not lend themselves to any scrutiny of detail; the reproductions are usually reduced, and the scale of measurement is rarely given. The direction of the threads cannot be followed in a reproduction. For this reason, researches into technique were limited to private collections, from which we have been able to illustrate specimens of nearly all the technical methods of old lace. Microphotography has not been employed, because the smallness of the picture makes it impossible to show more than the outline of a single bar. But the course of the threads is very important; for in the meshes and nets of bobbin lace it takes a characteristic pattern, which, where all the threads are alike in colour, it is impossible to follow without some indication. To this end, and in order to make the "hidden pattern" in all its complexity available, coloured drawings have been shown. A note on each drawing indicates the lace from which the example has been taken; the lace itself is shown in actual size. Once the technical pattern has been impressed on the eye by the enlarged illustration, it is as a rule easy to recognise in the lace itself.

In the last section an endeavour has been made to supplement the history of lace making, and to acquire an understanding of its relation to other activities.

The reproductions of lace analyses in detail illustrate the entire range of study in the three sections, namely, a general survey, an analytical comparison, and a summary of the history and development of lace-making. As, for technical reasons, it is desirable to avoid the insertion of text in the plates, the details of the analyses have been indicated in the index to the illustrations. These examples of lace have been distinguished by a special number, so that they may be referred to separately and not only by the Plate number.

GENERAL HISTORY OF LACE

By "lace" we understand a decorative material, intended for ornament, composed of fine threads (metal, silk, flax, cotton etc.), constructed by means of needles, bobbins, a crochet-hook or machinery when no separate fabric or net is used for the ground work. Materials produced by knotting, such as macramé, cannot be classified as "lace", any more than those produced by needlework on net (filet) or other fabric; such work belongs to the sphere of embroidery.

"Real lace" is one produced by hand either with a needle or with bobbins.

The term "old lace" is used by me to describe any real lace produced under the artistic, and social conditions prevailing up to the French Revolution. The latest record of old lace is doubtless that made at Valenciennes in 1840 for the Duchess of Nemours by Mlle. Glairo, then 66 years of age, with the assistance of a few surviving lace-makers, most of whom were octogenarians (1). "Old lace" was nearly always made of linen thread, and very occasionally of silk.

At an early period of human development, plant fibres were used in the making of objects of utility and ornament. When it was found that fibres could be twisted to form threads, these threads were used in the making of nets and woven fabrics. In weaving, a number of threads, known as the warp, are fastened side by side in parallel lines; a single thread, called the woof, is then run in and out of the threads of the warp and at the end of the line the woof is run back through the warp in the same manner, until the fabric is complete. Whilst the borders parallel to the warp (selvedge) are automatically fastened off, the edges from which the threads of the warp hang down must be secured to prevent the fabric from unravelling. The earliest examples of weaving known were discovered in Egyptian tombs. These display an extraordinarily high degree of technical skill; here the edges were secured by oversewing with special threads, or by knotting the ends of the warp threads, and in either case extremely artistic and complicated methods were frequently employed (2). No records are extant which would lead us to suppose that this sewing and oversewing, which was extended to the reverse side of the fabric, and this knotting of loose threads, ever assumed in antiquity the form described above under the designation of "lace".

The high degree of skill of the ancient Egyptians in fine linen fabrics was lost in later centuries, although a love of fine materials and a tradition of their production was still maintained in the East.

The examples still in existence clearly show that, as the need arose in the East also for lighter materials ornamented by hand, the edges of linen fabrics were not only fastened off with the needle, but that hemstitching was added. This border became wider and more complicated; finally single threads were drawn out and cut away, and the remaining network of the original material was adorned with ornamental needlework.

---

(1) Malotet p. 60.   (2) Braulick: "Altägyptische Gewebe."

15

This was the origin of the forerunners of lace, drawnwork or cutwork, *Punto tirato*, *Punto tagliato* (Pl. 1 and 2, fig. 4) and the reticellas, *Punto a reticello* (Pl. 2, fig. 5).

Whilst in openwork single threads only were drawn out or cut away, in reticella the threads were withdrawn to a greater extent. The few remaining threads were connected by a pattern worked with the needle. *Punto a reticello* is, therefore, a more delicate form of openwork.

Finally, the woven material was done away with altogether. Leading lines were fixed on a firm foundation; these threads were strengthened by oversewing, and the spaces between them were filled in and adorned with a variety of stitches, according to the ornament desired. This was known as *Punto in aria*.

With this method, the art of lace-making had really come into being.

In openwork the ornament was confined, by the right-angles of its latticed background, to straight lines. In reticella there was greater freedom and it was possible to form circles and semi-circles. In *Punto in aria*, where the work was no longer restricted by any fabric, the transition to flowing lines and tendrils naturally followed.

In Italy any real lace, that is to say any lace worked with the needle without a background of fabric, was termed *punto in aria*. But "*punto in aria*" has also come to denote the earliest type of needle point lace in its most simple technical form.

This "real *Punto in aria*," for which we have no other name, began by adopting the geometrical figures of reticella, but gradually evolved the narrow tendril design (Pl. 3—6).

In the 17th Century these tendrils became wider, and large flower designs in high relief were introduced. This was the *Punto tagliato a fogliamo*, or *Point gros de Venise* (Pl. 8, fig. 17). It was followed by Rosaline, or Rosellino lace, in which the tendrils and flowers were much reduced in size (Pl. 8, fig. 18), and by the lace recognised by the Italians as the genuine *Punto di Venezia*, the *Point plat de Venise* (Pl. 9).

In order to divert into France a proportion of the large sums of money which were flowing into Italy for her lace, and to promote the lace industry in France, Colbert founded, in 1665, a company having the sole rights for the production of lace for a space of ten years. Factories were opened in various places, the most important of which was at Alençon, and expert lace-makers were brought from Venice and Flanders to give instruction in their art. The French were content, at first, to make copies of Venetian lace. It was decreed that the imitations should be known as *Points de France*, and only an expert eye could distinguish between them and their models. In 1682 Colbert wrote to the manager at Alençon ". . . the chief defect is that none of the *points de France* are as firm or as white as the Venetian ones" (1).

After a time French needlelace changed in character. The makers sought to rival the bobbin lace of Flanders in delicacy and fineness. It reached its highest point of achievement in Alençon point and its varieties. Venice, by this time, had forfeited her supremacy and was herself imitating French lace.

The trimmings made of metal or silk and produced with the use of bobbins (Pl. 10, fig. 23), may be regarded as the forerunners of linen bobbin lace. These trimmings were in use long

---

(1) Ricci: "Trine ad ago", p. 27.

16

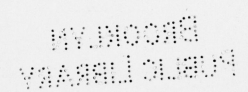

before lace was made. The origin of the technique of the bobbin is lost in obscurity but the method of interweaving threads is undoubtedly very old. Bobbin lace appears simultaneously with needle lace, and Italy was probably its land of origin also. Although Flanders lays claim to the distinction of having invented bobbin lace, the "*Neue Modellbuch,*" issued in 1561 and 1562 by Christoff Froschower of Zürich, supports Italy. In the introduction, translated by Dreger into High German, mention is made of "the art of bobbin lace, which was introduced into our country 25 years ago and is now much in use. It was brought by merchants for the first time from Venice and Italy in the year 1536."

In its earliest stages bobbin lace followed closely the patterns of needle lace, in its narrow lines, small points and geometrical figures (Pl. 11, fig. 24, 25), and later in its reticella motives (Pl. 11, fig. 26). When needle lace ornament resorted to a freer design, bobbin lace followed suit and continued to take needlework as its model until it attained its highest degree of development in Venice.

Venice took the lead in needle lace as far as Italy was concerned; no special characteristics were initiated in any other part of the country. The various classes of Italian needle lace, therefore, came to be known by their methods of production. The case of bobbin lace, however, was different. Milan and Genoa became the centres of this industry and the names of those towns were applied to the varieties of bobbin lace produced there.

Milanese bobbin lace (Pl. 26, 27) is distinguished by a narrow bobbin-made tape from which springs the ornamental design. The edging to the tape consists of a kind of hemstitch which is connected to the edging of the opposite strip by bars in the early examples, and later by network (1). The Genoese and other Italian laces of this period do not have this tape and the outline is formed by plaiting and interweaving.

Meanwhile, the technique of bobbin lace was reaching its highest degree of development in Flanders, and whilst France was taking the lead in needle lace, Flanders became the centre of production for the finest bobbin-made laces.

The old bobbin laces of Flanders with their large branching patterns (Pl. 140) were still under the influence of the *Points gros de Venise*, but later they assumed a more independent style. This development resulted in an elaborate technique which was employed in the making of three main types of lace:

Valenciennes, including Binche;

Mechlin (Malines) lace;

Brussels bobbin lace.

The old Flemish laces were made by two different processes. They were either worked in one piece with continuous threads (Pl. 25, fig. 46), or they were made of separately worked pieces put together (Pl. 140). These separate pieces were also made with bobbins. The early Flanders bobbin lace had no network ground and the patterns were joined by bars. The groundwork used in the later examples was joined to the edge of the pattern and consisted of the round Flemish mesh (Pl. 12, fig. 27).

(1) Ricci: "Trine a fuselli."

17

Valenciennes, Binche and Mechlin laces are all made in one piece; Brussels bobbin lace is made up of separate parts.

Valenciennes lace (Pl. 45, fig. 94, 95) is distinguished in particular by the close linen-stitch *(toilé)* in the pattern, which resembles a linen fabric. The threads of the *toilé* are parallel and perpendicular to the border of the lace. The edge of the pattern is separated from the background by a species of very narrow hemstitch. The patterns are on a network ground composed, in early Valenciennes lace, of various meshes, but in the later examples of the so-called round Valenciennes mesh. In the round Valenciennes mesh the threads are manipulated in the same way as in the round Flemish mesh; in the case of the Valenciennes mesh, however, the threads are drawn together so that the ground is closer than in the Flemish variety (Pl. 12, fig. 28).

Binche lace (Pl. 30, 31, 33) is closely related to Valenciennes. The linen-stitch is lighter and shades off less abruptly into the groundwork; the patterns are more blurred. The groundwork is usually powdered with a small star-shaped pattern known as *point de neige*.

The linen-stitch of Mechlin lace (Malines, Pl. 40, fig. 82) has the same texture as that of Valenciennes. The threads are parallel and perpendicular to the border. The patterns are edged with a coarser thread *(cordonnet, bourdon)*. The network ground is of various meshes in the early examples; in later specimens the net is that known as the *Eisgrond*, and is characteristic of Mechlin laces (Pl. 13, fig. 29).

In Brussels bobbin laces (Pl. 32) (1) the patterns may be executed by two different methods, either by linen-stitch *(toilé)*—in this case the threads are not parallel and perpendicular to the border, but follow the outline of the pattern—or by network *(gimp, grillé)*. In the network a number of warp threads follow the course of the bobbin from the left above to the right below, and a further number from the right above to the left below, the weft threads remaining horizontal (Pl. 49, fig. 103).

An effect of light and shade is achieved by the juxtaposition of the close texture of the linen-stitch and the open texture of the network.

The edge of the pattern is even more emphasised in Brussels than in Mechlin lace. The pattern is not outlined by a coarser thread, but by a narrow raised plaited line, known as raised work. After the lace has been completed, or after washing, it is restored by using a sharp bone or ivory stick to flatten the *toilé* and *grillé* and thus cause the raised work to stand out. Ignorant people are apt to smooth out Brussels and other bobbin laces, so that the raised work loses its effect.

In the early examples of Brussels bobbin lace the edges of the pattern are joined by bars. Later, a groundwork of net was worked round the pattern; this groundwork was occasionally in *point de neige*, but more often composed of the Brussels mesh, known by the Flemish name of "droschel" (Pl. 13, fig. 30).

In the latter half of the 18th century creative power in the art of lace-making died out. Technical skill survived for another generation, so long, that is to say, as those who were born about 1789, before the outbreak of the Great Revolution, were able to carry on a tradition inherited from their parents.

---

(1) "Brabançon" bobbin lace (Pl. 37) has the same technical characteristics as Brussels lace, but the patterns are not in such high relief.

DESCRIPTIVE SURVEY OF OLD LACE

Modern research in art and aesthetics has afforded us valuable help towards a descriptive analysis of lace; for the methods necessary to a comprehension of other materials have proved fruitful in lace also.

FUNDAMENTAL CONCEPTIONS ESSENTIAL TO THE DESCRIPTION OF LACE

The special character of any lace is determined by its three inherent properties, namely:—

Ornament;

Texture;

Technique.

By the texture of lace I wish here to imply the character of its structure as a whole.

When a portion of the structure stands out from the whole by reason of its formal design, this whole becomes divided into design and groundwork. The degree of this division lies between two widely opposed conditions.

On the one hand, the form or ornament stands out sharply with clearly defined contours; on the other, where the structure is diffused and merged in the whole, the form does not stand out from the groundwork and the contours are blurred (1).

Apart from the degree of division between the form and the background, the texture as a whole may be loose or compact in structure. A loose structure renders the texture pliant, transparent, delicate and light, a compact structure makes it dense and opaque.

Technique is concerned, in the first place, with the acquiring of the raw material (such as the flax fibres in old lace) and the production of fine threads by twisting these fibres together; then comes the manipulation of the needle or bobbin, and the use of the thread in making the fundamental elements of lace. In needle lace the fundamental elements consist of the various forms of buttonhole stitch, in bobbin lace of interweaving, plaiting and network.

Thus in technique we differentiate and combine the conceptions: the purely manual work of producing the material and the deliberate act of utilising this material, an act which is sometimes inspired by a definite mental attitude, finding expression as much in the individual method in carrying out the design as in the completed work itself.

The same thing applies to the conception of the technique of painting. This includes the production of the colours, in which in the course of time, important changes have been introduced, and the application of the colours to the surface to be painted. This application of the colours may also be manual work, but in its highest form it is a mental process behind which is the personality of the artist. The brushwork of the great masters is something peculiar to them, distinguishing one from the other and affording an important comparison between their personal methods and other contemporary painting.

(1) Sander: "Experimentelle Ergebnisse der Gestaltpsychologie," pp. 26, 27, 28.

The examination of technique cannot open the way to historical research unless both the material and the intellectual sides, and especially the latter, are taken into account, and until that technique is regarded not only as a craft but as an art. It is from this standpoint that we intend to study the technique of old lace.

As the execution of any technique depends on the nature of the material, we have laid particular stress on the nature of the threads and their production.

The consideration and description of ornament has its natural place in the main stages of development in the general history of lace. Definite evidence of the origin of certain forms at certain times and of their chronological sequence is to be found in pictures and examples of lace of which the date of origin is known.

The proof of chronological sequence in the development of texture is given by the simultaneous appearance in the same lace of certain peculiarities of structure and ornamental forms.

The chronological sequence of technique is shown by the coincidence of its different forms with the various forms of ornament and texture.

THE ESSENTIAL CHARACTERISTICS OF LACE

ORNAMENT

Forerunners of lace make their appearence as early as the 15th Century, in the form of small points or rounded scallops which follow and break up the edges of embroideries or cutwork. These borders are in simple designs of lines and half-circles carried out with the needle or with bobbins.

The first real lace came into use during the progressive 16th Century. Its designs were derived from the cutwork which had a right-angled network as its foundation, and therefore consisted in squares, right-angles, half circles, circles, geometrical figures and patterns reminiscent of a spider's web. The lace was usually made in one strip with applied scallops. Vertical and horizontal lines were emphasised throughout. The completed form was composed of independent parts of equal value placed side by side (Pl. 2, fig. 5; Pl. 11).

Later in the 16th Century, branchlike sprays and conventional flowers appeared beside the geometrical figures; a liking was also shown for representations of men and animals. The movement of the branches is never continuous, but constantly interrupted by a pause or suspension; the ornament is then repeated in reverse. On either side of the pause the design is shown symmetrically as in a mirror. In such patterns the upright and horizontal lines are still emphasised and the independence of the separate figures preserved, so that each one asserts itself within the borders of the whole (Pl. 4, 5, 6; 15, fig. 34).

The example fig. 34 from Vecellio's Book of Patterns (1) corresponds to a specimen of Brussels bobbin lace presented to the Archduke Albert and the Archduchess Isabella on the occasion of their entry into Brussels as Duke and Duchess of Brabant (Pl. 90).

(1) "Corona delle nobili et virtuose donne." Venice, Cesare Vecellio 1591.

20

Among the hundred or more patterns in Vecellio's "Corona" there is not a single example of a continuous, uninterrupted branch design.

Until the dawn of the 17th Century, needle lace and bobbin lace, both in the South and the North, progressed along the same lines. Needle lace took the lead and the patterns of bobbin lace followed suit.

From that time, however, there was development in various directions.

In Italy needle lace kept the lead and developed the branching patterns. Up to the middle of the 17th Century, when Italian lace attained its zenith, there are two separate and consecutive groups of lace to be distinguished in the development of design.

In the first group we find narrow, almost tentative branches, sometimes accompanied by figures of men and animals and by increasingly definite flower forms. The size of these accompanying forms is not always proportionate. The figures of men and animals have no fixed position and it is not uncommon to find them end to end. Symmetrical design and emphasis on the perpendicular gradually disappear and are replaced by the continuous branch design. According to Italian classification this is the "genuine *Punto in aria*" (1) (*Punto in aria propriamente detto*) (Pl. 3—6).

In the later groups, the *Point gros de Venise, Punto tagliato a fogliami* (Pl. 8, fig. 17), symmetrical pattern and stressing of the perpendicular are entirely abandoned. Wide, heavy branches with large flowers and leaves are spread in continous, flowing lines across the surface of the lace.

The later Rosaline lace (Pl. 8, fig. 18) and the *Point plat de Venise*, the "genuine *Punto di Venezia*" (*Punto di Venezia propriamente detto* (2)) (Pl. 9), has narrower tendrils which, at first, had the same continuous movement as the *Point gros de Venise*, but subsequently reverted to the recurring symmetrical pattern.

Bobbin lace assumed its own special characteristics in the Netherlands early in the 17th Century.

Reticella forms were used at first (Pl. 16, fig. 35), but before long the transition was made to plant motives. These motives did not consist, as in Italy, of branches or tendrils, but of symmetrical groups of leaves or blossoms, merely indicated at first (Pl. 17, fig. 36), but subsequently fully developed (Pl. 19, fig. 38).

This early development, the so-called "old Flanders bobbin lace" will henceforward be distinguished here by the designation "Rembrandt lace"; it is depicted in a number of that painter's works.

It must be specially noted that the designation "Rembrandt lace"—and Van Dyck and Velasquez lace for the two types that follow—is merely used as a distinguishing label. By the use of these names it is possible to refer in a single word to any one of the varieties of lace included in these three clearly defined types.

In the next stage of development, the groups of leaves are expanded into raised scallops with large leaf-like ornaments, whilst the symmetry of the pattern is still maintained (Pl. 20, Pl. 39). This type may be designated "Van Dyck lace", a name which is also to be found elsewhere.

In a third type the scallops are gradually rounded off until they disappear altogether. The pattern is closer, but the symmetrical arrangement still persists (Pl. 21, 22, 23).

---

(1) Ricci: "Trine ad ago," p. 21.   (2) Ricci: "Trine ad ago," p. 25.

The development shown in these last illustrations reaches its climax in the laces depicted by Velasquez in the portrait of Queen Maria Anna and in the numerous portraits of the Infanta Margareta. This type may therefore be distinguished by the name of "Velasquez lace."

In France and Belgium these three groups of lace are described by the collective designation of "Louis XIII."

In the closing period of these three stages of development both the needle lace of the South and the bobbin lace of the North reached their highest degree of technical execution.

On June 7th, 1660 the Kings of Spain and France met on the Ile des Faisans on the Bidassoa River. In Philip IV's suite was his daughter by his first marriage, the Infanta Maria Theresia, the future wife of Louis XIV. In Jeaurat's Cartoon at Versailles (Pl. 24, fig. 43), the solemn reception is depicted. Louis XIV is wearing the broad-branched Venetian needlelace (1). The Infanta is wearing the same robe and lace as that depicted by Velasquez in his portraits of Queen Maria Anna and the Infanta Margareta.

It appears that Mazarin (2) had already thought of promoting the lace industry in his own country by imitating the Venetian laces. He died in 1661. What he had imagined Colbert successfully accomplished. French lace reigned supreme, and the Flemish bobbin lace makers could not but be affected by an influence so near to them. At first France copied the Venetian models, with its wide branches and its contours in sharp relief. Flanders followed her example and produced the fourth type of "old Flemish bobbin lace" with its patterns of wide, continuous branches (Pl. 25, fig. 46; Pl. 90). The bobbin laces of Genoa and Milan had also developed on similar lines (Pl. 26, 133).

In describing and illustrating the laces produced during the first two-thirds of the 17th Century, it would be possible to summarize the different types by naming them after the artists in whose portraits the laces are recognisably portrayed. Lace now becomes more delicate. The ornament is usually worked on a net ground from which it stands out but little in relief. This style does not lend itself to precise pictorial reproduction, so that dates can no longer be ascertained by means of contemporary portraits.

Let us now make a survey of the subsequent development of ornament, bearing in mind the essential differences in form which have already been established—on the one hand, emphasis on the perpendicular and symmetry, on the other, in the place of symmetry, movement. It is then shown that three periods of symmetry and emphasised perpendicular alternate with three periods of movement.

Of these six periods, the first three fall in the reign of Louis XIV. We may call these three periods "Early Louis XIV," "Mid-Louis XIV" and "Late Louis XIV."

In Early Louis XIV we find the flowing tendrils in continuous movement. An innovation is made by the gradual introduction of a network ground, while the threads become increasingly fine. The early Valenciennes laces are particularly representative of this period (Pl. 28; Pl. 29, fig. 54).

---

(1) In her work, Mrs. Palliser gives a detailed illustration of the King's "canons" or kneelace, presumably taken from Jeaurat's cartoon.

(2) Palliser, 4th ed., pp. 151, 152.

Towards the end of the 17th Century a reaction has set in. The principle of uninterrupted movement has vanished. Central axes again appear on either side of which the ornament is repeated as in a mirror. The perpendicular is again accentuated. A symmetrical ornament with narrow tendrils assumes the characteristic *candelière* style. Round the motives, placed perpendicularly one above the other, sprays of flowers are grouped symmetrically and fill in the entire background (Pl. 29, fig. 55; Pl. 30). This is the Mid-Louis XIV period.

In Late Louis XIV, the tendency to movement again appears in lace ornament. Besides the continuous branching patterns there is a suggestion of the *candelière* style but instead of the more delicate patterns with their symmetrical arrangement of the earlier period, there are heavier and larger motives (Pl. 33, fig. 66; Pl. 34).

The next period is named the *Régence*. Here palm-leaf motives and flower patterns are opposed to each other in an attempt at symmetrical arrangement. Pointed or lozenge-shaped devices are freely used as central axes or fillings. Fan shapes and trellis work are frequently introduced. The flowers are represented more realistically (Pl. 35, 36, 37).

In the next period, Louis XV (Rococo), two tendencies are at work concurrently. The one has returned to the large branching patterns, and at the same time designs are produced in which the central line is stressed. Side by side with compact and closely designed work there appears a freer more loosely designed construction. Unsymmetrical motives have become the favourite ornaments, such as shell-like forms, animals, a variety of vessels, musical instruments, trophies and suchlike. The form of the pattern as a whole is frequently unsymmetrical (Pl. 38 to 46). The two examples of 1751 and 1759 (Pl. 175, 177) herald the approaching development. Individual sections have been detached from the ornament as a whole.

In the next period, Louis XVI, this breaking up of the pattern goes a stage further. Straggling tendrils are grouped round a central axis. Symmetry and the perpendicular predominate (Pl. 179).

Finally, even these meagre tendrils fade away, and small, separate motives are scattered at regular intervals over the groundwork. Ornament has disappeared and lace has become a spotted net.

This marks the end of the development of ornament in old lace. The new laces of the 19th Century initiated their development by the use of classical motives.

TEXTURE

In enumerating the fundamental conceptions essential to the analysis of lace, it was pointed out that the design stands out from the structure as a whole in varying degrees. On the one hand there is a distinct and sharply defined separation of the ornament from the background, and on the other a blurring of the contours and a merging of the ornament into the background.

We have considered the ornament itself and determined the different periods of its development. The survey that follows will show the relation of ornament to groundwork in these periods.

From the time when lace was first made until the close of the 16th and the beginning of the 17th Centuries, the ornament stands out from the background and is designed purely from a draughtsman's standpoint. The contours are sharply emphasised (Pl. 2, 3, 4, 5).

In the 17th Century, as we have seen, ornament developed differently in the South and the North. In the case of Italian needle lace the development led to continuous, uninterrupted branch designs, and the abandonment of symmetry and the perpendicular, in the northern bobbin lace it led to symmetrical design, sprays complete in themselves and the stressing of the perpendicular.

In texture also the development in the South and in the North was on opposing lines.

The Italian needle laces adhered to the rigid separation of design and background. Towards the close of their development the contours were emphasised even more sharply by the use of plastically raised patterns (Pl. 3—7; Pl. 8, fig. 17).

In the Flemish bobbin laces the ornamental patterns are gradually brought closer to one another until the background disappears entirely. Finally, lines and contours lose their significance and plastic lucidity is replaced by blurred outlines as in a painting. The whole design achieves its effect not by means of lines but by the use of light and shade. Thus arose, in due course, the Rembrandt, Van Dyck and Velasquez laces (Pl. 18—23).

In Early Louis XIV the ornaments in needle and bobbin laces were based on the same principle of movement, of continuous branch design. As regards texture, an attempt was clearly made in this period to break up the lines. The groundwork was absorbed by the design and the contours were blurred. An effect was sought not by means of lines and contours, as in drawing, but by lighter and darker shading, as in painting. The early stages of this development are to be found in the latest of the genuine Venetian laces, the *Points plat de Venise* and the Rosaline (Pl. 8, fig. 18; Pl. 9). Hitherto the bars had served to support and link up the whole, now they were adorned with small scallops and points and the groundwork began to be absorbed in the design. In this more elaborate form they had the effect of a kind of veil, making the contours seem less sharp. A further step on the same road was the introduction of a network ground. In the portrait of a woman by Jan Verspronck, dated 1653 (Pl. 21), this network is already to be seen and it reached its full development during this period. Ornamental nets were already highly developed in the Italian needle laces, and here, by their contrast to the raised work, they served to heighten the plastic effect. They now reached their fullest development in bobbin laces also, but, in this case, by means of various degrees of shading, they served to make the lines blurred and to break up the contours (Pl. 28, 29).

In the Mid-Louis XIV period the perpendicular line, symmetry, repose and equilibrium again predominate. The texture aims at separating the design from the background and making the contours prominent. Where a network ground is used the closely constructed ornament stands out from a more open network (Pl. 30).

Lace 2061 (Pl. 29, fig. 55) shows a transitional stage. The ornament is developed symmetrically after the candelabra design, but it is so interwoven with the background that it is hardly recognisable, and the effect produced is of a gleaming surface with, here and there, a lighter portion.

24

The ornament in the late Louis XIV period tends chiefly to movement. Here also, when a central arrangement and a symmetrical plan has been used, the texture makes no attempt to distinguish design from background. The large, symmetrical motives are placed so close together that the effect is achieved less by the prominence of lines and contours than by variations of light and shade (Pl. 32, 33, 34).

In the *Régence* period, when ornament again shows a tendency to symmetry, the texture aims chiefly at a fusion of the design and the ground (Pl. 37). But there are some examples in which the ornament stands out more clearly from the background (Pl. 38, fig. 75).

Just as the tendency in design, in the Louis XV (Rococo) period, fluctuates between the two opposites of symmetry and movement, so in the texture we find sometimes a sharp distinction between the pattern and the ground and a stressing of the contours, and sometimes a merging of the pattern and the ground, resulting in the blurred outlines of a painting (Pl. 39 to 46).

In the Louis XVI period emphasis of the perpendicular and symmetrical design go hand in hand with the sharply defined division between design and background. The network ground which is invariably employed becomes more and more delicate and permits what ornament remains to stand out in strong relief (Pl. 179, 180).

TECHNIQUE

a) MATERIAL

The Production of the Thread. The raw material of lace is linen fibre, the fibre of flax. Flax is a field plant, the stems of which grow to an approximate length of one yard. Each stem is composed of numerous, very fine, organic fibres, closely knitted together and enclosed within the cortex. The treatment of the flax stems for the purpose of obtaining the textile fabric aims at separating the fibres. The more thoroughly this separation is achieved, the finer will be the artificial linen fibres produced. The artificial fibres, however, always consist of a number of organic fibres.

Until about the middle of the 18th Century the spinning of the artificial fibres into threads was always carried out by hand. The material to be spun, the confused mass of fibres obtained after the process of separation, was wound loosely round the distaff. The fibres were drawn out of this distaff and twisted together. The first thread produced in this manner was fastened to the spindle, a small stick about 30 cm. long. Near the end of the spindle there was a wheel measuring about 3—4 cm. across, the whorl, which enabled the spindle to be kept revolving continuously. As the loosely hanging spindle was turned, the circular motion was communicated to the threads, and when the latter had attained a certain length they were wound round the spindle.

From the time of the ancient Egyptians until the middle of the 16th Century threads were produced solely by these methods. In 1530 Johann Jürgen of Watenbüttel, near Brunswick, invented the spinning-wheel. Before that time the spindle, hanging by its thread, had been

25

turned by hand. Now it was connected to a wheel which could be worked with the foot. In 1738 the first spinning machine was invented in England by Lewis Paul. This machine enabled all the processes hitherto carried out by hand, from the disentangling, preparation and arrangement of the fibres to the spinning and winding of the threads, to be done mechanically. The first spinning machine was worked in England in 1741.

The Fineness of the Thread. The degree of fineness of linen thread is expressed by a figure, or count, denoting the relation of its length to its weight. Local measures have been used occasionally as units of length and weight, but now-a-days the numbers or counts determined by English units of measurement are universally employed.

The count indicates the number of threads, each 300 yards long, required to make up an English pound in weight. The higher the figure of the count, that is the greater number of threads 300 yards long that go to the pound, the finer will be the thread (1). A continuous linen yarn of count 200 weighing one pound, is therefore 200 × 300 = 60.000 yards long. In count 100 the thread is only 30.000 yards long and, as the thread weighs the same, it must be twice as thick as the former count.

These units of thickness only apply to single-spun linen yarns. Different counts, giving a different relation of length to weight, are used for other raw materials such as cotton and wool. The numbers applied to commercial lace and sewing threads have nothing to do with the English counts; the latter refer only to the single-spun thread, the primary yarn.

At the present time, nothing but twists are employed in lace making and sewing, that is, threads formed of two or more primary yarns twisted together.

Until a few years ago linen yarn of counts 300 to 400 were still produced by machinery, but it is apparently impossible now to obtain commercially threads of a higher count than 240.

It is scarcely possible now-a-days to produce by hand counts of 60—70.

The degree of tenuity of the threads employed in the making of the old laces can be fairly accurately calculated if the width of the thread is ascertained and compared with the width of the threads of which the number is known. On Pl. 76A four primary, machine-made yarns are shown one below the other; the numbers of these threads are stated by the respective makers to be 60, 100, 210, 300. To these is added an old hand-made thread the number of which is to be calculated. The measured widths of the respective threads are 190, 135, 105, 90, 45 μ (2).

If I take count 300 with a width of 90 μ as the basis of comparison the widths of the numbers

	60	100	210
work out at	201,2	156	107,4 μ
According to measurement the widths were	190	135	105 μ

the theoretical and actual measurements are practically identical. The old handmade thread works out at a count of 1200.

On page 76a the method of calculation is shown in greater detail.

---

(1) 1 yard measures 91.439 cm.; 1 lb. weighs 453.6 g.
(2) 1 μ = 1/1000th mm.

26

Owing to the variations in density, threads of the same volume may have different weights, but the calculations given above show that, with their help, an approximate estimate can be arrived at.

If 111 threads of count 300 machine-made yarn are placed side by side close together they occupy a space of one centimetre (nearly $^2/_5$ or $\cdot$ 4 of an inch); it takes 222 threads of the old hand-made threads to occupy the same space. Threads even finer still are to be found in the old laces; and up to the present machinery has produced nothing so fine.

August Braulik (1) examined over 300 specimens of woven fabrics in Theodor Graf's collection at Vienna, which had been found in ancient Egyptian tombs. This examination showed that in ancient Egypt the cultivation and use of flax and the art of spinning and weaving was on a very high plane for over 2000 years, until about 1000 B.C. A woven fabric taken from the mummy of the High Priest Masahirta of the 21st Dynasty about 1000 B.C., had 130 warp threads in the space of one centimetre. Examples from the 22nd to the 26th Dynasties and from the Graeco-Roman period in Egypt have quite coarse threads, and it is rare to find a count as high as 70.

Special research would be required to establish whether periods occurred between the later years of antiquity and the 17th Century in which skill in the working of flax reverted to the high level attained by the ancient Egyptians.

The laces of the 16th and early 17th Centuries are not remarkable for the special fineness of their threads, which are, for the most part, of counts lower than 100. The finer threads did not appear until the first half of the 17th Century had gone by, and then they developed almost abruptly. The old Flemish bobbin laces of the fourth type (Pl. 140) still have comparatively coarse threads. The bobbin laces of the Early Louis XIV period, practically contemporaneous, have threads far finer than count 300. It was as though the most intensive culture of flax and the production of thread of the most extreme fineness had been discovered all over again, and the art remained on the same high plane until the beginning of the 19th Century. Dr. Alois Herzog states that, according to Karmarsch-Hartig, half a kilogram of a linen weave was sold in Paris in 1825 for 1530 franks (2). It had the metric number 1319 (equivalent to a linen count of 2198 and a width of $35\,\mu$).

b) NEEDLE AND BOBBIN

The technique of the needle in the production of lace is fundamentally different to that of the bobbin.

With the needle a single thread is taken from stitch to stitch, from one point to another. In bobbinwork a number of threads, each one crossing over and under another, pursue an unbroken course through the lace.

Needle lace is an expression of the principle of repose, of limitation and finiteness; every stitch is a pause, a sustained note. In bobbinwork movement is predominant; theoretically, the number of threads is infinite and the movement perpetual.

(1) A. Braulik: "Altägyptische Gewebe." Stuttgart 1900.

(2) In 1884 a thread fetching 3000 fr. a pound had become a rarity, the most that was paid for a pound of the finest thread being 2400 fr. Malotet, p. 58.

c) THE TECHNIQUE OF NEEDLE LACE

There is only one essential element in needle lace, the button-hole stitch. In the 16th Century laces, where it serves to strengthen the outline of the ornament, we find it in its simplest form.

Later the stitch was varied, and, by a combination of its different forms, web-like grounds and the complicated, ornamental network used in the Venetian laces, were fashioned (Pl. 7, 8, 9).

A net-work ground was introduced in needle lace at the close of the 17th and the beginning of the 18th Century, at a later date, therefore, than in bobbin lace. This network consists of loosely joined button-hole stitches. Fig. 98 of Pl. 47 shows it in its original form.

The meshes of the simple needle-worked ground were also strengthened by having a thread wound round them or by being closely oversewn with button-hole stitch.

The 18th Century brought with it no important addition to the technique of needle lace.

d) THE TECHNIQUE OF BOBBIN LACE

Twisting and Crossing. In bobbin work the threads are wound round small staves or bobbins; the free ends of the threads are then fastened side by side to the pillow. The worker selects four bobbins, takes a pair in each hand and carries out two movements: twisting and crossing. In twisting the right hand thread of each pair of bobbins is laid over the left; in crossing the left of the two central threads is laid over the right (Pl. 47, fig. 99). The single twist and cross is called a half-stitch. The stitch is completed by carrying out the twisting and crossing movements twice. Repeated twisting and crossing produces plaiting. In all *passements* and bobbin laces the inner threads of the plait of four threads are always crossed and the outer threads are twisted, that is to say, in the inner threads the upper one runs from left to right and in the outer threads the upper one runs from right to left.

Bobbinwork consists solely of these two movements. When the number of stitches required by the pattern have been made, two other pairs of bobbins are picked up, and so on. The foundations of bobbin lace—the stitches, plaits, woven grounds and meshes—depend on a correct selection of the bobbins.

Simple bars. Until the end of the 16th Century bobbin laces consisted almost exclusively of simple stitches and four-threaded plaits. Then patterns were introduced, in the form of square or curved woven designs (Pl. 47, fig. 100).

In the first half of the 17th Century the technique of the linen-stitch was further developed. Threads interlaced at right angles formed a close fabric. The details of the pattern composed of this closely woven fabric were connected by twisted threads, bars or ornamental ties (Pl. 24, fig. 43; Pl. 114).

About the middle of the 17th Century bobbin lace adopted the branching designs of the Venetian laces (Pl. 25, fig. 46; Pl. 133). Sometimes, owing to the backward swing of the tendrils, it is necessary to join the part of the branch that is turned backwards to a completed portion of the lace. For this purpose the *Point de raccroc* (Pl. 48, fig. 101) is used. At the point where the portion A, in course of production, has to be joined to the completed portion B the nearest thread of a pair of bobbins *a* is drawn with a crochet hook sufficiently far through a loop of the completed work to enable the bobbin of thread *b* to be put through this noose. The two threads are then pulled tight and are thus joined to the loop in the completed portion, as shown in the illustration. Thread *a* is under and thread *b* is over the loop, but they are crossed on its inner edge. Here pure bobbinwork in one continuous line is abandoned; the bobbins require assistance from another instrument, the crochet hook. In pure bobbinwork there are never more than two threads over one another; but at the point of "accrochage" there are four threads on three planes over one another. By the use of the *Point de raccroc* it is possible to make bobbin lace out of separate pieces.

Both Flemish and Italian bobbin laces make use of these aids and are found in two forms, either worked in one continuous piece (Pl. 25, fig. 46), or put together from different pieces (Pl. 140). Brussels bobbin lace is also made up of different pieces. Valenciennes, Binche and Mechlin preserve the form of the pure bobbin lace in one piece. The laces made in one piece are worked on a rigid pillow; those composed of different pieces are made on a round pillow which the worker can revolve.

Fancy nets. Fancy network was introduced at the same time as the tendril patterns.

In type 4 of the Flemish bobbin laces (Pl. 140) the basic forms of almost all fancy nets used in the later bobbin laces are to be found. These consist of:

(1) *Grillé* or Lattice work.

(2) Double *grillé*.

(3) Spiders or cobwebs.

(4) The five-holed stitch.

(5) Point de neige.

(6) "Armure".

(1) Simple *grillé* (Pl. 49, fig. 103) is sometimes used as an ornamental filling (Pl. 30, fig. 56, 57, 58). It is mainly used in Brussels and sometimes in Mechlin lace in conjunction with linen-stitch, to give the desired effect of light and shade to the fabric-like texture of the ornaments.

(2) Double *grillé* (Pl. 49, fig. 104) is used in the Flemish laces worked in one piece (Pl. 25, fig. 46).

(3) Spiders or cobwebs are to be found in a variety of forms, particularly in Type 4 of the Flemish laces, which are made up of different pieces. In this variety most of the threads on the same side branch out, either to the right or left, after they have entered the mesh.

In speaking of right and left and of the upper and lower sides of lace, the direction is taken from the standpoint of the laceworker. The bobbins move from above downwards. Fig. 102 of Pl. 48 shows a detail of a spider mesh from the lace in Pl. 29, fig. 55.

(4) The five-holed stitches first appear in the fancy nets of Flemish lace. From the Early Louis XIV period onwards they are frequently used to form a groundwork (Pl. 50, 51, 52).

They are generally known indiscriminately as "Five-holed stitches". There are no old names for the different varieties, and we have here distinguished them as five-holed stitches (i), (ii) and (iii).

(i) Modern names: Double virgin ground, *maille flamande*, or *maille à cinq trous* (Pl. 50, fig. 105). The pairs of threads run together from the left above to the right below and from the right above to the left below forming four whole stitches in each mesh and connecting the meshes by one whole stitch. The open space is round.

(ii) Modern names: Slavonic virgin ground, or *Réseau de la dentelle de Flandre moderne* (Pl. 50, fig. 106).

The threads of the pairs of bobbins do not run together. Each thread runs independently through the mesh. Of the eight threads composing the mesh four run outwards across to right and left, two run straight downwards, and two run downwards alternately in a vertical and horizontal direction. The open space is square. This stitch is used as a fancy net in the old Flemish laces and as a groundwork and fancy net in the Early Louis XIV laces. Pl. 51, fig. 107 and Pl. 52, fig. 109 show two variations of this stitch.

(iii) Modern names: Virgin ground or maiden's net, *Point à la vierge* (Pl. 51, fig. 108).

The pairs of threads run together in a slanting direction. The meshes are formed of four whole stitches, and are joined by half-stitches. The open space is square. These meshes first appear in the Louis XVI period. Mrs. Palliser only found one mention of the name *dentelle à la Vierge*, and that was in the inventory made in 1785 after the death of Louis-Philippe, Duke of Orleans.

(5) *Point de neige*, or *fond de neige*, is frequently found either as a fancy net or as a network ground in Early Louis XIV laces. It consists of star-shaped stitches placed regularly or irregularly over the ground. In the description that follows the designation "star" has been used.

Fond de neige was used in great variety in old laces; the illustrations show most of the forms employed. If the stars are regarded as isolated stitches they resolve themselves into three types.

(i) The linen-stitch star (1) *a—d* (Pl. 53, fig. 110).

(ii) Shell star *e—i* (Pl. 53, fig. 111).

(iii) Bud-star *k—o* (Pl. 53, fig. 112).

The relation of the art of bobbin lace-making to space is represented by the direction of the threads in the ornament and is combined with a relation to time in the actual manipulation of the threads, the continouus movement and the consecutive patterns. Regarded from this standpoint, therefore, it is possible, in describing it, to make use of the terms of that abstract art, music.

The various forms of *fond de neige* appearing in the laces here reproduced are depicted in Pl. 53—60, 63—65.

Fig. 113, Pl. 54 shows bud stars in the Brussels laces 302 and 305 (Pl. 34, fig. 67).

From each mesh two pairs of threads run vertically downwards, two pairs run to the right and two pairs to the left, both in a slanting direction.

If we regard each thread as a voice which, altering in pitch as it progresses, makes a melody, and if the horizontal rows of meshes are regarded as bars, then we can see how two pairs of voices, the green threads, sing a melody of two bars which is repeated again and again. In bar 2.

---

(1) The designations "linen stitch star," "shell-star" and "bud star" are not in general use and are merely employed here to distinguish one from the other.

two new pairs of voices, the white threads, introduce the same melody. This is the simple canon form. Every two pairs sing the same melody, not simultaneously, but one after the other. The red threads make the accompaniment, and repeat the same musical figure from bar to bar.

Fig. 114, Pl. 54. Bud stars in the Brussels lace 305 (Pl. 42, fig. 85).

All the pairs turn outwards to right and left of each row of meshes.

Every two pairs sing a melody lasting through four bars. In each of these four bars another two pairs begin the melody over again. The pair of blue threads marked I in the above illustration are followed in bar 2 by the red pair II, in bar 3 by the yellow pair III and in bar 4 by the green pair IV. In bar 5 the blue pair start the melody again.

Every mesh, that is, every harmonious figure produced by the concerted singing of the pairs of threads, consists of six pairs. Each pair takes part in the formation of the mesh itself in three out of the four bars, and forms the connection between two meshes in one bar. The yellow pair takes its share in the formation of the figure in bars A and B, pauses in the next bar C, appears again in figure D, and then begins the melody over again.

Fig. 115, Pl. 55. Shell stars in the Mechlin lace 103, and in Binche 203, 204, 205 (Pl. 40, fig. 81; Pl. 31, fig. 60; Pl. 31, fig. 61; Pl. 33, fig. 65).

All the pairs of threads run vertically downwards.

Every mesh consists of six pairs. A red and a green pair sing the same melody of two bars, one being a bar behind the other. Two white pairs form a figure of three bars; they sing the same melody, but one is two bars behind the other. Two blue pairs form the same figure as the white but a bar behind. The yellow pairs are the accompaniment and each in turn accentuates a bar.

Fig. 116, Pl. 55. Shell-stars in lace 110 (Pl. 42, fig. 86).

The pairs forming the meshes follow the same direction as in fig. 115. The ground covered is larger because independent pairs of threads form a hexagonal frame to each separate mesh.

Fig. 117, Pl. 56. Bud-stars in the Brussels bobbinlaces 305, 3034 (Pl. 42, fig. 85; Pl. 32, fig. 62).

The meshes consist of six pairs of threads, three of which run outwards to the right and three to the left.

In the drawing a number of threads on the right side are only indicated, so as to make the course of the others clearer. A yellow and a red pair sing the same melody of three bars, the red being one bar behind. In bar 1. the two pairs unite to form the mesh, in bars 2. and 3. they pursue one another, in bar 4. they catch each other up again, and so on. This form is the *caccia*, the chase, or the *fuga*, the flight. Whilst the yellow and red pairs go from right to left, the green and blue pairs describe the same figure from left to right. The white pairs, five and six, form the accompaniment.

Fig. 118, Pl. 56. Linen-stitch stars in the Mechlin lace 108 (Pl. 43, fig. 87).

Each mesh consists of six pairs of threads. Five pairs, yellow, green, blue, violet and red, sing the same melody in canon through five bars, slowly moving to the left. A white pair moves vertically downwards in accompaniment, accentuating every other bar. Another white pair moves to the right and accentuates every bar.

Fig. 119, 120, Pl. 57; fig. 121, 122, Pl. 58, show similar movements.

Fig. 128, Pl. 63, 64. Linen stitch stars in the Binche lace 203 (Pl. 31, fig. 60).

Two threads, shown as dotted lines, run vertically downwards. They unite in one bar, pursue one another in the next, meet again in the third, and so on. They sing the same melody in canon through two bars. Twelve white threads follow each other in the same melody, brought out by the black thread, through twelve bars. Independent, separate threads form a diamond-shaped framework. The stars in this lace look like spots put in with a brush, an effect produced by the fact that the threads running into the mesh from above are only twisted once whilst those running downwards out of the mesh have a double twist.

Fig. 113—123, 128, 129 are examples of the canon, or imitative method.

Fig. 125, 130, 131 (Pl. 60, 67, 68) show how technique is applied to texture. In the Binche lace 2061 (Pl. 29, fig. 55) the ornament is in the regular, symmetrical, "candelabra" style of the Mid-Louis XIV period (Pl. 67, fig. 130). The variation of open and close-textured surfaces has blurred the lines and achieved the effect of brush-work (Pl. 68, fig. 131). In fig. 125, Pl. 60, the narrow tendrils are composed of four parallel threads. Different circular shell-stars are arranged symmetrically in such a manner that on either side of the central line the same pattern appears at corresponding places (Pl. 67, fig. 130).

(6) *Armure* (1). This is a loosely woven net made up of single threads in half stitches.

Its most usual varieties are shown in figures 127, 132, 133 of Pl. 62, 69.

The *Armure* Fig. 127 in the Binche 2061 (Pl. 29, fig. 55) and the Armure fig. 132 in the Mechlin lace 103 (Pl. 40, fig. 81) consist of eight threads.

The *Armure* fig. 133 in the laces fig. 89, 90, Pl. 43 consists of twelve threads.

The *Armure* with twelve threads (fig. 133) is often confused with the spider, but they can easily be distinguished from one another because the axis of the spider runs in the same direction as the bobbins, whilst the axis of the *armure* runs horizontally.

The *fond triangulaire* fig. 135 of Pl. 70 in the Mechlin lace 102 (Pl. 40, fig. 80) and the *fond triangulaire* fig. 134 of Pl. 70 in the Mechlin lace 105 (Pl. 38, fig. 75) are halfway between the spider and the *Armure*.

Groundnets. In the 18th Century the different bobbin laces began to specialise in their own particular grounds. Brussels lace adopted the *droschel* ground (Pl. 13, fig. 30), Mechlin the *Eisgrond* (Pl. 13, fig. 29) and Valenciennes the Valenciennes ground with the round mesh (Pl. 12, fig. 28), in which the direction of the threads is similar to that of the round Flemish mesh (Pl. 12, fig. 27).

The round Valenciennes mesh is so-called to distinguish it from the square Valenciennes ground which was introduced in the 19th Century (Pl. 71, fig. 136, 137), and is formed of a series of plaits.

---

(1) I am indebted to Mme. Paulis for the information that the name "armure" is not generally applied to a particular mesh, but is used to denote certain methods of weaving the threads; thus we have "armure satin" or "armure serge". I have used the word "armure" here to distinguish certain meshes because I could not find another name for them.

A more open net, the double ground (Pl. 72, fig. 138), is found in the *Régence* and Louis XV periods, and was frequently used in Louis XVI Mechlin lace. In the Late Louis XIV period the double ground was sometimes combined with small square-shaped patterns (Pl. 34, fig. 67) and at a later date geometrically arranged squares were often placed on a double ground (Pl. 72, fig. 139).

In the last half of the 18th Century new groundnets were introduced in the laces of Antwerp and Lille. As in Mechlin lace, these grounds were worked round the pattern in a coarser thread.

In Antwerp lace (Pl. 73, fig. 140) the groundnet is composed of a series of whole stitches. Pairs of threads run vertically downwards and are crossed by pairs of threads slanting to the right and left (Pl. 73, fig. 141). This ground is known as *fond Chant*, or *Point de Paris*.

In Lille lace the groundnet is formed by single threads running downwards and from right to left and from left to right (Pl. 76, fig. 149).

In the Louis XV period there was a tendency to imitate needle-point with bobbinwork. The light net of the Brussels bobbin laces Pl. 44, fig. 91, 92 and Pl. 45, fig. 93 is based on the principle of the simple needle-worked ground (Pl. 47, fig. 98). The meshes are made by *Point de raccroc* (Pl. 48, fig. 101; Pl. 61, fig. 126).

The combining of needle and bobbin work in the same lace was introduced in the Louis XIV period; this method finds its most characteristic expression in the Brussels laces of the 19th Century.

THE DEVELOPMENT OF STYLE IN LACE

PERIODS

Hitherto we have considered the three components of lace and their various forms individually. It was found that in certain periods the ornamental patterns of laces assumed certain similar characteristics distinguishing them from the ornaments of other periods. We then saw how texture and technique are evolved in the groups of lace which are assigned by their patterns to the different periods.

If we now consider ornament, texture and technique combined as a whole, we find that the many different forms of lace can not only be divided into a chronological sequence, but that they alternate rhythmically between the opposite styles represented by the terms classical and baroque.

Two main periods stand out in which these styles predominate: the one, from the early days of lace-making until the close of the 16th Century, and the other in the first part of Louis XIV's reign.

A severely symmetrical form predominates in the laces of the 16th Century. Independent parts are brought into harmony with the whole; when released from the whole these parts retain their individual significance. The geometrical pattern is indicative of the principle of repose, of self-sufficiency. A movement is no sooner begun than it is arrested or suspended. The diversion of the movement reinstates symmetry and repose (ornament). The lines and contours are quite distinct from the ground, which is on a second and lower plane (texture). The needle takes the thread from one point of suspension to the other. The bobbins are limited to plaiting and linenstitch. The plaiting takes the threads vertically downwards, the linenstitch up and down and across (technique). This period is uniformly classical in form (Pl. 2, fig. 5; Pl. 14, 15, 90).

In the laces of the Early Louis XIV period the principle of repose and limitation is replaced by that of movement, freedom from limitation, and growth. The flowing movement is continued in perpetuity. The conceptions of vertical and horizontal have lost their significance. Instead of symmetry there is recurrence. The ground is no longer on a separate plane but sinks into the pattern, thus causing the contours to be blurred and the pattern indistinct. Instead of lines, the eye is caught by lighter and darker patches. The separate parts have lost their independence and are merged in the whole. The bobbins no longer seek to achieve definition and symmetry by leading the thread vertically, but take it diagonally into the sphere of the indefinite. The lines develop into an inexhaustible profusion of patterns. Ornament, texture and technique combine to form typical examples of full baroque (Pl. 28; Pl. 29, fig. 54).

These two periods may be termed the classical and the full baroque periods in lacemaking.

In the first half of the 17th Century occur unrelated formations; unrelated in a twofold sense. In the first place the ornaments and the texture of the laces of this period represent the extremes of the classical and baroque styles, and secondly, these extremes change places in the North and South.

34

In the South the ornament goes through a transition stage into the baroque. In this transition stage symmetry and emphasis on the perpendicular are still retained. Figures of men and animals frequently occur; in making use of them no particular attention is paid to their orientation or their relation to one another. The tendrils are narrow and wavering and seem as though reluctant to indulge in the full swing of their movement. Their mannerism is typical like the thin, radiating lines of water in the fountains of Wurzelbauer of Nuremberg, Hubert Gerhart and Adriaen de Vries (1) (Pl. 3—6) (2).

The tendrils gradually become wider, freer and heavier and develop into a completely baroque style of ornament (Pl. 7; Pl. 8, fig. 17). The texture, however, remains classical. The contours stand out sharply and at the highest point of this development the draughtsmanship of the lines is given a plastic quality by being raised in relief, thus causing the ground to sink back still further.

In the North the ornament remains classical and the texture becomes baroque. In the ornament, symmetry and emphasis on the perpendicular predominate; the whole consists of a combination of separate parts. The texture seeks to blur lines and contours, to rob details of their individuality and to merge them in the general effect, until finally the ornament is entirely subsidiary to the texture and there remains nothing but an effect of light and shade, as in a painting (Pl. 22, 23; Pl. 25, fig. 45).

In this fusion of contradictory tendencies, classical purity of line and draughtsmanship gains the ascendance in the South and baroque impressionism in the North, thus clearly showing how the development of style in lace is influenced by its technique. The needle tends to produce clear-cut plastic lines; the bobbins tend to blurred outlines and effects of light and shade.

The development of style in lace between the classical and full baroque can be summarized thus:

In the South a classical period is followed by one of conventionalised design, then by the Early baroque period, the *Points gros de Venise* with its baroque ornaments and classical texture, and finally by the full baroque of the Italian needlepoint, the early Rosellino lace (Pl. 124).

In the North, between the classical and full baroque periods, there is a period of early baroque in which the increasingly baroque character of the texture overshadows the classical ornament.

These periods in the development of style in lace do not coincide chronologically with the corresponding periods in art, but occur later.

---

(1) Pinder: "Das Problem der Generation," p. 57/58.

(2) Concerning this group of laces, M. Schuette ("Alte Spitzen," 3rd ed., p. 113) says: "The delicate, somewhat tapering drawing, with the round stems, and the realistic lilies, cyclamen, carnations and sunflowers, is common to them all; some show a Persian influence in the elongated oval medallions. No doubt they were all produced in the same workroom, which is to be sought in Venice." E. Ricci ("Trine ad ago," p. 21) says: "*Punto in aria*, which, by virtue of its noble and discreet beauty and its pure draughtsmanship, is the most Italian of all laces, expresses this art in the highest degree. Laces afterwards became richer and more delicate, but they were never more perfect in style, in simple richness of design and graceful simplicity of execution than those laces which are known as 'real *Punto in aria*.'"

Generations of artists and denomination of styles

Classic / Baroque	The generations are in the prime of life towards					
Quattrocento	1490	1490	Charles VIII. 1483–1498		Henry VII. 1485–1509	
Botticelli 1446		1500				
Michelangelo 1475 Classic I	1515	10	Louis XII. 1498–1515	Maximilian I. 1493–1519		
Raffael 1483–1520 Classic II	1525	20				
Andrea del Sarto 1486		30	François I. 1515–1547	Charles V. 1516–1556	Henry VIII. 1509–1547	
Parmeggianino 1504	1540	40				
		50			Edward VI	Tudor
Tintoretto 1518 Mannerism.	1555	60	Henry II. 1547–1559		1547–1553 Mary 1553–1558	
P. Breughel d. Ä. 1525	1565	70	François II. 1559–1560 Charles IX. 1560–1574	Philipp II. 1556–1598	Elisabeth 1558–1603	
		80	Henry III.			
Greco 1547	1590	90	1574–1589			
		1600	Henry IV.			
Rubens 1577—1640		10	1589–1610	Philipp III. 1598–1621	James I. Stuart 1603–1625	Jacobean
Franz Hals 1580 Full Baroque	1620	20				
Velasquez / van Dyck 1599		30	Louis XIII.			
Rembrandt 1606—1669	1640	40	1610–1643		Charles I. 1625–1649	
Ter Borch 1627				Philipp IV. 1621–1665		
Murillo 1618	1650	50	Régence			
Françoise Badar 1624—1677		60	Anne d'Autriche		Cromwell	
		70			Charles II. 1660–1685	
Vermeer van Delft 1635 I. Late Baroque	1680	80	Louis XIV.		James II. 1685–1689	
		90	1661–1715 geb. 1638		William III. Orange 1689–1702	
Rigaud 1659 II. Late Baroque	1700	1700				
Schlüter 1664		10	Régence Phil. d'Orléans 1715–1723		Anne Stuart 1702–1714	Queen Anne
Watteau 1684 III. Late Baroque		20			George I. Hannover 1714–1727	
D. Zimmermann 1685 Régence	1725	30				
Chardin 1699 IV. Late Baroque	1740	40			George II. 1727–1760	Georgian
Liotard 1704						
Tiepolo 1696 Cuvilliés 1698 Rokoko		50	Louis XV.			
Fragonard 1732 V. Late Baroque	1760	60	1723–1774			
Romney 1734	1770	70				
Classicism		80	Louis XVI.		George III. 1760–1820	
David 1748	1790	90	1774–1793			
Carstens 1754						
Canova 1757		1800				

36

The classical period in art occurs at the beginning of the 16th Century, that of lace in the last two-thirds of the Century. Mannerism occurs in the 16th Century, lace has its period of early baroque and mannerism in the first half of the 17th Century. The full baroque period in lace only began when full baroque in art was dying out.

The belated adjustment of lace to the style of its day may be accounted for by the fact that its character depended on the generations who, when their influence was predominant, were already advanced in age and were still preoccupied with the problems of an earlier period. The old laces were produced, for the most part, in convents and communities in which the directors and forewomen were old women who clung to tradition.

The table on p. 36 contrasts the succession of generations of artists given by Pinder (1) with the succession of different styles and their chronological order.

Full baroque in art ended with the death of Rubens in 1640; Velasquez died twenty years later; in 1661 Louis XIV came to the throne. The full baroque period in lace begins about the same time. We already have the large branching designs, and before long the texture becomes entirely baroque in character.

In considering ornament we found that the development of lace could be divided into six phases dating from the beginning of Louis XIV's reign; namely, Early, Mid, and Late Louis XIV, *Régence*, Louis XV and Louis XVI. We have seen that in the Early Louis XIV period lace adopted the full baroque style, so we may call the periods that follow numbers 1 to 5 of the Late baroque style.

The 1st Late baroque style in lace, of the Mid Louis XIV period, tends to symmetry and emphasis of the perpendicular. In the *candelière* style delicate tendrils are grouped round a central axis. Even where the movement is continuous the tendrils are narrow and far apart. It is a recurrence of mannerism. The texture has become more open and the outlines stand out from the ground (Pl. 9; Pl. 30, fig. 56, 57, 58). The Valenciennes and Binche bobbin laces of this period are particularly worthy of note; here the pattern or the ground is made of delicate tendrils consisting of only four threads running parallel to one another (Pl. 60, fig. 125). The tendrils in the early laces of this kind are still in continuous movement; the central axis is introduced later (2) (Pl. 29, fig. 55; Pl. 30).

The 2nd Late baroque style of the Late Louis XIV period tends to a repetition of full baroque. The forms are heavier than in the previous style; the ornaments are closer together and the outlines less significant; the ground merges in the pattern (Pl. 31—34).

In the *Régence* period, that of the 3rd Late baroque style, there is a reversion to the 1st Late baroque. But in the symmetrical grouping round a vertical axis the delicate tendrils are replaced by heavier motives. The texture tends to be more baroque. The clearcut effect of the ornament is weakened by the shading of the surfaces (Pl. 35—37; Pl. 38, fig. 75).

---

(1) Pinder: "Das Problem der Generation."

(2) The high position in Italian lace given by E. Ricci to "*punti in aria propriamente detto*" (see footnote to p. 35), seems to me the suitable position in bobbin laces for this class of lace. With the later Valenciennes lace of the 18th Century, they are the highest expression of the idea of bobbin lace.

The 4th Late baroque or rococo style, in the Louis XV period (Pl. 38—46) has two tendencies; beside the flowing movement of the baroque style there appears repose and symmetry. In the texture a sharp distinction between design and ground alternates with delicate shading and a blurred, indistinct pattern.

The 5th Late baroque style, of the Louis XVI period, reverts to numbers 3 and 1. In the texture the ground stands away from the design and the ornament is clearly defined. The parts renew their independent existence. It is the transition to the classical (Pl. 179).

In the arts, a wave advances in rhythmical movements from classicism to full baroque; shorter ripples then go back to classicism. As we have seen, the development of lace follows the same course.

ATTRIBUTION OF STYLE AND DATE

The history of lace is anonymous. No names are connected with individual pieces of work. In attempting to make a summary of the laces in separate groups and to assign them to certain periods, there is practically no other guide than the characteristics of the laces themselves. Hence, it is impossible to avoid mistakes; later examples may be assigned to earlier periods or earlier examples to later periods. If the date of origin of a piece of lace is documented, it does not necessarily follow that its style will coincide with the period of its production; the worker may have belonged to the previous generation, or it may represent the early work of a generation to come.

If we use pictorial representations in assigning a date, it must be remembered that laces belonging to an earlier period are often included in such pictures. The important thing is to ascertain what laces were already in existence at that particular date. The frequent appearance of similar laces in portraits of the same period, as in the 17th Century, only proves that during that time certain laces were widely distributed.

The name of a lace does not always imply the place of origin. In the various towns and schools, besides their own speciality, laces were produced after the pattern and method practised in other towns. Bobbin-workers would move from place to place and take drawings and directions with them, to be used as occasion arose.

The names of the different laces indicate special distinguishing characteristics. The various styles and periods did not succeed one another by a definite series of steps but by gradual transition and accompanied by both older and newer forms.

THE PART PLAYED BY PERSONALITY. FRANÇOISE BADAR

Art, however defined, is the work of individuals, the expression of all the permanent and temporary conditions which have combined at the time of their activity to make up the characteristics of their art. In addition to such conditions as nationality, family, birthplace, age and environment, the period itself has its influence. In its effect on those born at about the same time, this influence groups them together as being faced with the same problems (Pinder). Each individual artist solves these problems in his own way. If he is one of the really great, his particular way will leave its mark on the period and generation, and the names of such artists are honoured in the history of art.

In the anonymous history of lace it seems useless to attempt to connect the main developments of style with any one person, apart from Colbert, who indirectly gave the impulse to the high degree of development of lace-making in France. Nevertheless, one name has come down to us, which is intimately bound up with the highest point in the art of lace-making, the full baroque period. That name is Françoise Badar.

She was born at Valenciennes in 1624. In 1639 she went to Antwerp where she learnt bobbin-work. She returned to Valenciennes in 1649 and set up a school of needlework for the employment of the women of the district. Her activities gave an extraordinary impetus to the lace industry in Valenciennes. In 1665 she undertook the organisation of the lace school at Le Quesnoy founded by Colbert, and directed it until 1669. She then returned to Valenciennes, where she died in 1677 (1).

After her death bobbin lace in Valenciennes did not maintain the high level to which she had brought it. Mechlin and Brussels laces became successful rivals and overshadowed the Valenciennes.

Françoise Badar carried on her work for thirty years and we may assume that her influence left its mark on the laces of that time. According to the year of her birth, she comes between the generations of Ter Borch and Vermeer van Delft. Her period is still under the influence of the wave of the full baroque style in art. It has already been shown (p. 22) how, in 1660 on the Ile des Faisans, the Italian laces having baroque ornament and classical texture coincided with Flemish laces having classical ornament and baroque texture. Whilst Flemish lace soon displays the large branching designs and classical texture of Italian lace (Pl. 25, fig. 46; Pl. 140), Valenciennes lace displays at the same time a baroque style in its highest form of development (Pl. 28). The creation of the full baroque style in bobbin lace and the impulse towards enrichment of its technical forms may well be attributed to the influence of a strong personality. In 1677 Valenciennes, hitherto a Flemish town, was incorporated into France by Louis XIV as the dower of his Spanish wife. Françoise Badar died in the same year.

If we take the influence of Françoise Badar into consideration, we may find that some hitherto unanswered questions as to whether certain laces should be assigned to Valenciennes or Binche could be answered.

Hitherto, only the round-meshed Valenciennes lace of the 18th Century and the square-meshed lace of the 19th Century have been definitely classed as "Valenciennes". Various names have been given to the earlier Valenciennes laces with their fancy nets and different meshes. Either all laces of this kind having no round mesh in the ground have been placed in the Binche

---

(1) Maria-Therèse Horion, a sister in the Order of the Holy Family, wrote the life of Françoise Badar from notes left by the latter. The work was printed at Liège in 1726 and is now in the Library at Valenciennes. Detailed stories of her life are to be found in the works of Mabille de Poncheville and Malotet.

category, or they have been called "Valenciennes made after Binche lace." The earlier Valenciennes laces, with their unity of style and finished technique, mark the zenith of the art of bobbin lace-making. The assumption that they appeared not later than 1677 is supported by the circumstance of the decline of Valenciennes lace after the death of François Badar. Their chronological position would thus be fixed as between the middle of the 17th Century and the 1st late baroque period of lace, the period of the *candelière*. It is easy to believe that, during Françoise Badar's lifetime and under her influence, the not very distant town of Binche produced the same or similar kinds of lace as those produced at Valenciennes. Subsequently, Binche lace retained the character it had acquired from the early Valenciennes, thus going in the opposite direction to the Valenciennes lace of the 18th Century. With the production of its own special round-meshed ground net, this latter took on a new aspect and became the most costly and sought-after lace for the purpose of personal adornment.

CONCLUSION

We have distinguished the peculiarities of style in lace by the terms generally used to describe the various features of classical and baroque art. This is justified in so far that the brief space of time between the beginning and the end of the making of old lace occurs during those periods in art known as classical and baroque. Exactly the same differences may be found, however, in earlier works of art which have no connection with our classical and baroque styles.

Classical and baroque are, in the widest sense, opposite poles, between which artistic feeling and effort is always and everywhere active.

Of the many expressions employed in the modern study of art in order to make these opposites comprehensible, the terms North and South are the most suitable to describe the development of lace. Just as bobbin laces owe their highest development to the northern spirit and are essentially an expression of northern feeling, so needle laces are essentially an expression of the South.

The author has endeavoured in this work clearly to distinguish from one another the different periods in the history of lace. A study of the subject led to the grouping together of similar kinds. These groups vary in a rhythmical sequence, and an attempt has been made to compare their progress with a similar rhythmical sequence in the arts so that they may find their place in the scheme of the history of art. In lace the beat of the pulsations towards the two opposites, classical and baroque, is retarded.

In considering technique we dwelt on the subject of the material, the threads, as a specially distinguishing medium, and we found that, in spite of all ingenious inventions, machinery cannot achieve the results obtained by the patient work of the hand.

In ancient Egypt and in Flanders at the time when old lace was made, it appears that the finest yarns were produced by selecting single flax fibres according to their length, smoothness and delicacy and twisting them together with the hand. The primary threads thus obtained were then more firmly twisted by means of the spindle or spinning-wheel.

40

Mural paintings in the tombs of Beni Hasan.
From L. Klebs: „Die Reliefs und Malereien des Mittleren Reichs".

41

This method is portrayed in ancient Egyptian paintings. In illustrations a, b, c on p. 41 (1), the three standing figures on the right show the method of using the spindle. Each of them is using two spindles simultaneously; she lets the primary thread from the container slip over her raised left hand and twists it with the pendant spindle. The spindles are set in motion either with the right hand alone, or by rubbing the right hand on the upper part of the thigh. The central figure is working with four primary threads, both the others with two. The containers from which the primary threads run sometimes stand behind the spinners, so that the workers need not trouble about the finished threads except to give them the necessary twist.

Luise Klebs (2) describes the action of the women kneeling behind the three standing figures as follows: "The Egyptian spinner often has her spinning material prepared beforehand. For this purpose, women sit on the ground and smooth the separate fibres and twist them together in one continuous fibre. Possibly only the longest and best fibres are selected for very delicate fabrics. These unspun threads are then wound into a ball and placed in a pot; the actual spinning material consists of two or more of these balls, which take the place of the distaff, so that two or more continuous fibres are spun together." In the Beni Hassan pictures the first three kneeling women on the right are manipulating small heaps of flax lying in front of and behind them, whilst the fourth is holding a bundle of fibres in her left hand from which she appears to be drawing single fibres.

There are no representations or exact descriptions of the production in Flanders of the finest lace threads. A notice (3) exists announcing the opening in Valenciennes on July 3rd, 1722 of a saleroom for laces and lace yarns at the "maison dite l'Hôpital de la Charité." Young girls were employed in making these goods: "Les unes aux dites dentelles, et les autres à filer le lin. De sorte que l'on trouve aussi continuellement dans cette maison un magazin de filets crus, propres à retordre, ou à faire toutes sortes de toiles, batistes et linons." In 1763 (4) a certain J. B. Comtesse settled in Valenciennes as a "fabricant de fil retors à Douai". "Comtesse se procurait du fil brut chez les marchands filtiers du pays. Les dentellières de Valenciennes réclamaient un fil fin, pas trop retors, uni et plat, alors que celles d'Alençon exigeaient un fil retors, ni cotonneux, ni cassant, parcequ'elles jetaient leurs fuseaux et frappaient leurs dentelles bien plus fort qu'en Flandre, ce qui détordait le fil." Thus, the "filets crus" or the "fil brut" were distinguished from the "fil retors". That by a "fil retors" a single and not a twisted thread is implied, is shown by the fact that it might be "pas trop retors" (in the case of Valen-

---

(1) Percy E. Newberry: "Beni Hassan," vol. ii, Plate XIII. A clearer drawing of the three figures on the extreme right appears in Louise Klebs, "Reliefs und Malereien des mittleren Reichs." Illus. 92 after Cailliaud, "Recherches sur les arts et les métiers," Paris 1831 (illus. a, c.). There is a similar illustration in Newberry, vol. ii, Plate IV (fig. b). Other representations of spinning occur in the paintings from El Berscheh and on a tomb of the Middle Kingdom at Thebes reproduced in N. J. Davies, "The Tomb of Antefoker," 1920, and in Davies, "Five Theban Tombs," vol. XXXVII. Dr. Wolf of the Egyptian College of Leipzig University, informs me that the tombs at Beni Hassan have now fallen into decay. There are no photographs of their paintings and they cannot now be obtained. The Tomb of El Berscheh described by Newberry was destroyed by an earthquake.

(2) L. Klebs: "Die Reliefs und Malereien des mittleren Reichs," p. 17.

(3) André Mabille de Poncheville: "La dentelle à la main en Flandre," p. 76.

(4) A. Malotet: "La dentelle de Valenciennes," p. 46.

ciennes) or "retors" (in the case of Alençon). Moreover, there are no twisted threads in the old Valenciennes and Alençon laces. It may be supposed, therefore, that fine threads were produced in Flanders for the old laces in the same manner as the linen threads were produced in ancient Egypt. This is the only method by which it would seem to be possible to make the extremely fine threads consisting of a small number of flax fibres (1).

These threads were almost insubstantial and yet so strong that the sensitive fingers of the worker of those days could manipulate at one time a number of such threads weighed down by the bobbins. To make a piece of Valenciennes for a cap about 20 centimetres wide, over 1200 bobbins were required, and a pair of ruffles took the lace-maker a year to complete, working fifteen hours a day (Malotet, p. 51, 52).

Modern attempts to imitate old bobbin work fail principally because the worker has to make use of the stiff and somewhat coarse machine-made twists. Even the coarser of the old bobbin-laces were made of soft, pliable, hand-spun threads; this pliability cannot be attained by machinery. The technique of needle-lace maintained the tradition somewhat longer, but the machine-made threads added to the stiffness which is always present to a certain extent in needle-lace.

Our enquiry has thus led us to one certain conclusion, and that is that the making of old lace cannot recur. With the disappearance of the conditions necessary to its production, it has become a thing of the past.

Once we have realised that old lace is a relic of a vanished civilisation it becomes obvious that we must save what remains to us from destruction. A certain proportion has been preserved in museums, but probably the greater part is scattered throughout the world and is gradually sinking into decay, its value as the irreplaceable legacy of a bygone age totally unrecognised.

---

(1) The hand-made thread shown on Plate 76 A consists of seven fibres.

INDEX AND SUMMARY OF ILLUSTRATIONS(1)

---

(1) The arrow on the drawings for pillow lace points downwards in the direction of the progressive bobbin work.

44

Plate 25	Fig. 44. Flemish pillow lace. Second third of 17th Century. Van Dyck lace. — Fig. 45. Flemish pillow lace. Middle of 17th Century. Velasquez lace. — Fig. 46. Flemish pillow lace. Last third of 17th Century. Worked in one piece. Plaited *brides* join the edges of the ornament. — A Flemish pillow lace of the same period, made up of separate pillow-worked patterns. See Plate 140.
Plate 26	Fig. 47. Milan pillow lace. Fritz Iklé Collection, reduced. The ornament with its richly decorated mesh stands out in clear relief from the *réseau* without being joined up by *brides*. — Fig. 48. Part of lace shewn in fig. 47, original size.
Plate 27	Fig. 49. Milan pillow lace. From Countess Valerie Luxburg. Palermo, reduced. — Fig. 50. Part of lace shewn in fig. 49, original size. The ornamental parts are here connected by a *réseau*, the mesh of which is composed like the round Flemish and round Valenciennes mesh. Plate 12, figs. 27 and 28. In the Milan lace Plate 26 the edgings of the pillow made tape are separate in their backwards swing. The gaps are filled with decorative net. In the Milan lace, Plate 27, the borders of the pillow made tape are closed onto each other in the backwards swing. The scrolls of the lace therefore consist of two parts of the same tape formed one after the other, and joined up in the scroll by *Point de raccroc*. (Plate 48. Fig. 101.)
Plate 28	Fig. 51. 17th Century Valenciennes lace, original size. Fritz Iklé Collektion, High Baroque pillow lace. — Fig. 52. 17th Century Valenciennes lace, original size. From Frau Andree, Berchtesgaden. High Baroque pillow lace. — Fig. 53. 17th Century Valenciennes lace, original size. High Baroque pillow lace.
Plate 29	Fig. 54. 17th Century Valenciennes lace, original size. High Baroque pillow lace. — Fig. 55. Binche 2061, original size. 1. Late Baroque, middle Louis XIV period. The *réseau* consists of four-threaded sprays with annulated shell devices, see Plate 60. Decorative nets: (a) *Armure*, see Plate 62. (b) spider-work see Plate 48, fig. 102. Illustration of ornament, see Plate 67. Illustration of texture see Plate 68.
Plate 30	Fig. 56. Binche. From Baroness Speidel-Pocci Berlin, original size, 1. Late Baroque, mid-Louis XIV period. The *réseau* is composed of four-thread tendrils with ring-shaped shell devices, similar to the lace shewn in fig. 55. — Fig. 57. Binche. Fritz Iklé Collection, original size. 1. Late Baroque, mid-Louis XIV period. *Réseau:* reinforced *fond a la vierge*, see Plate 50, fig. 105. — Fig. 58. Binche, original size. 1. Late Baroque. Mid-Louis XIV period. *Réseau:* reinforced *fond à la vierge*, see Plate 50, fig. 105.
Plate 31	Fig. 59. Binche 202, original size. 2. Late Baroque, end of Louis XIV period. *Réseau:* reinforced *fond vierge*, see Plate 50, fig. 105. Decorative net: *Point de neige*. (a) Toilé stars linked by expanded *brides*, see Plate 58, fig. 121; (b) Toilé stars with lozenge-shaped framework made from the threads of the mesh, see Plate 59, fig. 123. — Fig. 60. Binche 203, original size. 2. Late Baroque. End of Louis XIV period. *Réseau:* reinforced *fond à la vierge*, see Plate 50, fig. 105. Decorative net work: *Point de neige*. (a) Toilé stars with lozenge-shaped framework composed of separate threads, see Plate 63/64; (b) Shell devices connected by simple *brides*, see Plate 55, fig. 115. — Fig. 61. Binche 204, original size. 2. Late Baroque. End of Louis XIV period. *Réseau: Point de neige*. (a) Shell devices arranged asymmetrically, see Plate 59, fig. 124; (b) Shell devices with simple *bride* connection, see Plate 55, fig. 115.
Plate 32	Fig. 62. Brussels pillow lace 3034, original size. 2. Late Baroque. End of Louis XIV period. *Point de neige*. (a) Bud design connected by simple *brides*, see Plate 56, fig. 117. — Fig. 63. Brussels pillow lace 3031, original size. 2. Late Baroque. End of Louis XIV period. *Point de neige*. (a) Bud design joined up by simple *brides*, see Plate 56, fig. 117. — Fig. 64. Brussels pillow lace 3033, original size, 2. Late Baroque. End of Louis XIV period. *Point de neige*, a bud device joined up by simple *brides*, see Plate 56, fig. 117.
Plate 33	Fig. 65. Binche 205, original size. 2. Late Baroque. End of Louis XIV period. *Point de neige*. (a) Shell devices joined up by simple *brides*, see Plate 55, fig. 115; (b) Shell devices linked up by complicated *brides*, amongst them a rudimentary spray made by four parallel threads. — Fig. 66. Brussels pillow lace with "*bride*-ground". Cathedral Church at Eichstätt. Reduced. 2. Late Baroque. End of Louis XIV period. Breadth 61 cm. Photograph by Bavarian State Office for the Preservation of Ancient Monuments, Munich. In Mrs. Palliser's History of Lace, 4th Ed. p. 146 rather similar lace from the Victoria and Albert Museum, London, is illustrated. Breadth 66 cm. It was a present from Mme. de Maintenon to Fénélon, Archbishop of Cambrai 1695—1715.
Plate 34	Fig. 68. Brussels pillow lace. 302. Two lace lappets sewn together to make a *jabot*. Reduced. 2. Late Baroque. End of Louis XIV period. — Fig. 67. Part of lace shewn in Fig. 66, original size. *Point de neige:* bud design joined by simple *brides*, see Plate 54, fig. 113.

Plate 35   Fig. 69. Brussels pillow lace from the Wittelsbach christening treasure. Reduced. 3. Late Baroque. Regency period. Breadth 59 cm. Photograph by the Residenzmuseum, Munich. — Fig. 70. Part of lace shewn in fig. 69, original size. *Réseau:* round Flemish mesh, see Plate 12, fig. 27. Decorative net work: five hole meshes 1 and 2, see Plate 50.

Plate 36   Fig. 72. Brussels pillow lace 261, original size. 3. Late Baroque. Regency period. *Réseau:* round Flemish mesh, see Plate 12, fig. 27. Decorative net work: (a) *fond à la vierge*, slavonic pattern with full twistings between the meshes, see Plate 52, fig. 109. — (b) *fond à la vierge*, Slavonic pattern with double-twisted threads, see Plate 51, fig. 107. — (c) Reinforced *fond à la vierge*, see Plate 50, fig. 105. Between the meshes half-twisted and double-twisted threads. — Fig. 71. Brussels pillow lace. Cathedral Church at Eichstätt. Reduced. 3. Late Baroque Regency Period. Breadth 59 cm. Photograph by Bavarian State Office for Preservation of Ancient Monuments. Munich.

Plate 37   Fig. 73. Brabant pillow lace from the Wittelsbach christening treasure. Reduced. 3. Late Baroque. Regency. Breadth 38 cm. Photograph by the Residenzmuseum, Munich. — Fig. 74. Part of lace shewn in fig. 73, original size.

Plate 38   Fig. 75. Mechlin lace 105. Original size. 3. Late Baroque. Regency. *Réseau: Point de neige. Toilé* devices in double framework, lozenge-shaped and circular, made of single individual threads and threads from the mesh, see Plate 65/66, fig. 129. — Decorative net work: (a) *Fond triangulaire*, see Plate 70, fig. 134. — Fig. 76. Brussels pillow lace from the Wittelsbach christening treasure. Greatly reduced. 4. Late Baroque. Breadth 58 cm, length 414 cm. Photograph by the Residenzmuseum, Munich.

Plate 39   Fig. 78. Part of lace illustrated in fig. 76, slightly reduced. The ground is composed partly of *brides picotées*, partly of pillow work nets in imitation of needlepoint ground-mesh, see Plate 66, fig. 129. The decorative nets shew an abundance of different patterns. — Fig. 77. Part of lace in fig. 76, original size.

Plate 40   Fig. 79. Binche 201. Original size. 4. Late Baroque. Rococo. *Réseau:* (a) *Point de neige.* Shell devices connected unsymmetrically by *brides.* — (b) Squares made up of plaits and *brides picotées.* — Fig. 80. Mechlin lace 102. Original size. 4. Late Baroque. Rococo. *Réseau:* (a) Round Valenciennes mesh, see Plate 12, fig. 28. — (b) *Point de neige. Toilé* devices with square-shaped framework of independent pairs of threads, see Plate 58, fig. 122. Decorative net: (c) *Fond triangulaire*, see Plate 70, fig. 135. — The lace has the strong thread round the pattern as in Mechlin lace, the ground mesh of Valenciennes, and the general character of Binche. — Fig. 81. Mechlin lace 103. Original size. 4. Late Baroque. Rococo. *Réseau:* (a) *Point de neige.* Shell devices connected by simple *brides*, see Plate 55, fig. 115. — (b) *Armure*, see Plate 69, fig. 132. — Fig. 82. Mechlin lace 107. Original size. 4. Late Baroque. Rococo. *Réseau:* Mechlin ground, see Plate 13, fig. 29. Decorative net: (a) *Point de neige. Toilé* devices connected by expanded *brides*, see Plate 57, fig. 120.

Plate 41   Fig. 84. Brussels pillow lace 304. Two lappets with narrow centre piece. Reduced. 4. Late Baroque. Rococo. — Fig. 83. Part of lace shewn in fig. 84, original size. *Réseau:* (a) Droschel ground, see Plate 13, fig. 30. — (b) *Point de neige.* Bud devices connected by simple *brides*, see Plate 56, fig. 117. — (c) Double *fond Torchon* with squares of *point d'esprit*, see Plate 72, fig. 139.

Plate 42   Fig. 85. Brussels pillow lace 305. Original size. 4. Late Baroque. Rococo. *Réseau:* (a) Droschel ground, see Plate 13, fig. 30; (b) *Point de neige.* Bud devices connected by simple *brides*, see Plate 56, fig. 117. (c) Bud devices connected by simple *brides*, see Plate 54, fig. 114. — Fig. 86. Mechlin lace. 110. Original size. Child's bonnet. With a small piece of Binche insertion. 4. Late Baroque. Rococo. *Réseau* in the Binche: (a) *Point de neige.* Shell devices with hexagonal-shaped framework from separate pairs of threads, see Plate 55, fig. 116. *Réseau* in the Mechlin lace, centre piece (b) Mechlin ground, see Plate 13, fig. 29. *Réseau* in the lace edging (c) reinforced *fond à la vierge* see Plate 50, fig. 105. Decorative net (d) *Point de neige. Toilé* devices with lozenge-shaped *framework* composed from the threads of the mesh, se Plate 59, fig. 123.

Plate 43   Fig. 87. Mechlin lace 108. Original size. 4. Late Baroque. Rococo. *Réseau:* (a) Mechlin ground see Plate 13, fig. 29. Decorative net (b) *Point de neige. Toilé* devices connected by expanded *brides*, see Plate 56, fig. 118. — Fig. 88. Brussels pillow lace 306. Original size. 4. Late Baroque. Rococo. *Réseau:* (a) Droschel ground, see Plate 13, fig. 30. Decorative net (b) *Toilé* devices connected by expanded *brides* see Plate 57, fig. 119. — Figs. 89. 90. Mechlin pillow lace. From Frau Julius Schmits, Elberfeld. Original size. 4. Late Baroque. Rococo. *Réseau*, twelve-threaded *armure*, see Plate 69, fig. 133.

Plate 44   Fig. 91. Brussels pillow lace from Frau Elisabeth Wolff-Merck, Munich. Reduced. 4. Late Baroque. Rococo. Length 206 cm, breadth 81 cm. — Fig. 92. Part of lace shewn in fig. 91. Original size. The

46

ground, from which the ornament and figurative patterns stand out in relief, has various shadings. The darker parts consist of the pillow-worked imitation of the needlepoint ground, see Plate 61, fig. 126, the lighter parts of the Droschel ground, see Plate 13, fig. 30.

47

48

BIBLIOGRAPHY

1. LACES

Mrs. Bury Palliser: "A History of Lace," 3rd ed. London, 1875 (1st ed. 1864).

Ernest Lefébure: "Broderies et Dentelles." Paris, 1887.

Alan S. Cole: Hand-made Laces. London, 1890.

Tina Frauberger: "Handbuch der Spitzenkunde." Leipzig, 1894.

Dr. M. Dreger: "Entwicklungsgeschichte der Spitze." Vienna, 1901.

Mrs. Bury Palliser: "A History of Lace." Entirely revised, rewritten, and enlarged under the editorship of M. Jourdain and Alice Dryden. 4th ed. London, 1902.

M. Jourdain: "The Connoisseur." October 1905; November 1905; October 1907; March 1908.

M. Jourdain: "Old Lace." London, 1908.

Elisa Ricci: "Antiche Trine Italiane, Trine ad Ago." Bergamo, 1908.

Elisa Ricci: "Antiche Trine Italiane, Trine a Fuselli." Bergamo, 1911.

Mrs. Lowes: "Chats on Old Lace and Needlework." London, 1908.

E. van Overloop: "Matériaux pour servir à l'histoire de la dentelle en Belgique." Brussels, 1908—1914.

E. van Overloop: "La Dentelle. Guide du visiteur." Guide to the Brussels Museum of Lace. 1914.

A. Mabille de Poncheville: "La dentelle à la main en Flandre." Valenciennes, 1911.

Marie Schuette: "Alte Spitzen." On the occasion of the Exhibition at the Leipzig Museum of Industrial Arts. 1912.

Marie Schuette: "Alte Spitzen." A Handbook for Collectors and Amateurs. Berlin, 1914.

Thérèse de Dillmont: "Encyklopädie der weiblichen Handarbeiten." Mühlhausen.

Madame L. Paulis: "La Dentelle aux fuseaux." Part 1. "Dentelles à fil continu." I. Cluny. Brussels, 1921.

Charlier de Lantsheere: "Trésor de l'art dentellier." Brussels, 1922.

Mrs. Head: "The Lace and Embroidery Collector." London, 1922.

A. Malotet: "La Dentelle à Valenciennes." Paris, 1927.

2. TECHNIQUE

Aug. Braulick: "Altägyptische Gewebe." Stuttgart, 1900.

Dr. Alois Herzog: "Die Unterscheidung der Flachs- und Hanffaser." Berlin, 1926.

M. Lehmann: "Die Spinnerei." Leipzig, 1911.

Gustav Schradin: "Garne und Stoffe." Stuttgart, 1927.

3. PSYCHOLOGY OF FORM

Friedrich Sander: "Experimentelle Ergebnisse der Gestaltpsychologie." Report of the Xth Congress on Experimental Psychology at Bonn, 1927. Jena, 1928.

Friedrich Sander: "Über Gestaltqualitäten." Eighth International Psychological Congress. Groningen, 1926.

4. HISTORY

A. Riegl: "Textilkunst." In the "Geschichte der technischen Künste," edited by Bruno Bucher. Third volume, XVI. Leipzig, 1893.

Percy E. Newberry: "Beni Hassan." Part II. London, 1894.

W. M. Flinders Petrie: "Qurneh." London, 1909.

Wilhelm Worringer: "Formprobleme der Gotik." Ed. 8—12. Munich, 1920.

Peter Jessen: "Der Ornamentstich." Berlin, 1920.

Peter Jessen: "Meister des Ornamentstiches." A selection from four centuries.

Heinrich Wölfflin: "Kunstgeschichtliche Grundbegriffe." 5th ed. Munich, 1921.

Luise Klebs: "Die Reliefs und Malereien des mittleren Reiches." Heidelberg, 1922.

Josef Strzygowski: "Die Krisis der Geisteswissenschaften." Vienna, 1923.

Wilhelm Pinder: "Das Problem der Generation in der Kunstgeschichte Europas." Berlin, 1926.

Wilhelm Pinder: "Kunstgeschichte nach Generationen." Reprint from the collective work "Zwischen Philosophie und Kunst," Leipzig, 1926.

Rudolf Berliner: "Ornamentale Vorlageblätter des 15. bis 18. Jahrhunderts." Leipzig, 1926.

THE PLATES

Tafel 1
Abb. 1. Durchbrucharbeit, 16. Jahrhundert, in natürlicher Größe. — Abb. 2. Durchbrucharbeit
Italien 16. Jahrhundert. Sammlung Leopold Iklé, verkleinert. — Abb 3. Durchbrucharbeit
verkleinert.

Plate 1
Fig. 1. *Punto tagliato*, 16th Century, original size. — Fig. 2. *Punto tagliato*. Italy 16th Century. Leopold Iklé
Collection, reduced. — Fig. 3. *Punto tagliato*, reduced.

Planche 1
Fig. 1. Point coupé, XVIᵉ siècle, grandeur naturelle. — Fig. 2. Point coupé, Italie, XVIᵉ siècle. Collection
Léopold Iklé. Figure réduite. — Fig. 3. Point coupé. Figure réduite.

Tavola 1
Fig. 1. Falsatura a punto tagliato, secolo XVI, in grandezza naturale. — Fig. 2. Punto tagliato; Italia, secolo
XVI. Raccolta Leopold Iklé, impiccolita. — Fig. 3. Punto tagliato, impiccolita.

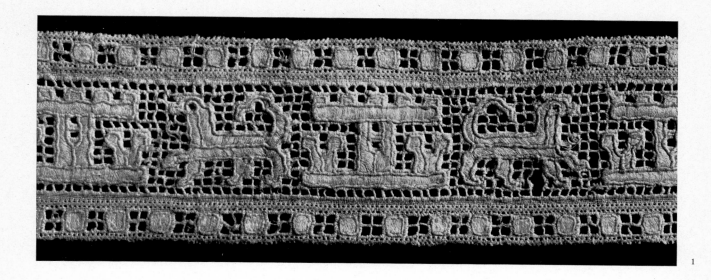

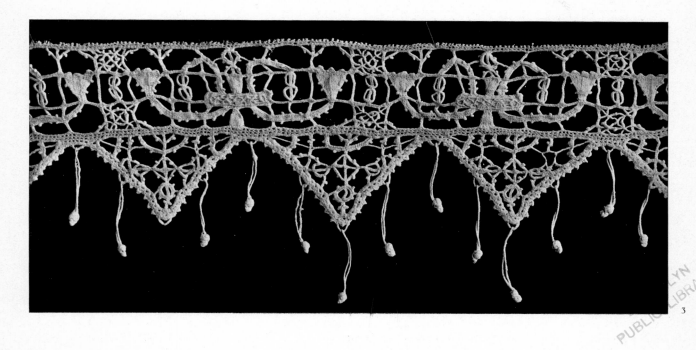

Tafel 2
Abb. 4. Teilstück der Durchbrucharbeit Abb. 3, in natürlicher Größe. — Abb. 5. Retticella.

Plate 2
Fig. 4. Part of *Punto tagliato* from Fig. 3, in original size. — Fig. 5. *Punto a reticello.*

Planche 2
Fig. 4. Fragment du point coupé de la fig. 3, mais en grandeur naturelle. — Fig. 5. Dentelle reticella.

Tavola 2
Fig. 4. Particolare del punto tagliato fig. 3, in grandezza naturale. — Fig. 5. Falsatura e punto a reticello.

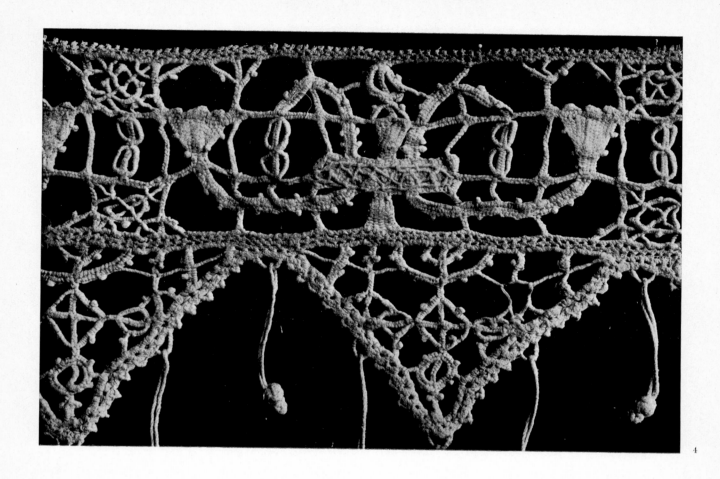

4

5

Tafel 3

Abb. 6. Nähspitze. Punto in aria. Sammlung Fritz Iklé, natürliche Größe. — Abb. 7. Nähspitze. Punto in aria. Sammlung Fritz Iklé, verkleinert.

Plate 3

Fig. 6. Needlepoint lace. *Punto in aria*. Fritz Iklé Collection, original size. — Fig. 7. Needlepoint lace. *Punto in aria*. Fritz Iklé Collection, reduced.

Planche 3

Fig. 6. Dentelle à l'aiguille. Punto in aria. Collection Fritz Iklé. En grandeur naturelle. — Fig. 7. Dentelle à l'aiguille. Punto in aria. Collection Fritz Iklé. Figure réduite.

Tavola 3

Fig. 6. Punto in aria. Raccolta Fritz Iklé, grandezza naturale. — Fig. 7. Punto in aria. Raccolta Fritz Iklé, impiccolita.

6

7

3

Tafel 4

Abb. 8. Nähspitze. Punto in aria. Sammlung Fritz Iklé, verkleinert. — Abb. 9. Die Spitze Abb. 8 in natürlicher Größe.

Plate 4

Fig. 8. Needlepoint lace. *Punto in aria*. Fritz Iklé Collection, reduced. — Fig. 9. The lace shewn in fig. 8, in original size.

Planche 4

Fig. 8. Dentelle à l'aiguille. Punto in aria. Collection Fritz Iklé. Figure réduite. — Fig. 9. La dentelle de la fig. 8, mais en grandeur naturelle.

Tavola 4

Fig. 8. Punto in aria. Raccolta Fritz Iklé, impiccolita. — Fig. 9. Merletto della fig. 8 in grandezza naturale.

8

9

4

Tafel 5

Abb. 10. Nähspitze. Punto in aria. Sammlung Fritz Iklé, verkleinert. — Abb. 11. Spitze Abb. 10 in natürlicher Größe.

Plate 5

Fig. 10. Needlepoint lace. *Punto in aria*. Fritz Iklé Collection, reduced. — Fig. 11. The lace shewn in fig. 10 in original size.

Planche 5

Fig. 10. Dentelle à l'aiguille. Punto in aria. Collection Fritz Iklé. Figure réduite. — Fig. 11. La dentelle de la fig. 10, mais en grandeur naturelle.

Tavola 5

Fig. 10. Punto in aria. Raccolta Fritz Iklé, impiccolita. — Fig. 11. Merletto della fig. 10 in grandezza naturale.

10

11

Tafel 6

Abb. 12. Nähspitze. Punto in aria. Sammlung Fritz Iklé, verkleinert. — Abb. 13. Nähspitze. Punto in aria. Sammlung Fritz Iklé, verkleinert. — Abb. 14. Nähspitze. Punto in aria. Sammlung Fritz Iklé, verkleinert.

Plate 6

Fig. 12. Needlepoint lace. *Punto in aria*. Fritz Iklé Collection, reduced. — Fig. 13. Needlepoint lace. *Punto in aria*. Fritz Iklé Collection, reduced. — Fig. 14. Needlepoint lace. *Punto in aria*. Fritz Iklé Collection, reduced.

Planche 6

Fig. 12. Dentelle à l'aiguille. Punto in aria. Collection Fritz Iklé. Figure réduite. — Fig. 13. Dentelle à l'aiguille. Punto in aria. Collection Fritz Iklé. Figure réduite. — Fig. 14. Dentelle à l'aiguille. Punto in aria. Collection Fritz Iklé. Figure réduite.

Tavola 6

Fig. 12. Punto in aria. Raccolta Fritz Iklé, impiccolita. — Fig. 13. Punto in aria, Raccolta Fritz Iklé, impiccolita. — Fig. 14. Punto in aria. Raccolta Fritz Iklé, impiccolita.

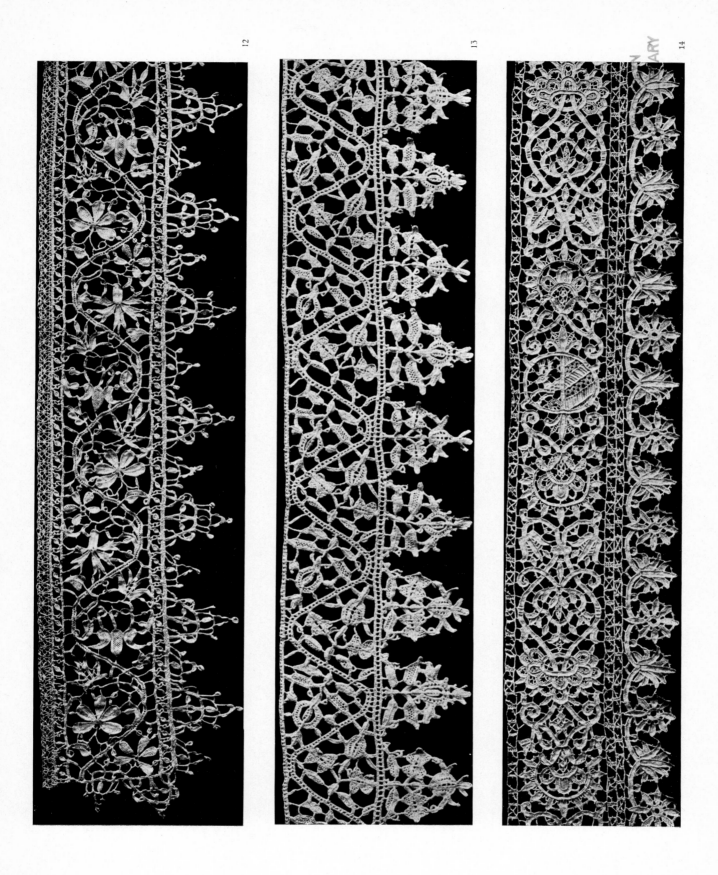

Tafel 7

Abb. 15. Nähspitze. Punto tagliato a fogliami, mit schwachem Relief, Sammlung Fritz Iklé. — Abb. 16. Nähspitze. Punto tagliato a fogliami, mit schwachem Relief. Sammlung Fritz Iklé.

Plate 7

Fig. 15. Needlepoint lace. *Punto tagliato a fogliami*, with low relief. Fritz Iklé Collection. Fig. 16. Needlepoint lace. *Punto tagliato a fogliami*, with low relief. Fritz Iklé Collection.

Planche 7

Fig. 15. Dentelle à l'aiguille. Punto tagliato a fogliami, faible relief. Collection Fritz Iklé. — Fig. 16. Dentelle à l'aiguille. Punto tagliato a fogliami, faible relief. Collection Fritz Iklé.

Tavola 7

Fig. 15. Punto tagliato a fogliami, con sottile rilievo, Raccolta Fritz Iklé. Fig. 16. Punto tagliato a fogliami con sottile rilievo. Raccolta Fritz Iklé.

15

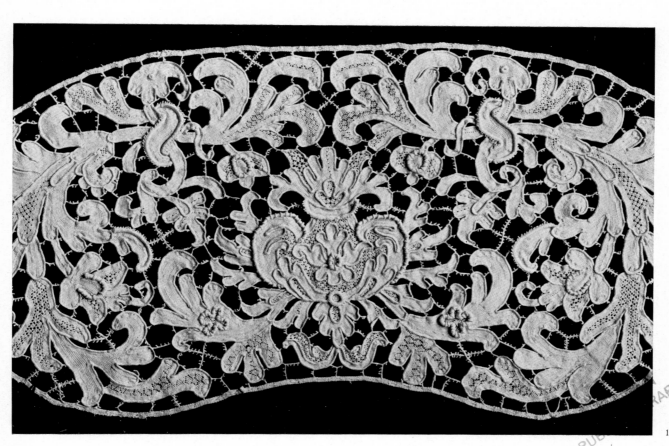

16

7

Tafel 8
Abb. 17. Nähspitze. Punto tagliato a fogliami, mit starkem Relief, natürliche Größe, Sammlung Fritz Iklé. — Abb. 18. Nähspitze, Rosaline, natürliche Größe, Sammlung Fritz Iklé.

Plate 8
Fig. 17. Needlepoint lace. *Punto tagliato a fogliami*, with strong relief, original size. Fritz Iklé Collection. —
Fig. 18. Needlepoint lace. *Rosellino*, original size. Fritz Iklé Collection.

Planche 8
Fig. 17. Dentelle à l'aiguille. Punto tagliato a fogliami, fort relief, en grandeur naturelle. Collection Fritz
Iklé. — Fig. 18. Dentelle à l'aiguille. Rosellino, en grandeur naturelle. Collection Fritz Iklé.

Tavola 8
Fig. 17. Punto tagliato a fogliami, con forte rilievo, grandezza naturale, raccolta Fritz Iklé. — Fig. 18.
Trina adago, Rosellino, grandezza naturale, raccolta Fritz Iklé.

17

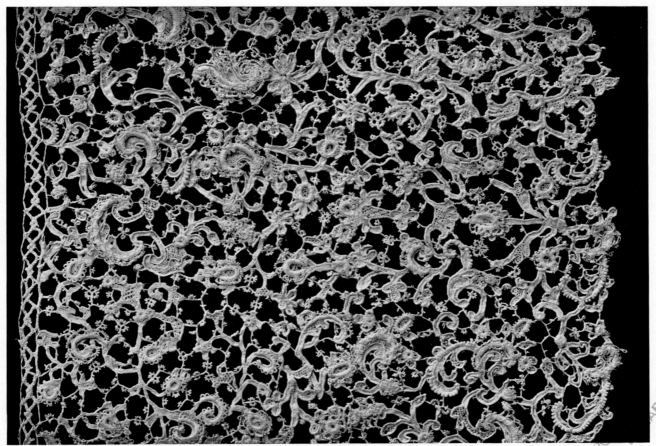

18

8

Tafel 9

Abb. 19. Nähspitze, Point plat de Venise, verkleinert. Sammlung Fritz Iklé. — Abb. 20. Teilstück der Spitze Abb. 19 in natürlicher Größe.

Plate 9

Fig. 19. Needlepoint lace. *Point plat de Venise*, reduced. Fritz Iklé Collection. — Fig. 20. Part of lace shewn in fig. 19 in original size.

Planche 9

Fig. 19. Dentelle à l'aiguille. Point plat de Venise. Figure réduite. Collection Fritz Iklé. — Fig. 20. Fragment de la dentelle de la fig. 19, mais en grandeur naturelle.

Tavola 9

Fig. 19. Punto di Venezia, impiccolita. Raccolta Fritz Iklé. — Fig. 20. Una parte della trina della fig. 19, in grandezza naturale.

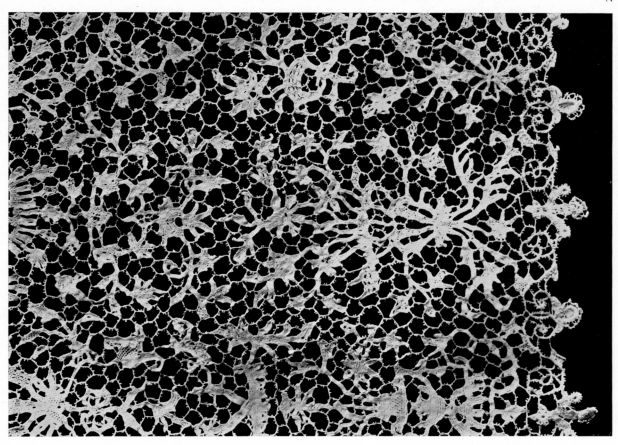

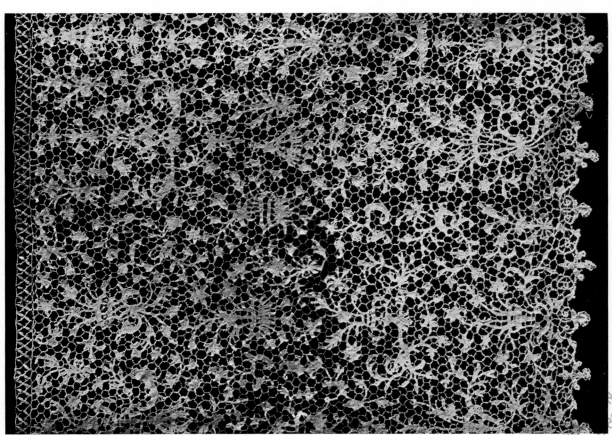

9

Tafel 10

Abb. 21. Nähspitze, Alençon in natürlicher Größe. — Abb. 22. Nähspitze, Alençon in natür=
licher Größe. Die Stege des Grundnetzes sind dicht mit Knopflochstichen besetzt. —
Abb. 23. Posamenterien. Klöppelarbeit, natürliche Größe.

Plate 10

Fig. 21. Needlepoint lace. Alençon, original size. — Fig. 22. Needlepoint lace. Alençon, original size. The
brides of the meshed ground are heavily trimmed with button=hole stitch. — Fig. 23. Passementeries, pillow
work, original size.

Planche 10

Fig. 21. Dentelle à l'aiguille. Point d'Alençon en grandeur naturelle. — Fig. 22. Dentelle à l'aiguille. Point
d'Alençon en grandeur naturelle. Les brides du fond de réseau sont garnies de points de boutonnière
serrés. — Fig. 23. Passementerie. Ouvrage aux fuseaux en grandeur naturelle.

Tavola 10

Fig. 21. Trina adago, Alençon, in grandezza naturale. — Fig. 22. Alençon in grandezza naturale. Le orlature
della rete son provviste di punto ad occhiello. — Fig. 23. Passamanterie. Lavoro a fuselli, grandezza naturale.

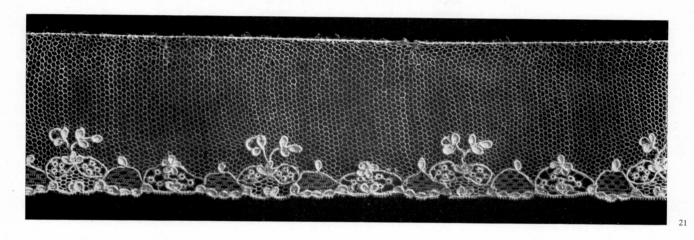

21

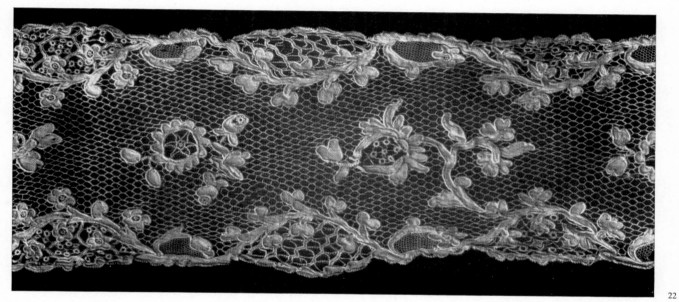

22

23

10

Tafel 11
Abb. 24. Klöppelzacken, natürliche Größe. — Abb. 25. Klöppelzacken, natürliche Größe.
— Abb. 26. Klöppelzacken, natürliche Größe.

Plate 11
Fig. 24. Pillow work scallops, original size. — Fig. 25. Pillow work scallops, original size. — Fig. 26. Pillow work callops, original size.

Planche 11
Fig. 24. Dentelle aux fuseaux en grandeur naturelle. — Fig. 25. Dentelle aux fuseaux en grandeur naturelle. — Fig. 26. Dentelle aux fuseaux en grandeur naturelle.

Tavola 11
Fig. 24. Dentellature a fuselli, grandezza naturale. — Fig. 25. Dentellature a fuselli, grandezza naturale. — Fig. 26. Dentellature a fuselli, grandezza naturale.

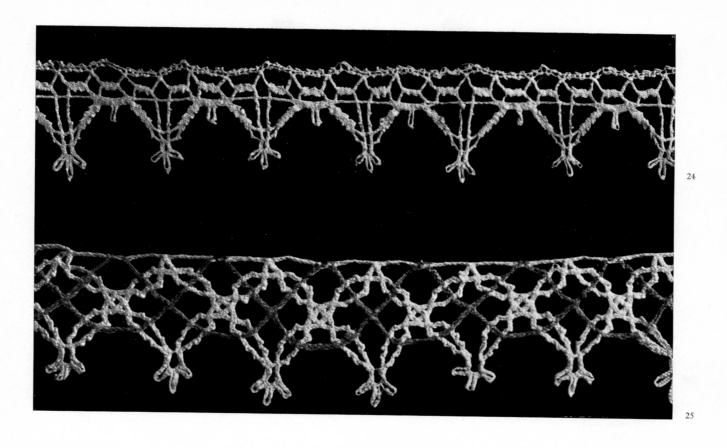

24

25

26

11

Tafel 12
Abb. 27. Runde flandrische Masche. — Abb. 28. Runde Valenciennesmasche.

Plate 12
Fig. 27. Round Flemish mesh. — Fig. 28. Round Valenciennes mesh.

Planche 12
Fig. 27. Maille ronde flamande. — Fig. 28. Maille ronde de Valenciennes.

Tavola 12
Fig. 27. Maglia rotonda di Fiandra. — Fig. 28. Maglia rotonda di Valenciennes.

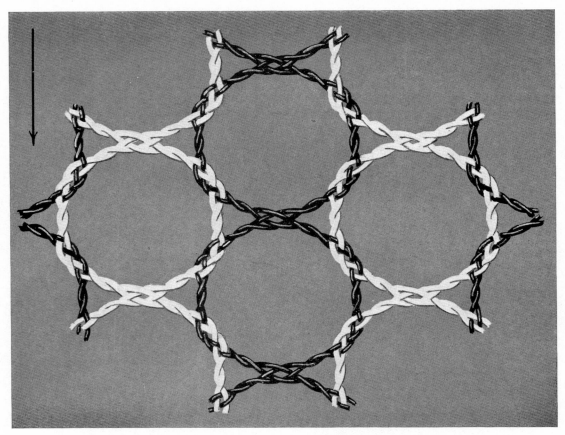

27

28

Tafel 13
Abb. 29. Mechelner Grund. Eisgrond. — Abb. 30. Droschelgrund.

Plate 13
Fig. 29. Mechlin *réseau*. Eisgrond. — Fig. 30. Droschel *réseau*.

Planche 13
Fig. 29. Le réseau de Malines. L' «Eisgrond». — Fig. 30. Le réseau Droschel.

Tavola 13
Fig. 29. Fondo di Malines. Eisgrond. — Fig. 30. Fondo Droschel.

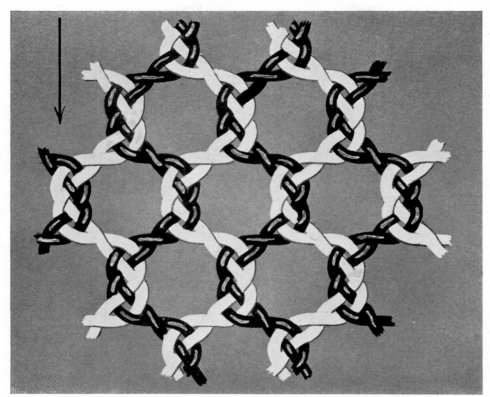

29

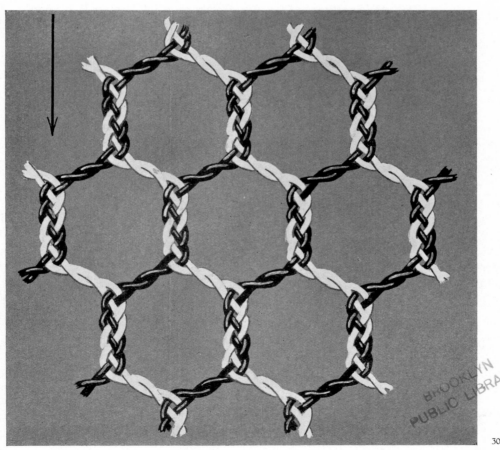

30

13

Tafel 14

Abb. 31. Muster aus Cesare Vecellio „Corona delle nobili et virtuose donne", Venedig 1591. — Abb. 32 dgl.

Plate 14

Fig. 31. Pattern from Cesare Vecellio "Corona delle nobili et virtuose donne". Venice 1591. — Fig. 32 ditto.

Planche 14

Fig. 31. Dessin de Cesare Vecellio «Corona delle nobili et virtuose donne», Venise, 1591. — Fig. 32 Id.

Tavola 14

Fig. 31. Disegno tolto dalla «Corona delle nobili e virtuose donne» di Cesare Vecellio, Venezia 1591. — Fig. 32 idem.

31

32

14

Tafel 15
Abb. 33, 34. Muster aus Cesare Vecellio „Corona delle nobili et virtuose donne", Venedig 1591.
Eine in der Art des Musters Abb. 34 ausgeführte Klöppelspitze. s. Tafel 90.

Plate 15
Fig. 33 ditto. Fig. 34. ditto. For a pillow lace carried out in the same way as this pattern see Plate 90.

Planche 15
Fig. 33 Id. — Fig. 34. Id. — Une dentelle aux fuseaux exécutée dans le genre de ce patron. Cf. Pl. 90.

Tavola 15
Fig. 33 idem. Fig. 34 idem. Una trina a fuselli eseguito nel genere di questo disegno. Vedasi Tavola 90.

33

34

15

Tafel 16
Abb. 35. Rubens. Jaqueline von Caestre, um 1617/1618. Brüssel, Photogr. Bruckmann.
Klöppelspitze in den Formen der Reticella.

Plate 16
Fig. 35. Rubens. Jaqueline de Caestrie, ca. 1617/1618. Brussels. Photo Bruckmann. Pillow lace in the
Reticella style.

Planche 16
Fig. 35. Rubens. Jacqueline de Caestrie, vers 1617/1618. Bruxelles. Photogr. Bruckmann. Dentelle aux
fuseaux genre reticella.

Tavola 16
Fig. 35. Rubens. Jacqueline di Caestrie, verso il 1617—1618. Bruxelles. Fotografia Bruckmann. Trina
a fuselli su disegno per reticello.

16

Tafel 17
Abb. 36. Gerard Doufeet. Weibliches Bildnis, um 1617. München. Potogr. Klöppelspitzen mit Andeutung von symmetrischen Blatt= oder Blütenformen.

Plate 17
Fig. 36. Gerard Doufeet. Feminine portrait, about 1617. Munich. Pillow lace with suggestion of symme= trical leaf= or flower designs.

Planche 17
Fig. 36. Gérard Doufeet. Portrait de femme, vers 1617. Munich. Dentelles aux fuseaux avec esquisse de fleurs et feuilles disposées avec symétrie.

Tavola 17
Fig. 36. Gerard Doufeet. Ritratto di donna, verso il 1617. Monaco di Baviera. Trine a fuselli con accenni di fiori e fogliami simmetrici.

36

17

Tafel 18
Abb. 37. Paulus Moreelse. 1571—1638. Weibliches Bildnis. Berlin. Photogr. Hanfstängel.
Klöppelspitzen. Die Zacken nehmen ausgeprägtere Pflanzenformen an.

Plate 18
Fig. 37. Paulus Moreelse. 1571—1638. Feminine portrait. Berlin. Photo Hanfstängel. Pillow lace. The
scallops develop distinctly to plant motifs.

Planche 18
Fig. 37. Paulus Moreelse. 1571—1638. Portrait de femme. Berlin. Photogr. Hanfstängel. Dentelle aux
fuseaux. Les motifs commencent á prendre des formes végétales.

Tavola 18
Fig. 37. Paulus Moreelse. 1571—1638. Ritratto di donna. Berlino. Fotografia Hanfstängel. Trine a fuselli.
Le punte assumono una più spiccata forma di piante.

37

18

Tafel 19
Abb. 38. Rembrandt. Weibliches Bildnis 1633. Braunschweig. Photogr. Bruckmann. Klöppel=
spitze mit regelmäßig ausgebildeten, um senkrechte Achsen gruppierten Blattmotiven.

Plate 19
Fig. 38. Rembrandt. Feminine portrait 1633. Brunswick. Photo Bruckmann. Pillow lace with regularly
developed leaf motifs grouped on perpendicular axes.

Planche 19
Fig. 38. Rembrandt. Portrait de femme, 1633. Brunswick. Dentelle aux fuseaux. Motif: feuilles formées
régulièrement et groupées autour d'axes verticaux.

Tavola 19
Fig. 38. Rembrandt. Ritratto di donna 1633. Braunschweig. Trina a fuselli con motivi di fogliami
regolarmente sviluppati su assi verticali.

38

19

Tafel 20
Abb. 39. Van Dyck. Karl I. von England, um 1632. Dresden. Klöppelspitzen mit weitaus≠ladenden Zacken, um senkrechte Achsen gruppierte Blattmotive.

Plate 20
Fig. 39. Van Dyck. Charles I of England, about 1632. Dresden. Pillow lace with widely projecting scallops, leaf motifs grouped on perpendicular axes.

Planche 20
Fig. 39. Van Dyck. Charles Ier d'Angleterre, vers 1632. Dresde. Dentelles aux fuseaux à dents en large saillie. Motif: feuilles groupées autour d'axes verticaux.

Tavola 20
Fig. 39. Van Dyck. Carlo I d'Inghilterra verso, il 1632. Dresda. Trine a fuselli con dentellatura larga e con motivi di fogliami regolarmente sviluppati su assi verticali.

39

20

Tafel 21
Abb. 40. Jan Verspronk. Weibliches Bildnis, um 1653 München. Klöppelspitze, um senkrechte Achsen gruppierte Pflanzenmotive. Die Teile des Ornamentes sind durch eine Art Grund=netz miteinander verbunden.

Plate 21
Fig. 40. Jan Verspronk. Feminine portrait, about 1653. Munich. Pillow lace with plant motifs grouped on perpendicular axes. The parts of the ornament are connected by a kind of *réseau*.

Planche 21
Fig. 40. Jan Verspronck. Portrait de femme, vers 1653. Munich. Dentelle aux fuseaux. Motif: formes végé=tales groupées autour d'axes verticaux. Les parties de l'ornementation sont reliées entre elles par une sorte de fond de réseau.

Tavola 21
Fig. 40. Jan Verspronk. Ritratto di donna verso il 1653. Trine a fuselli, motivi di piante aggruppati attorno ad assi verticali. Le parti ornamentali sono congiunte fra di loro mediante una specie di rete di fondo.

40

21

Tafel 22
Abb. 41. Velasquez. Maria Anna von Österreich, um 1658/1660. Madrid. Die Textur der Spitzen ist so dicht, daß die Zeichnung des Ornaments verschwindet. Die Art dieser Spitzen gibt Tafel 25 Abb. 45 wieder: Um senkrechte Achsen angeordnete Pflanzenmotive sind ganz nahe aneinandergerückt.

Plate 22
Fig. 41. Velasquez. Maria Anna of Austria, ca. 1658/1660. Madrid. The texture of the lace is so close that the design of the ornament disappears. Plate 25, fig. 45 shews this type of lace: plant motifs about perpendicular axes are worked quite close together.

Planche 22
Fig. 41. Vélasquez. Marie Anne d'Autriche, vers 1658—1660. Madrid. La texture est si serrée que les contours de l'ornementation disparaissent. La pl. 25, fig. 45 montre le genre de ces dentelles. Des formes végétales disposées autour d'axes verticaux se rapprochent étroitement.

Tavola 22
Fig. 41. Velasquez. Maria Anna d'Austria, verso il 1658—1660. Madrid. Trine a fuselli.

41

22

Tafel 23

Abb. 42. B. van der Helst. Weibliches Bildnis. 1649. München. Pinakothek. Photogr. Hanf=
stängel. Klöppelspitzen. Siehe Bemerkung zu Tafel 22.

Plate 23

Fig. 42. B. van der Helst. Feminine portrait. 1469. Munich. Photo Hanfstängel. Pillow lace. See remark
to Pl. 22.

Planche 23.

Fig. 42. B. van der Helst. Portrait de femme. 1649. Munich. Photogr. Hanfstängel. Dentelle aux fuseaux
et remarque à la planche 22.

Tavola 23

Fig. 42. B. van der Helst. Rittratto di donna. 1649. Monaco di Baviera. Fotografia Hanfstängel. Trine
a fuselli. Ved. osserv. Tavola 22.

42

23

Tafel 24
Abb. 43. Jeaurat. Zusammenkunft der Könige von Spanien und Frankreich auf der Fasanen=
insel 1660.

Plate 24
Fig. 43. Jeaurat. Meeting of the King of France and King of Spain on the Ile des Fasanes 1660.

Planche 24
Fig. 43. Jeaurat. La rencontre des rois d'Espagne et de France dans l'île des faisans, 1660.

Tavola 24
Fig. 43. Jeaurat. Convegno dei Re di Spagna e di Francia nell'Isola dei Fagiani. 1660.

24

Tafel 25

Abb. 44. Flandrische Klöppelspitze. Zweites Drittel 17. Jahrhunderts, Van-Dyck-Spitze. — Abb. 45. Flandrische Klöppelspitze. Mitte 17. Jahrhundert. Velasquez-Spitze. — Abb. 46. Flandrische Klöppelspitze. Letztes Drittel 17. Jahrhunderts. In einem Zuge gearbeitet.

Plate 25

Fig. 44. Flemish pillow lace. Second third of 17th Century. Van Dyck lace. — Fig. 45. Flemish pillow lace. Middle of 17th Century. Velasquez lace. — Fig. 46. Flemish pillow lace. Last third of 17th Century. Worked in one piece.

Planche 25

Fig. 44. Dentelle flamande aux fuseaux. Deuxième tiers du XVIIe siècle. Dentelle de Van Dyck. — Fig. 45. Dentelle flamande aux fuseaux. Milieu du XVIIe siècle. Dentelle de Vélasquez. — Fig. 46. Dentelle flamande aux fuseaux. Dernier tiers du XVIIe siècle. Faite d'une pièce.

Tavola 25

Fig. 44. Trina a fuselli di Fiandra. Secondo terzo del Sec. XVII. Trina Van Dyck. — Fig. 45. Trina a fuselli di Fiandra. Metà del Sec. XVII. Trina Velasquez. — Fig. 46. Trina a fuselli di Fiandra. Ultimo terzo del Sec. XVII. Tutto d'un pezzo.

44

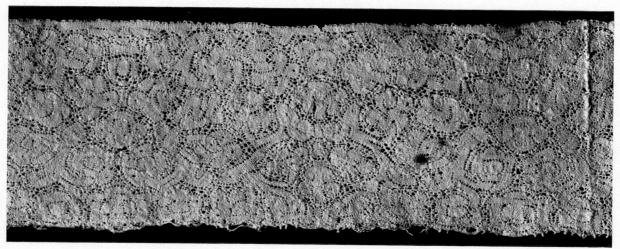

45

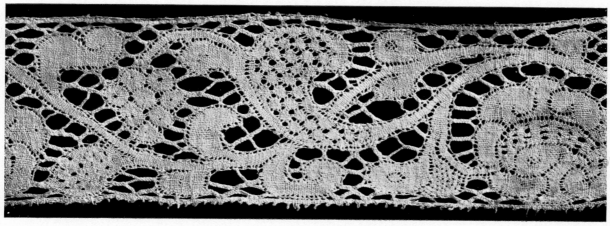

46

25

Tafel 26
Abb. 47. Mailänder Klöppelspitze. Sammlung Fritz Iklé, verkleinert. Das mit Ziernetzen reich=
gefüllte Ornament hebt sich ohne Stegverbindung klar vom Grunde ab. — Abb. 48. Teilstück der Spitze
Abb. 47, in natürlicher Größe.

Plate 26
Fig. 47. Milan pillow lace. Fritz Iklé Collection, reduced. The ornament with its richly decorated mesh
stands out in clear relief from the ground without being joined up by *brides*. — Fig. 48. Part of lace
shewn in fig. 47, original size.

Planche 26
Fig. 47. Dentelle de Milan aux fuseaux. Collection Fritz Iklé. Figure réduite. L'ornementation bien remplie
par des réseaux d'ornement se détache nettement du fond sans aucune barette. — Fig. 48. Fragment
de la dentelle de la fig. 47, mais en grandeur naturelle.

Tavola 26
Fig. 47. Trina a fuselli di Milano. Raccolta Fritz Iklé, impiccolita. — Fig. 48. Particolari della trina fig. 47,
in grandezza naturale.

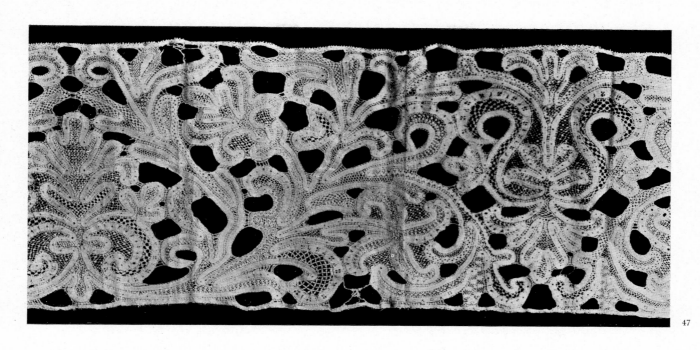

47

48

26

Tafel 27
Abb. 49. Mailänder Klöppelspitze. Von Gräfin Valerie Luxburg, Palermo. Verkleinert.—Abb. 50.
Teilstück der Spitze Abb. 49 in natürlicher Größe.

Plate 27
Fig. 49. Milan pillow lace. From Countess Valerie Luxburg, Palermo. Reduced. — Fig. 50. Part of lace
shewn in fig. 49, original size.

Planche 27
Fig. 49. Dentelle de Milan aux fuseaux. Provenant de Madame la Comtesse Valerie Luxburg, de Palerme.
Figure réduite. — Fig. 50. Fragment de la dentelle fig. 49, mais en grandeur naturelle.

Tavola 27
Fig. 49. Trina a fuselli di Milano. Della contessa Valeria Luxburg, Palermo. Impiccolita. — Fig. 50. Pezzo
della trina fig. 49 in grandezza naturale.

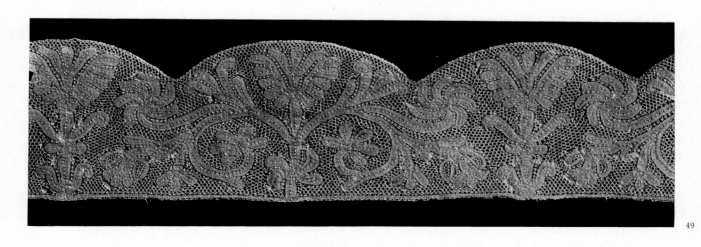

49

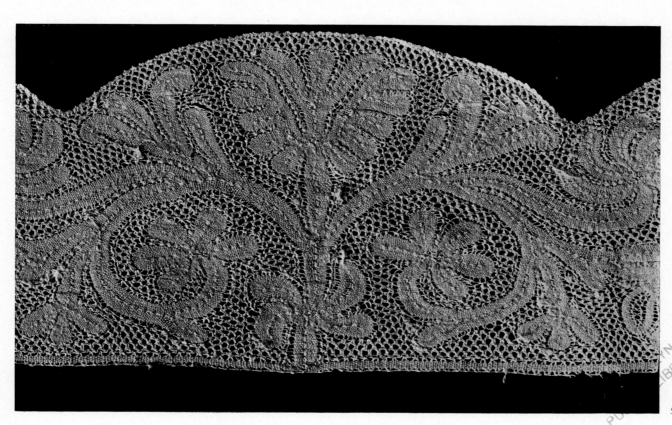

50

27

Tafel 28

Abb. 51. Valenciennesspitze 17. Jahrhunderts, in natürlicher Größe. Sammlung Fritz Iklé. Hochbarock der Klöppelspitze. — Abb. 52. Valenciennesspitze 17. Jahrhunderts, in natürlicher Größe. Von Frau Andree, Berchtesgaden. Hochbarock der Klöppelspitze. — Abb. 53. Valenciennesspitze 17. Jahrhunderts, in natürlicher Größe. Hochbarock der Klöppelspitze.

Plate 28

Fig. 51. 17th Century Valenciennes lace, original size. Fritz Iklé Collection. High Baroque pillow lace. — Fig. 52. 17th Century Valenciennes lace, original size. From Frau Andree, Berchtesgaden. High Baroque pillow lace. — Fig. 53. 17th Century Valenciennes lace, original size. High Baroque pillow lace.

Planche 28

Fig. 51. Dentelle de Valenciennes. XVIIᵉ siècle. Grandeur naturelle. Collection Fritz Iklé. Haut baroque de la dentelle aux fuseaux. — Fig. 52. Dentelle de Valenciennes. XVIIᵉ siècle. Grandeur naturelle. Provenant de Madame Andree, de Berchtesgaden. Haut baroque de la dentelle aux fuseaux. — Fig. 53. Dentelle de Valenciennes. XVIIᵉ siècle. Grandeur naturelle. Haut baroque de la dentelle aux fuseaux.

Tavola 28

Fig. 51. Trina di Valenciennes, Secolo XVII, in grandezza naturale. Raccolta Fritz Iklé. Pieno barocco dei trine a fuselli. — Fig. 52. Trina di Valenciennes, Secolo XVII, in grandezza naturale. Della signora Andree, Berchtesgaden. Pieno barocco dei trine a fuselli. — Fig. 53. Trina di Valenciennes, Sec. XVII, in grandezza naturale. Trina a fusilli in pieno barocco.

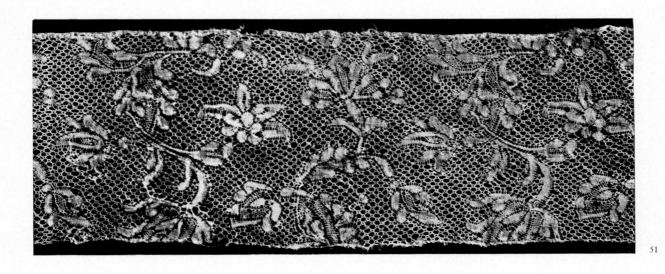

51

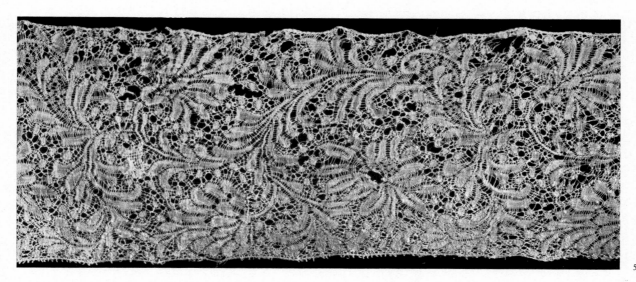

52

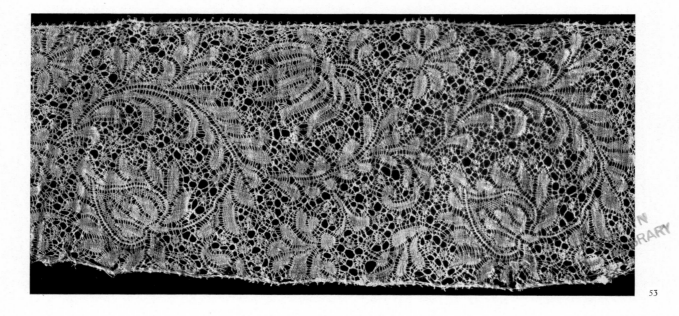

53

Tafel 29

Abb. 54. Valenciennesspitze 17. Jahrhunderts, in natürlicher Größe. Hochbarock der Klöppelspitze. — Abb. 55. Binche 2061, natürliche Größe. 1. Spätbarock, Mitte Louis XIV.

Plate 29

Fig. 54. 17th Century Valenciennes lace, original size. High Baroque pillow lace. — Fig. 55. Binche 2061, original size. 1. Late Baroque, middle Louis XIV period.

Planche 29

Fig. 54. Dentelle de Valenciennes. XVIIe siècle. Grandeur naturelle. Haut baroque de la dentelle aux fuseaux. — Fig. 55. Binche 2061 en grandeur naturelle. 1er baroque tardif de la dentelle. Milieu du Louis XIV.

Tavola 29

Fig. 54. Trina di Valenciennes, Sec. XVII, in grandezza naturale. Trine a fuselli in pieno barocco. — Fig. 55. Binche 2061, grandezza naturale. 1. Tardo barocco, metá Luigi XIV.

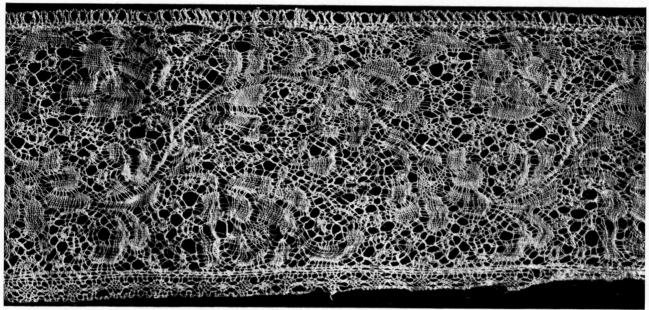

54

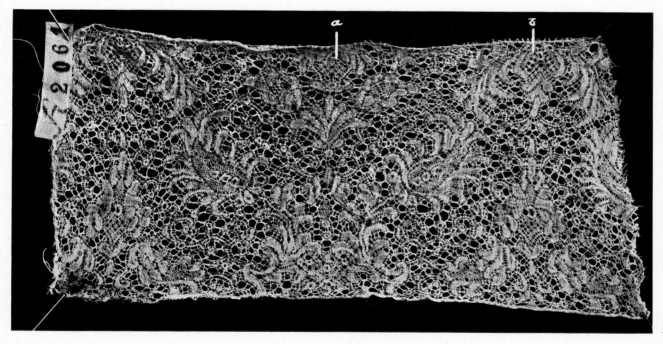

55

29

Tafel 30
Abb. 56. Binche. Von Baronin Speidel‹Pocci, Berlin, natürliche Größe. 1. Spätbarock, Mitte Louis XIV. — Abb. 57. Binche. Sammlung Fritz Iklé› natürliche Größe. 1. Spätbarock. Mitte Louis XIV. — Abb. 58. Binche, natürliche Größe. 1. Spätbarock. Mitte Louis XIV.

Plate 30
Fig. 56. Binche. From Baroness Speidel‹Pocci, Berlin, original size, 1. Late Baroque, mid‹Louis XIV period. — Fig. 57. Binche. Fritz Iklé Collection, original size. 1. Late Baroque, mid‹Louis XIV period. — Fig. 58. Binche, original size. 1. Late Baroque. Mid‹Louis XIV period.

Planche 30
Fig. 56. Binche. Appartenant à Madame la Baronne Speidel‹Pocci, de Berlin. Grandeur naturelle. 1er baroque tardif de la dentelle. Milieu du Louis XIV. — Fig. 57. Binche. Collection Fritz Iklé. Grandeur naturelle. 1er baroque tardif de la dentelle. Milieu du Louis XIV. — Fig. 58. Binche en grandeur naturelle. 1er baroque tardif de la dentelle, Milieu du Louis XIV.

Tavola 30
Fig. 56. Binche. Della baronessa Speidel‹Pocci, Berlino, grandezza naturale. 1. Tardo barocco, metà Luigi XIV. — Fig. 57. Binche. Raccolta Fritz Iklé, grandezza naturale. 1. Tardo barocco. Metà Luigi XIV. — Fig. 58. Binche, grandezza naturale. 1. Tardo barocco. Metà Luigi XIV.

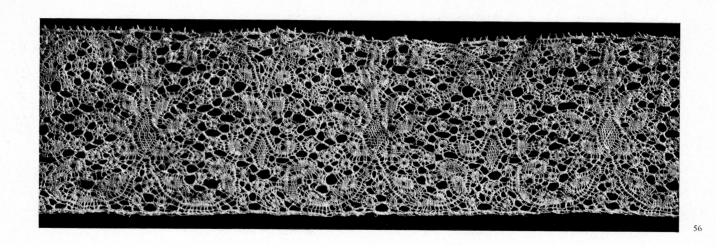

56

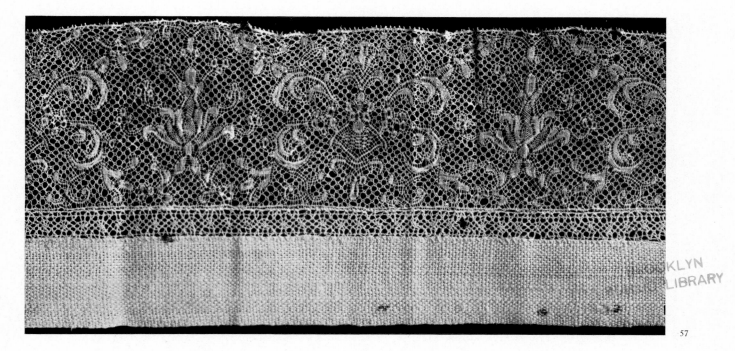

57

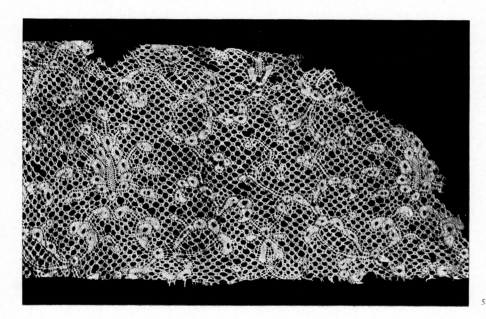

58

Tafel 31

Abb. 59. Binche 202, natürliche Größe. 2. Spätbarock. Ende Louis XIV. — Abb. 60. Binche 203, natürliche Größe. 2. Spätbarock. Ende Louis XIV. — Abb. 61. Binche 204, natürliche Größe. 2. Spätbarock. Ende Louis XIV.

Plate 31

Fig. 59. Binche 202, original size. 2. Late Baroque, end of Louis XIV period. — Fig. 60. Binche 203, original size. 2. Late Baroque. End of Louis XIV period. — Fig. 61. Binche 204, original size. 2. Late Baroque. End of Louis XIV period.

Planche 31

Fig. 59. Binche 202. Grandeur naturelle. 2e baroque tardif de la dentelle. Fin du Louis XIV. — Fig. 60. Binche 203 en grandeur naturelle. 2e baroque tardif de la dentelle. Fin du Louis XIV. — Fig. 61. Binche 204 en grandeur naturelle. 2e baroque tardif de la dentelle. Fin du Louis XIV.

Tavola 31

Fig. 59. Binche 202, grandezza naturale. 2. Tardo barocco. Fine Luigi XIV. — Fig. 60. Binche 203, grandezza naturale. 2. Tardo barocco. Fine Luigi XIV. — Fig. 61. Binche 204, grandezza naturale. 2. Tardo barocco. Fine Luigi XIV.

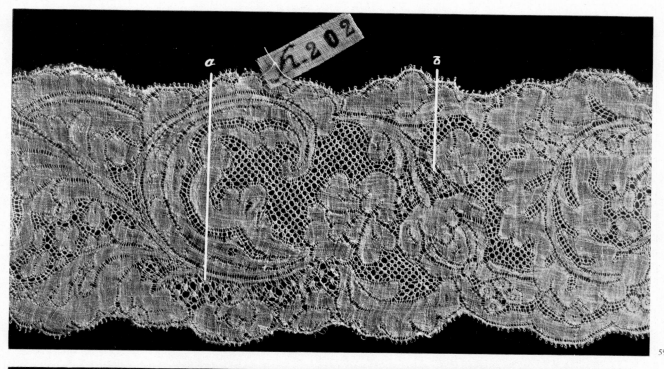

a　　5202　　*b*

59

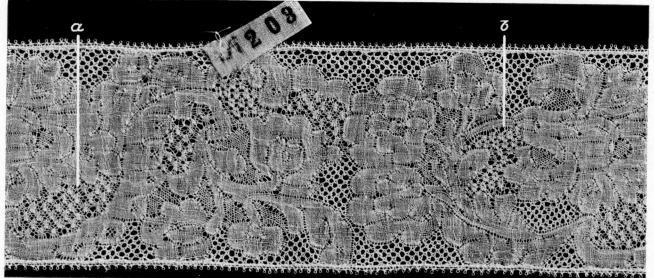

a　　5203　　*b*

60

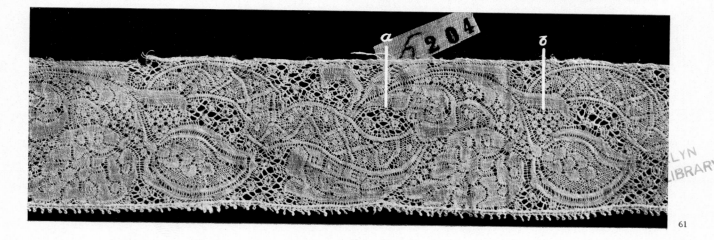

a　　5204　　*b*

61

31

Tafel 32
Abb. 62. Brüsseler Klöppelspitze 3034, natürliche Größe. 2. Spätbarock. Ende Louis XIV.
— Abb. 63. Brüsseler Klöppelspitze 3031, natürliche Größe. 2. Spätbarock. Ende Louis XIV.
— Abb. 64. Brüsseler Klöppelspitze 3033, natürliche Größe. 2. Spätbarock. Ende Louis XIV.

Plate 32
Fig. 62. Brussels pillow lace 3034, original size. 2. Late Baroque. End of Louis XIV period. — Fig. 63.
Brussels pillow lace 3031, original size. 2. Late Baroque. End of Louis XIV period. — Fig. 64. Brussels
pillow lace 3033, original size, 2 Late Baroque. End of Louis XIV period.

Planche 32
Fig. 62. Dentelle de Bruxelles aux fuseaux 3034. Grandeur naturelle. 2e baroque tardif de la dentelle.
Fin du Louis XIV. — Fig. 63. Dentelle de Bruxelles aux fuseaux 3031. Grandeur naturelle. 2e baroque
tardif, de la dentelle. Fin du Louis XIV. — Fig. 64. Dentelle de Bruxelles aux fuseaux 3033. Grandeur
naturelle. 2e baroque tardif de la dentelle. Fin du Louis XIV.

Tavola 32
Fig. 62. Trina a fuselli di Bruxelles 3034, grandezza naturale. 2. Tardo barocco. Fine Luigi XIV. — Fig. 63.
Trina a fuselli di Bruxelles 3031, grandezza naturale. 2. Tardo barocco. Fine Luigi XIV. — Fig. 64. Trina
a fuselli di Bruxelles 3033, grandezza naturale. 2. Tardo barocco. Fine Luigi XIV.

62

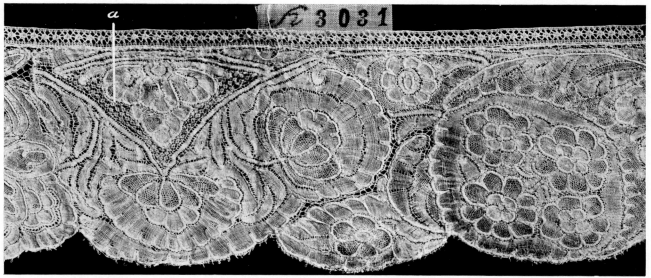

63

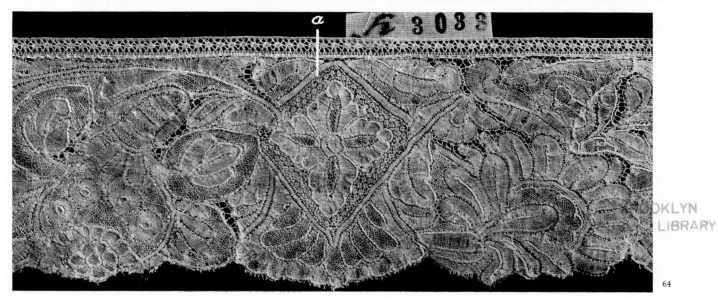

64

32

Tafel 33

Abb. 65. Binche 205, natürliche Größe. 2. Spätbarock. Ende Louis XIV. — Abb. 66. Brüsseler Klöppelspitze mit Steggrund. Domkirche in Eichstätt. Verkleinert. 2. Spätbarock. Ende Louis XIV. Breite 61 cm.

Plate 33

Fig. 65. Binche 205, original size. 2. Late Baroque. End of Louis XIV period. — Fig. 66. Brussels pillow lace with "bride-ground". Cathedral Church at Eichstätt. Reduced. 2. Late Baroque. End of Louis XIV period. Breadth 61 cm.

Planche 33

Fig. 65. Binche 205 en grandeur naturelle. 2ᵉ baroque tardif de la dentelle. Fin du Louis XIV. — Fig. 66. Dentelle de Bruxelles aux fuseaux avec fond à barrettes. Cathédrale d'Eichstätt. Figure réduite. 2ᵉ baroque tardif de la dentelle. Fin du Louis XIV. Largeur 61 c/m.

Tavola 33

Fig. 65. Binche 205, grandezza naturale. 2. Tardo barocco. Fine Luigi XIV. — Fig. 66. Trina a fuselli di Bruxelles con fondo ad orlatura. Duomo di Eichstätt. Impiccolita. 2. Tardo barocco. Fine Luigi XIV. Larghezza 61 cm.

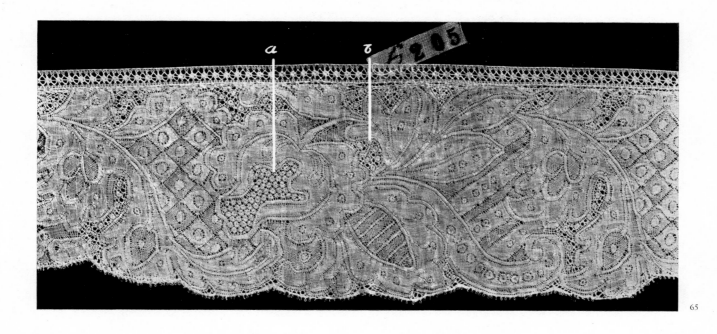

65

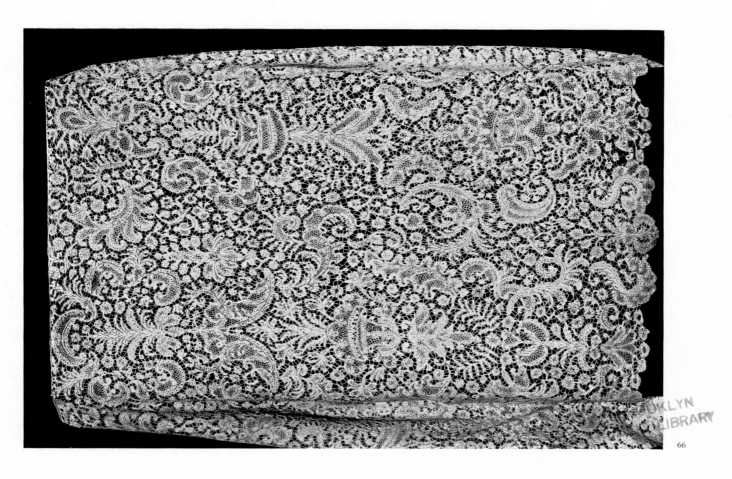

66

33

Tafel 34

Abb. 68. Brüsseler Klöppelspitze 302. Zwei zu einer Krawatte zusammengenähte Barben. Verkleinert. 2. Spätbarock. Ende Louis XIV. — Abb. 67. Teilstück der Spitze Abb. 68 in natür= licher Größe.

Plate 34

Fig. 68. Brussels pillow lace. 302. Two lace lappets shewn together to make a *jabot*. Reduced. 2. Late Baroque. End of Louis XIV period. — Fig. 67. Part of lace shewn in Fig. 68, original size.

Planche 34

Fig. 68. Dentelle de Bruxelles aux fuseaux 302. Deux barbes cousues en cravate. Figure réduite. 2e baroque tardif de la dentelle. Fin du Louis XIV. — Fig. 67. Fragment de la dentelle fig. 68, mais en gran= deur naturelle.

Tavola 34

Fig. 68. Trine a fuselli di Bruxelles 302. Due strisce di pizzi formanti una caratta. Impiccolita. 2. Tardo barocco. Fine Luigi XIV. — Fig. 67. Parte della trina fig. 68 in grandezza naturale.

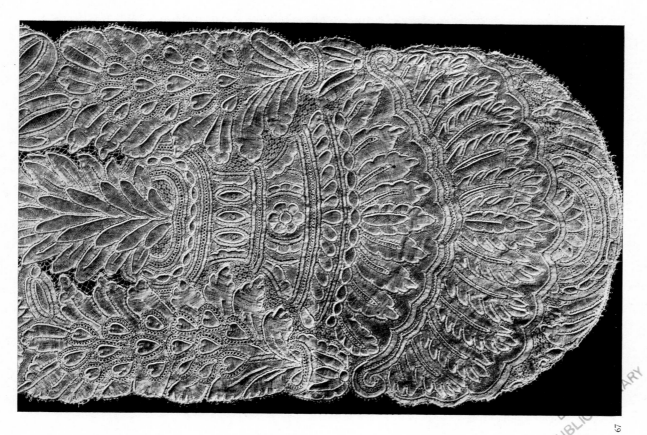

34

Tafel 35
Abb. 69. Brüsseler Klöppelspitze aus dem Wittelsbachischen Taufschatz. Verkleinert. 3.
Spätbarock. Régence. Breite 59 cm. Aufnahme vom Residenzmuseum, München. — Abb. 70.
Teilstück der Spitze Abb. 69 in natürlicher Größe.

Plate 35
Fig. 69. Brussels pillow lace from the Wittelsbach christening treasure. Reduced. 3. Late Baroque. Regency
period. Breadth 59 cm. Photograph by the Residenzmuseum, Munich. — Fig. 70. Part of lace shewn in
fig. 69, original size.

Planche 35
Fig. 69. Dentelle de Bruxelles aux fuseaux. Pièce du Trésor de baptême de la maison de Wittelsbach.
Figure réduite. 3e baroque tardif de la dentelle. Régence. Largeur 59 c/m. — Fig. 70. Fragment de la dentelle
fig. 69, mais en grandeur naturelle.

Tavola 35
Fig. 69. Trina a fuselli di Bruxelles del tesoro battesimale dei Wittelsbach. Impiccolita. 3. Tardo barocco.
Reggence. Larghezza 59 cm. Fotographia del Museo della Residenza, Monaco di Baviera. — Fig. 70. Parte
della trina fig. 69 in grandezza naturale.

69

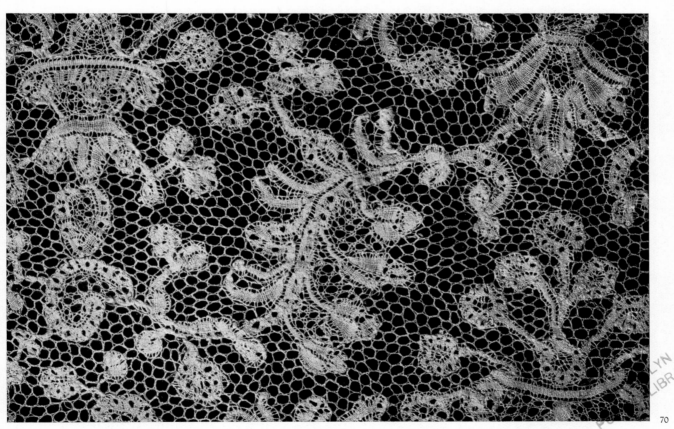

70

Tafel 36

Abb. 72. Brüsseler Klöppelspitze 261, natürliche Größe. 3. Spätbarock. Régence. — Abb. 71. Brüsseler Klöppelspitze. Domkirche in Eichstätt. Verkleinert. 3. Spätbarock. Régence. Breite 59 cm.

Plate 36

Fig. 72. Brussels pillow lace 261, original size. 3. Late Baroque. Regency period. — Fig. 71. Brussels pillow lace. Cathedral Church at Eichstätt. Reduced. 3. Late Baroque Regency Period. Breadth 59 cm.

Planche 36

Fig. 72. Dentelle de Bruxelles aux fuseaux 261. Grandeur naturelle. 3ᵉ baroque tardif. Régence. — Fig. 71. Dentelle de Bruxelles aux fuseaux. Cathédrale d'Eichstätt. Figure réduite. 3ᵉ baroque tardif de la dentelle. Régence. Largeur 59 c/m.

Tavola 36

Fig. 72. Trina a fuselli di Bruxelles 261, grandezza naturale. 3. Tardo barocco. Reggenze. — Fig. 71. Trina a fuselli di Bruxelles. Duomo di Eichstätt. Impiccolita. 3. Tardo barocco. Reggenze. Larghezza 59 cm. Fotographia del Landesamt bavarese per la manutenzione dei monumenti, Monaco di Baviera.

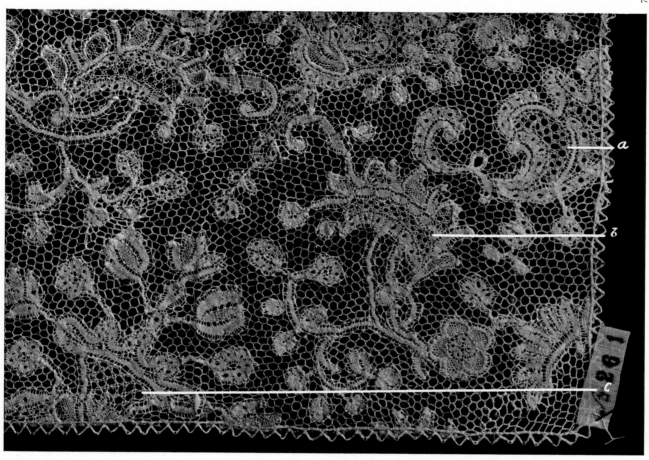

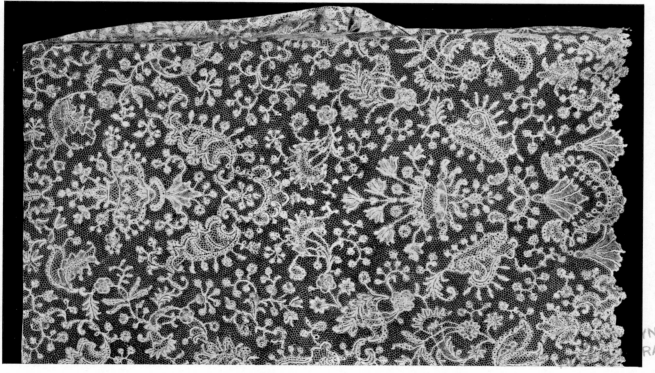

36

Tafel 37

Abb. 73. Brabanter Klöppelspitze aus dem Wittelsbachischen Taufschatz. Verkleinert. 3. Spätbarock. Régence. Breite 38 cm. — Abb. 74. Teilstück der Spitze Abb. 73 in natürlicher Größe.

Plate 37

Fig. 73. Brabant pillow lace from the Wittelsbach christening treasure. Reduced. 3. Late Baroque. Regency. Breadth 38 cm. — Fig. 74. Part of lace shewn in fig. 73, original size.

Planche 37

Fig. 73. Dentelle de Brabant aux fuseaux. Pièce du Trésor de baptême de la maison de Wittelsbach. Réduction. 3e baroque tardif de la dentelle. Régence. Largeur: 38 c/m. — Fig. 74. Fragment de la dentelle fig. 73, mais en grandeur naturelle.

Tavola 37

Fig. 73. Trina a fuselli del Brabante, appartenente al tesoro battesimale dei Wittelsbach. Impiccolita. 3. Tardo barocco. Reggenza. Larghezza 38 cm. Fotografia del Museo della Residenza, Monaco. — Fig. 74. Particolare di merletto della fig. 73, in grandezza naturale.

73

74

Tafel 38
Abb. 75. Mechelner Spitze 105. Natürliche Größe. 3. Spätbarock. Régence. — Abb. 76. Brüsseler
Klöppelspitze aus dem Wittelsbachischen Taufschatz. Stark verkleinert. 4. Spätbarock.
Rokoko. Breite 58 cm, Länge 414 cm.

Plate 38
Fig. 74. Mechlin lace 105. Original size. 3. Late Baroque. Regency. — Fig. 76. Brussels pillow lace from
the Wittelsbach christening treasure. Greatly reduced. 4. Late Baroque. Breadth 58 cm, length 414 cm.

Planche 38
Fig. 75. Dentelle de Malines 105 en grandeur naturelle. 3e baroque tardif de la dentelle. Régence. —
Fig. 75. Dentelle de Bruxelles aux fuseaux. Pièce du Trésor de baptême de la maison de Wittelsbach.
Figure très réduite. 4e baroque tardif de la dentelle. Rococo Largeur: 58 c/m. Longueur: 414 c/m.

Tavola 38
Fig. 75. Trina di Malines 105. Grandezza naturale. 3. Tardo barocco. Reggenza. — Fig. 76. Trina a fu=
selli di Bruxelles appartenente al tesoro battesimale dei Wittelsbach. Molto rimpiccolita. 4. Tardo barocco.
Roccocò. Larghezza 58cm, lunghezza 414 cm. Riprodotto dal Museo della Residenza, Monaco.

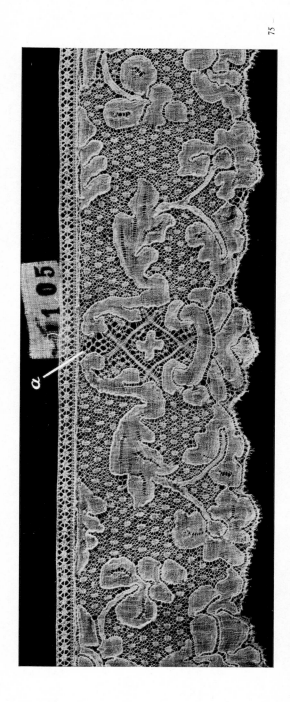

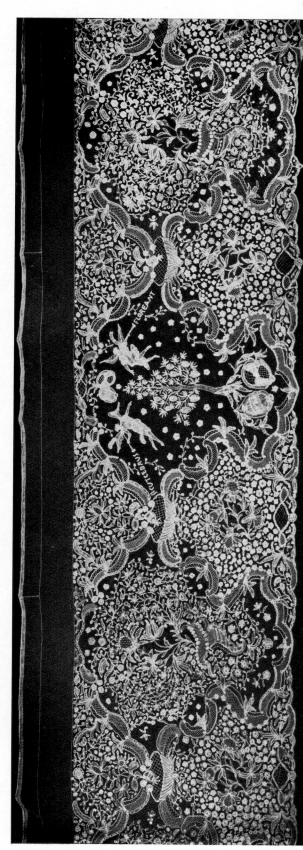

Tafel 39
Abb. 78. Teilstück der Spitze Abb. 76 mäßig verkleinert. — Abb. 77. Teilstücke der Spitze Abb. 76 in natürlicher Größe.

Plate 39
Fig. 78. Part of lace illustrated in fig. 76, slightly reduced. — Fig. 77. Part of lace in fig. 76, original size.

Planche 39
Fig. 78. Fragment de la dentelle fig. 76. Réduction modérée. — Fig. 77. Fragments da la dentelle fig. 76, mais en grandeur naturelle.

Tavola 39
Fig. 78. Parte della trina fig. 76, un poco impiccolita. — Fig. 77. Particolari della trina fig. 76, in grandezza naturale.

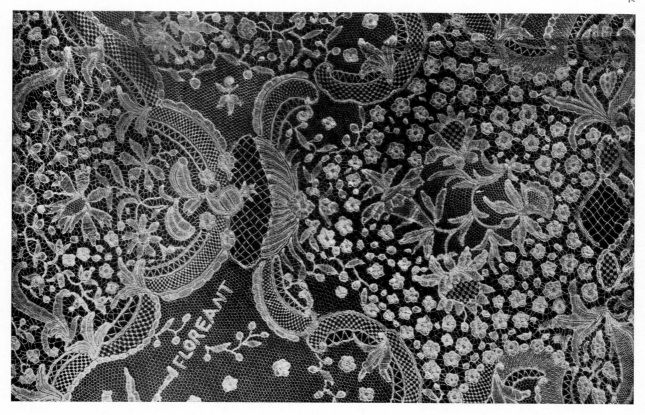

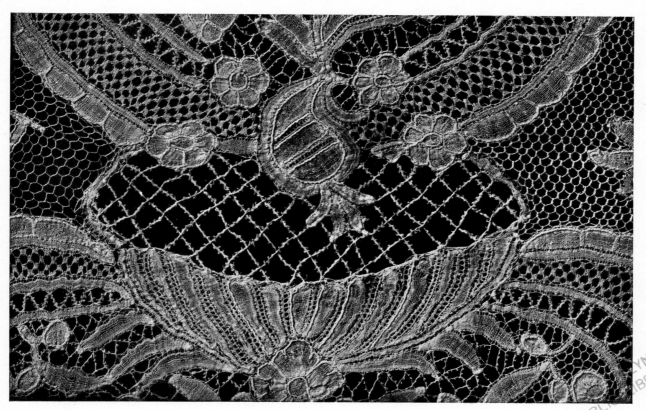

Tafel 40

Abb. 79. Binche 201. Natürliche Größe. 4. Spätbarock. Rokoko. — Abb. 80. Mechelner Spitze 102. Natürliche Größe. 4. Spätbarock. Rokoko. — Abb. 81. Mechelner Spitze 103. Natürliche Größe. 4. Spätbarock. Rokoko. — Abb. 82. Mechelner Spitze 107. Natürliche Größe. 4. Spät=barock. Rokoko.

Plate 40

Fig. 79. Binche 201. Original size. 4. Late Baroque. Rococo. — Fig. 80. Mechlin lace 102. Original size. 4. Late Baroque. Rococo. — Fig. 81. Mechlin lace 103. Original size. 4. Late Baroque. Rococo. — Fig. 82. Mechlin lace 107. Original size. 4. Late Baroque. Rococo.

Planche 40

Fig. 79. Binche 201 en grandeur naturelle. 4e baroque tardif de la dentelle. Rococo. — Fig. 80. Dentelle de Malines 102 en grandeur naturelle. 4e baroque tardif de la dentelle. Rococo. — Fig. 81. Dentelle de Malines 103 en grandeur naturelle. 4e baroque tardif de la dentelle. Rococo. — Fig. 82. Dentelle de Malines 107 en grandeur naturelle. 4e baroque tardif de la dentelle. Rococo.

Tavola 40

Fig. 79. Binche 201. Grandezza naturale. 4. Tardo barocco. Roccocò. — Fig. 80. Merletto di Malines 102. Grandezza naturale. 4. Tardo barocco. Roccocò. — Fig. 81. Merletto di Malines 103. Grandezza naturale. 4. Tardo barocco. Roccocò. — Fig. 82. Merletto di Malines 107. Grandezza naturale. 4. Tardo barocco. Roccocò.

79

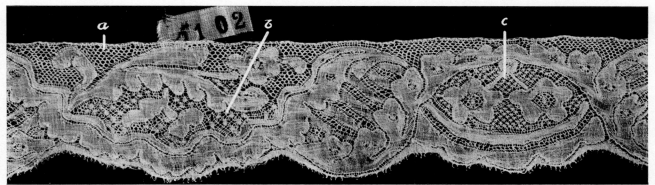

80

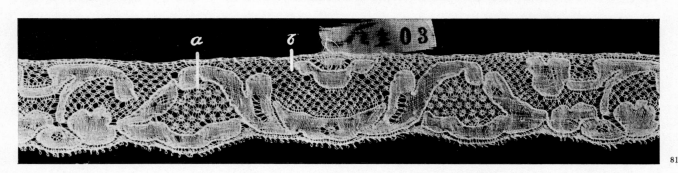

81

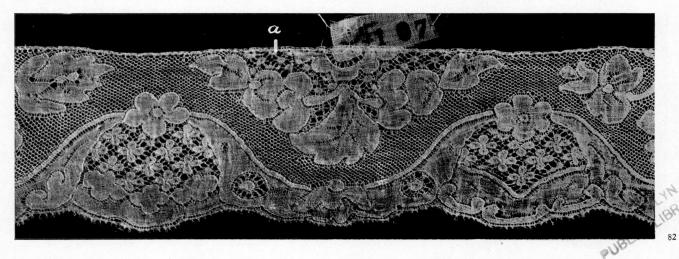

82

40

Tafel 41
Abb. 84. Brüsseler Klöppelspitze 304. Zwei Barben mit schmalem Mittelstück. Verkleinert.
4. Spätbarock. Rokoko. — Abb. 83. Teilstück der Spitze Abb. 84 in natürlicher Größe.

Plate 41
Fig. 84. Brussels pillow lace 304. Two lappets with narrow centre piece. Reduced. 4. Late Baroque. Rococo.
— Fig. 83. Part of lace shewn in fig. 84, original size.

Planche 41
Fig. 84. Dentelle de Bruxelles aux fuseaux 304. Deux barbes avec étroite pièce du milieu. Figure réduite.
4e baroque tardif de la dentelle. Rococo. — Fig. 83. Fragment de la dentelle fig. 84, mais en grandeur
naturelle.

Tavola 41
Fig. 84. Merletto a fuselli di Bruxelles 304. Due striscie di merletti con pezzo centrale ristretto. Impic=
colita. 4. Tardo barocco. Roccocò. — Fig. 83. Particolare del merletto della fig. 84, grandezza naturale.

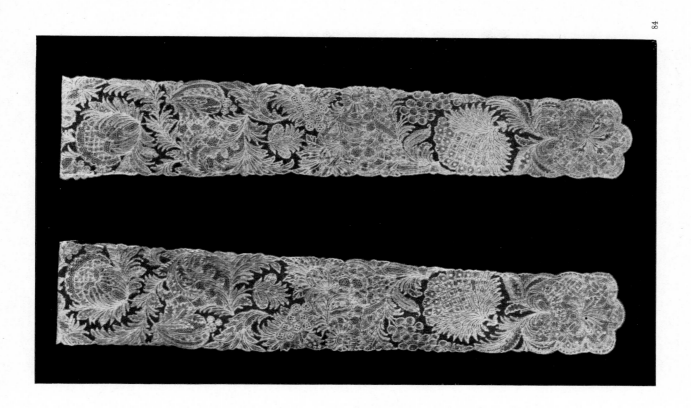

41

Tafel 42
Abb. 85. Brüsseler Klöppelspitze 305. Natürliche Größe. 4. Spätbarock. Rokoko. — Abb. 86.
Mechelner Spitze 110. Natürliche Größe. Kinderhäubchen. Ein kleines Stück von Binche ein=
gesetzt. 4. Spätbarock. Rokoko.

Plate 42
Fig. 85. Brussels pillow lace 305. Original size. 4. Late Baroque. Rococo. — Fig. 86. Mechlin lace 110.
Original size. Child's bonnet. With a small piece of Binche insertion. 4. Late Baroque. Rococo.

Planche 42
Fig. 85. Dentelle de Bruxelles aux fuseaux 305 en grandeur naturelle. 4e baroque tardif de la dentelle.
Rococo. — Fig. 86. Dentelle de Malines 110 en grandeur naturelle. Bonnet d'enfant. Un petit entre=deux
en dentelle de Binche. 4e baroque tardif de la dentelle. Rococo.

Tavola 42
Fig. 85. Merletto a fuselli di Bruxelles 305. Grandezza naturale. 4. Tardo barocco. Roccocò. — Fig. 86.
Merletto di Malines 110. Grandezza naturale. Cuffia da bambino. Inserito un piccolo pezzo di Binche.
4. Tardo barocco. Roccocò.

85

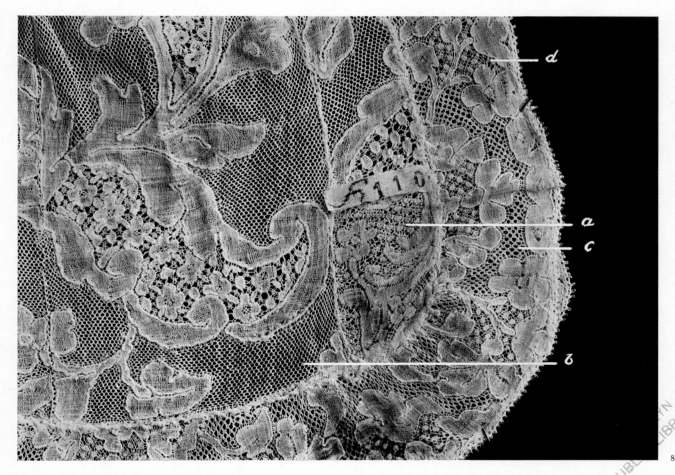

86

42

Tafel 43

Abb. 87. Mechelner Spitze 108. Natürliche Größe. 4. Spätbarock. Rokoko. — Abb. 88. Brüsseler Klöppelspitze 306. Natürliche Größe. 4. Spätbarock. Rokoko — Abb. 89. 90. Mechelner Klöppel= spitzen. Von Frau Julius Schmits, Elberfeld. Natürliche Größe. 4. Spätbarock. Rokoko.

Plate 43

Fig. 87. Mechlin lace 108. Original size. 4. Late Baroque. Rococo. — Fig. 88. Brussels pillow lace 306. Original size. 4. Late Baroque. Rococo. — Figs. 89. 90. Mechlin pillow lace. From Frau Julius Schmits, Elberfeld. Original size. 4. Late Baroque. Rococo.

Planche 43

Fig. 87 Dentelle de Malines 108 en grandeur naturelle. 4e baroque tardif de la dentelle. Rococo. — Fig. 88. Dentelle de Bruxelles aux fuseaux 306 en grandeur naturelle. 4e baroque tardif de la dentelle. Rococo. — Fig. 89. 90. Dentelle de Malines aux fuseaux. Provenant de Madame Julius Schmits, d'Elber= feld. En grandeur naturelle. 4e baroque tardif de la dentelle.

Tavola 43

Fig. 87. Merletto di Malines 108. Grandezza naturale. 4. Tardo barocco. Roccocò. — Fig. 88. Merletto a fuselli di Bruxelles 306. Grandezza naturale. 4. Tardo barocco. Roccocò. — Fig. 89. 90. Merletti a fuselli di Malines, della Signora Julius Schmits, Elberfeld. Grandezza naturale. 4. Tardo barocco. Roccocò.

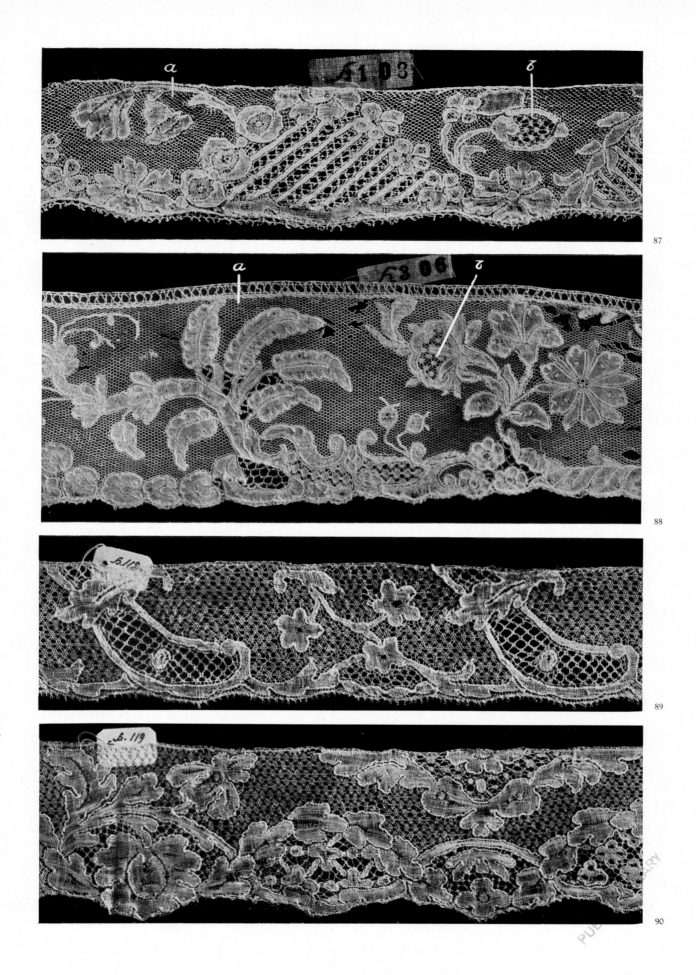

87

88

89

90

43

Tafel 44
Abb. 91. Brüsseler Klöppelspitze von Frau Elisabeth Wolff=Merck, München. Verkleinert.
4. Spätbarock. Rokoko. — Abb. 92. Teilstück der Spitze Abb. 91 in natürlicher Größe.

Plate 44
Fig. 91. Brussels pillow lace from Frau Elisabeth Wolff=Merck, Munich. Reduced. 4. Late Baroque. Rococo.
— Fig. 92. Part of lace shewn in fig. 91. original size.

Planche 44
Fig. 91. Dentelle de Bruxelles aux fuseaux. Appartenant à Madame Elisabeth Wolff=Merck, de Munich.
Figure réduite. 4e baroque tardif de la dentelle. Rococco. — Fig. 92. Fragment de la dentelle fig. 91, mais
en grandeur naturelle.

Tavola 44
Fig. 91. Merletto a fuselli di Bruxelles della Signora Elisabeth Wolff=Merck, Monaco. Impiccolita. 4. Tardo
barocco. Roccocò. — Fig. 92. Particolare del merletto fig. 90 in grandezza naturale.

91

92

44

Tafel 45
Abb. 93. Brüsseler Klöppelspitze. Teilstück eines Haubendeckels. Natürliche Größe. 4. Spät=
barock. Rokoko. — Abb. 94. 95. Valenciennesspitzen mit der runden Masche. Natürliche
Größe. 4. Spätbarock. Rokoko.

Plate 45
Fig. 93. Brussels pillow lace. Part of the crown of a cap. Original size. 4. Late Baroque. Rococo. — Figs. 94.
95. Valenciennes lace with round mesh. Original size. 4. Late Baroque. Rococo.

Planche 45
Fig. 93. Dentelle de Bruxelles aux fuseaux. Fragment d'un fond de bonnet. En grandeur naturelle. 4e baro=
que tardif. Rococo. — Fig. 94. 95. Dentelles de Valenciennes avec la maille ronde. En grandeur naturelle.
4e baroque tardif de la dentelle. Rococo.

Tavola 45
Fig. 93. Merletto a fuselli di Bruxelles. Particolare della parte superiore di una cuffia. Grandezza naturale.
4. Tardo barocco. Roccocò. — Fig. 94. 95. Merletti Valenciennes con maglie rotonde. Grandezza naturale.
4. Tardo barocco. Roccocò.

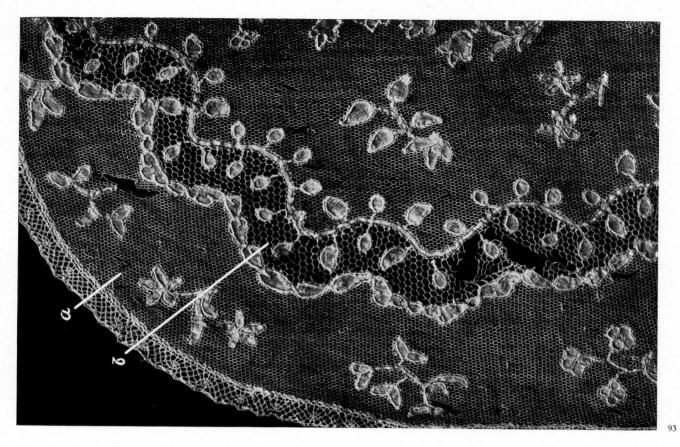

93

94

95

45

Tafel 46

Abb. 96. Valenciennesspitze mit der runden Masche. Haubendeckel. Verkleinert. 4. Spät=
barock. Rokoko. — Abb. 97. Teilstück der Spitze Abb. 96 in natürlicher Größe.

Plate 46

Fig. 96. Valenciennes lace with round mesh. Crown of a cap. Reduced. 4. Late Baroque. Rococo. — Fig. 97.
Part of lace shewn in fig. 96, original size.

Planche 46

Fig. 96. Dentelle de Valenciennes avec la maille ronde. Fond de bonnet. Figure réduite. 4e baroque
tardif de la dentelle. Rococo. — Fig. 97. Fragment de la dentelle fig. 96, mais en grandeur naturelle.

Tavola 46

Fig. 96. Merletto Valenciennes con maglia rotonda. Parte superiore di cuffia. Impiccolita. 4. Tardo barocco.
Roccocò. — Fig. 97. Particolare del merletto fig. 96 in grandezza naturale.

96

97

46

Tafel 47

Abb. 98. Einfacher Nadelgrund. — Abb. 99. Die Klöppelschläge. — Abb. 100. Der Formen=
schlag. Point d'esprit.

Plate 47

Fig. 98. Simple needlepoint ground. — Fig. 99. Bobbin work. — Fig. 100. *Point d'Esprit.*

Planche 47

Fig. 98. Fond simple à l'aiguille. — Fig. 99. Les passées. — Fig. 100. Les points d'esprit.

Tavola 47

Fig. 98. Fondo semplice ad aghi. — Fig. 99. Intrecci a fuselli. — Fig. 100. Intreccio foggiato Point d'esprit.

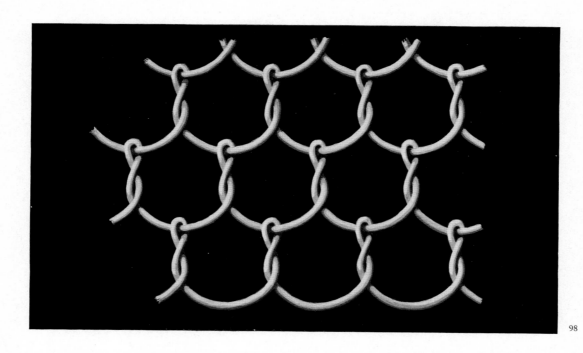

98

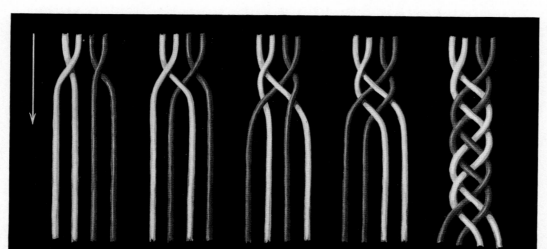

99

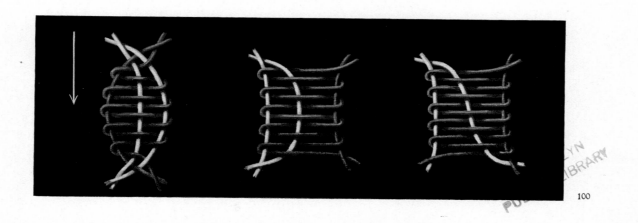

100

47

Tafel 48

Abb. 102. Spinnen aus der Binche 2061. Tafel 29, Abb. 55. — Abb. 101. Point de raccroc.

Plate 48

Fig. 102. Spiderwork from the Binche 2061. Plate 29, fig. 55. — Fig. 101. *Point de raccroc.*

Planche 48

Fig. 102. Araignées de la Binche 2061 de la pl. 29, fig. 55. — Fig. 101. Le point de raccroc.

Tavola 48

Fig. 102. Trama del merletto Binche. Tav. 29, fig. 55. — Fig. 101. Point de Raccroc (punto raccroc).

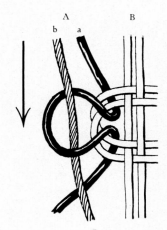

101

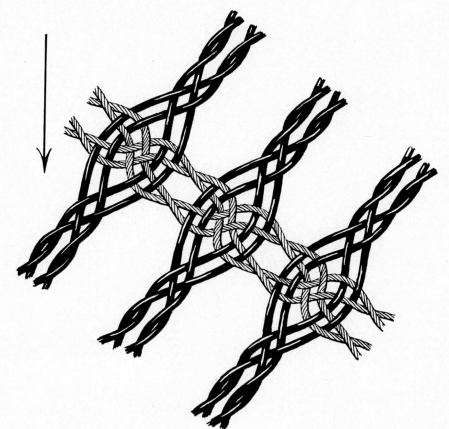

102

48

Tafel 49
Abb. 103. Einfacher Gitterschlag oder Netzschlag. Grillé. — Abb. 104. Doppelter Gitterschlag.

Plate 49
Fig. 103. Simple trellis or net work. Grillé. — Fig. 104. Double trellis netting.

Planche 49
Fig. 103. Le point grillé simple. — Fig. 104. Le double point grillé.

Tavola 49
Fig. 103. Semplice intreccio a graticola od a rete. Grillé. — Fig. 104. Doppio intreccio a graticola.

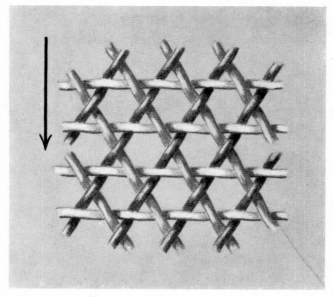

103

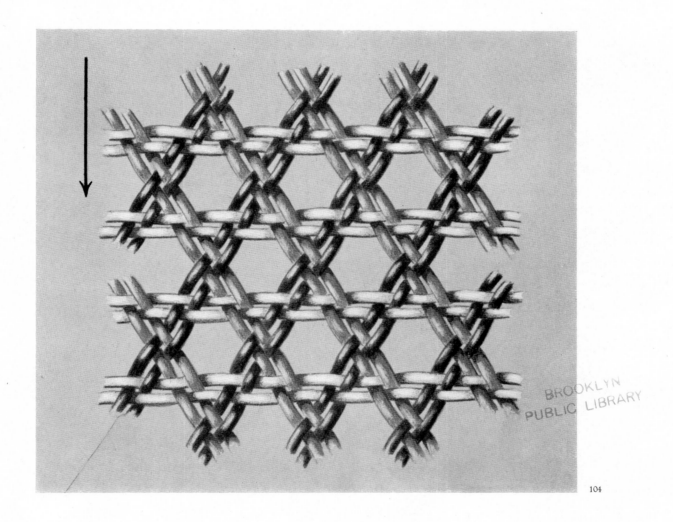

104

49

Tafel 50

Abb. 105. Fünflöchrige Masche 1. Verstärkter Jungferngrund. Doppel=Ziergrund. Maille flamande. Maille à cinq trous. — Abb. 106. Fünflöchrige Masche 2. Jungferngrund, slawische Musterung. Réseau de la dentelle de Flandre moderne.

Plate 50

Fig. 105. Five=hole mesh 1. Reinforced ground mesh. Double decorative ground mesh. *Maille flamande. Maille à cinq trous.* — Fig. 106. Five=hole mesh 2. *Fond à la vierge.* Slavonic pattern. *Réseau de la dentelle de Flandre moderne.*

Planche 50

Fig. 105. La maille à cinq trous 1. La maille flamande. — Fig. 106. La maille à cinq trous 2. Réseau de la dentelle de Flandre moderne.

Tavola 50

Fig. 105. Maglia 1 a cinque fori. Fondo vergine rinforzato. Maglia fiamminga. — Fig. 106. Maglia 2 a cinque fori. Fondo vergine, motivo slavo. Réseau de la dentelle de Flandre moderne.

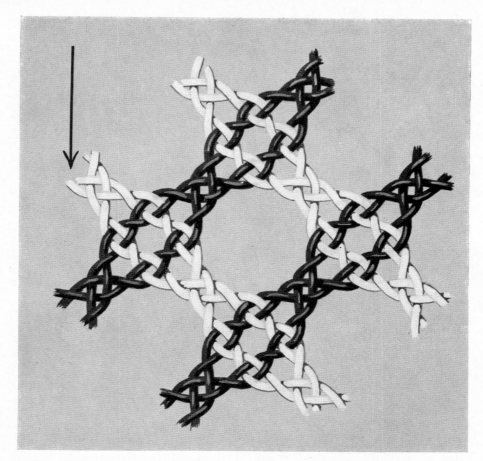

105

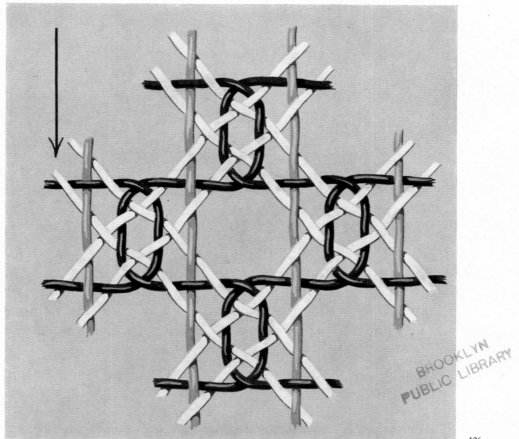

106

Tafel 51

Abb. 107. Fünflöchrige Masche 2a. Jungferngrund, slawische Musterung, mit doppelt ge=
drehten Fäden. — Abb. 108. Fünflöchrige Masche 3. Jungferngrund. Fond à la vierge.

Plate 51

Fig. 107. Five=hole mesh 2a. *Fond à la vierge.* Slavonic pattern, with double-twisted threads. — Fig. 108.
Five=hole mesh 3. *Fond à la vierge.*

Planche 51

Fig. 107. La maille à cinq trous 2a, à fils tournés deux fois. — Fig. 108. La maille à cinq trous 3. Fond
à la Vierge.

Tavola 51

Fig. 107. Maglia 2a a cinque fori. Fondo vergine, motivo slavo, a fili doppie torcigliati. — Fig. 108. Maglia
3 a cinque fori. Fondo vergine. Fond à la vierge.

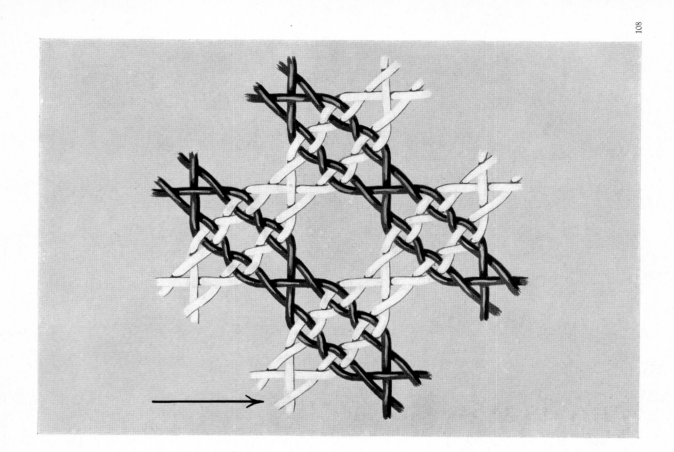

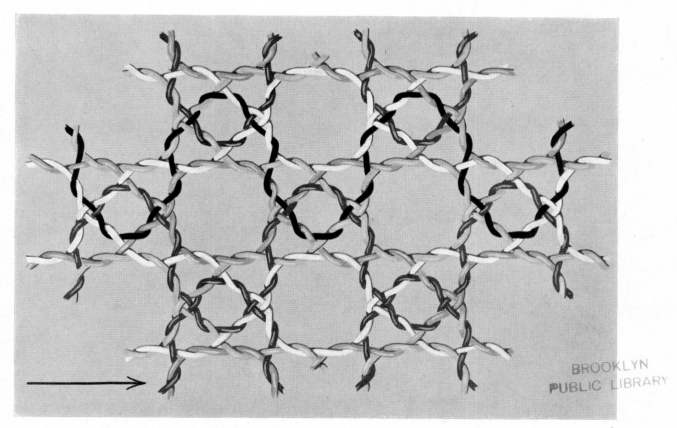

51

Tafel 52

Abb. 109. Fünflöchrige Masche 2b. Jungferngrund, slawische Musterung, mit Ganzschlägen zwischen den Maschen.

Plate 52

Fig. 109. Five-hole mesh 2b. *Fond à la vierge*, Slavonic pattern, with full twistings between the meshes.

Planche 52

Fig. 109. La maille à cinq trous 2b. Les mailles sont reliées les unes aux autres par des passées complètes.

Tavola 52

Fig. 109. Maglia 2b a cinque fori. Fondo vergine, motivo slavo, con intrecci completi fra le maglie.

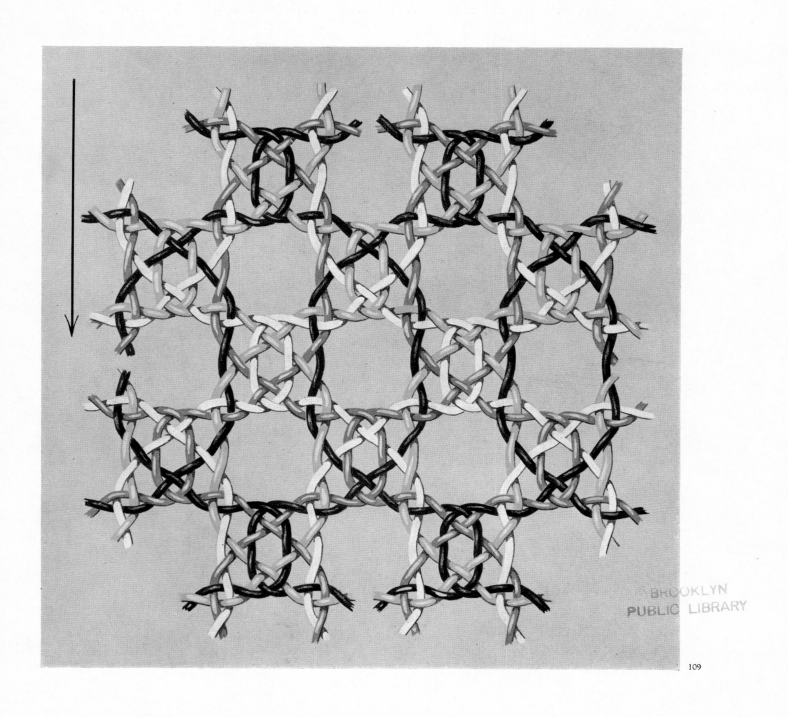

109

52

Tafel 53
Abb. 110. Leinenschlagsterne a—d. — Abb. 111. Muschelsterne e —i. — Abb. 112. Knospen=
sterne k—o.

Plate 53
Fig. 110. *Toilé* devices a—d. — Fig. 111. Shell devices e—i. — Fig. 112. Bud devices k—o.

Planche 53
Fig. 110. Etoiles au point de toile a—d. — Fig. 111. Etoiles rocaille e—i. — Fig. 112. Etoiles en bourgeon k—o.

Tavola 53
Fig. 110. Stelle intrecciate a—d. — Fig. 111. Stelle a conchiglia e—i. — Fig. 112. Stella a boccio k—o.

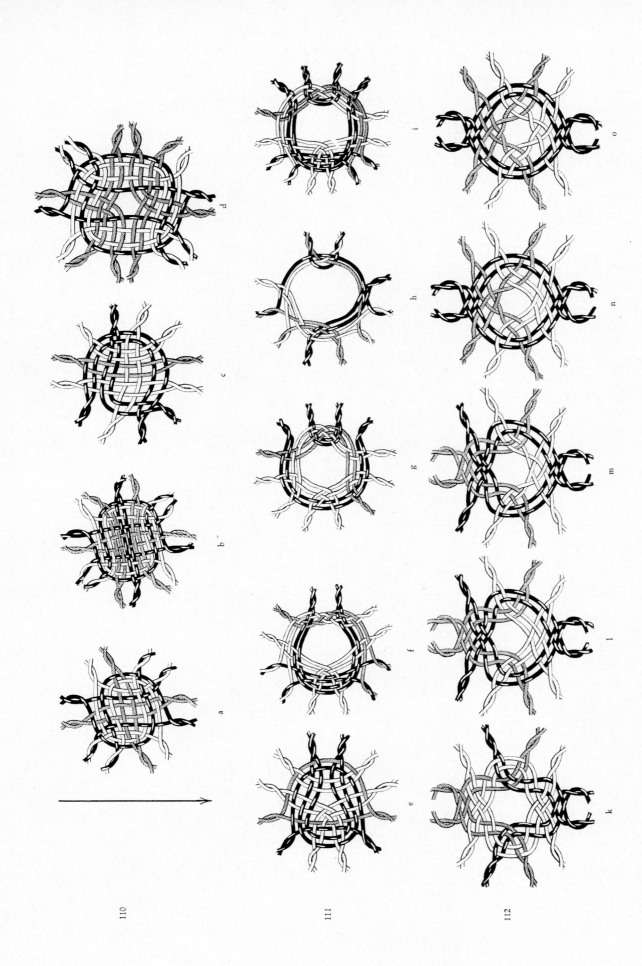

d

c

b

a

i

h

g

f

e

o

n

m

l

k

110

111

112

53

Tafel 54

Abb. 113. Knospensterne o (Tafel 53, Abb. 112) mit einfacher Stegverbindung. Beschreibung S. 30. — Abb. 114. Knospensterne k (Tafel 53, Abb. 112) mit einfacher Stegverbindung. Beschreibung S. 31.

Plate 54

Fig. 113. Bud devices o. (Plate 53, fig. 112) connected by simple *brides*. Description see p. 30. — Fig. 114. Bud devices k (Plate 53, fig. 112) connected by simple *brides*. Description see p. 31.

Planche 54

Fig. 113. Etoiles en bourgeon o (Planche 53, fig. 112) reliées entre elles par des brides simples. Description p. 30. — Fig. 114. Etoiles en bourgeon k (Planche 53, fig. 112.) reliées entre elles par des brides simples. Description p. 30.

Tavola 54

Fig. 113. Stelle a boccio o (tavola 53, fig 112) con collegamento ad orlatura semplice. Descrizione a pag. 30. Fig. 114. Stelle a boccio k (tavola 53, fig. 112) con collegamento ad orlatura semplice. Descrizione a pag. 31.

54

Tafel 55

Abb. 115. Muschelsterne e (Tafel 53, Abb. 111) mit einfacher Stegverbindung. Beschreibung S. 31. — Abb 116. Muschelsterne e (Tafel 53, Abb. 111) mit Stegverbindung und sechsgliedriger Umrahmung aus selbständigen Fadenpaaren gebildet. Beschreibung S. 31.

Plate 55

Fig. 115. Shell devices e (Plate 53, fig. 111) connected by simple *brides*. Description see p. 31. — Fig. 116. Shell devices e (Plate 53, fig. 111) connected by *brides* with hexagonal framework composed of independent pairs of threads. Description see p. 31.

Planche 55

Fig. 115. Etoiles rocaille e (Planche 53, fig. 111) reliées entre elles par des brides simples. Description p. 31. — Fig. 116. Etoiles rocaille e (Planche 53, fig .111) reliées entre elles par des brides; encadrement à six membres formé de paires de fils indépendantes. Description p. 31.

Tavola 55

Fig. 115. Stella a conchiglia e (tavola 53, fig. 111) con collegamento ad orlatura semplice. Descrizione a pag. 31. — Fig. 116. Stelle a conchiglia e (tavola 53, fig. 111) con collegamento ad orlatura ed incorniciatura a sei segmenti costituita da coppie di fili indipendenti. Descrizione a pag. 31.

55

Tafel 56
Abb. 117. Knospensterne n (Tafel 53, Abb. 112) mit einfacher Stegverbindung. Beschreibung
S. 31. — Abb. 118. Leinenschlagsterne a (Tafel 53, Abb. 110) mit erweiterter Stegverbindung.
Beschreibung S. 32.

Plate 56
Fig. 117. Bud devices n (Plate 53, fig. 112) connected by simple *brides*. Description see p. 31. — Fig. 118.
Toile devices a (Plate 53, fig. 110) connected by expanded *brides*. Description see p. 32.

Planche 56
Fig. 117. Etoiles en bourgeon n (Planche 53, fig. 112) reliées entre elles par des brides simples. Description p. 31. — Fig. 118. Etoiles au point de toile a (Planche 53, fig. 110) reliées entre elles par des brides
élargies. Description p. 31.

Tavola 56
Fig. 117. Stelle a boccio n (tavola 53, fig. 112) con collegamento ad orlatura semplice. Descrizione a pag. 31. —
Fig. 118. Stelle intrecciate a (tavola 53, fig. 110) con collegamento ad orlatura ampliato. Descrizione a pag. 32.

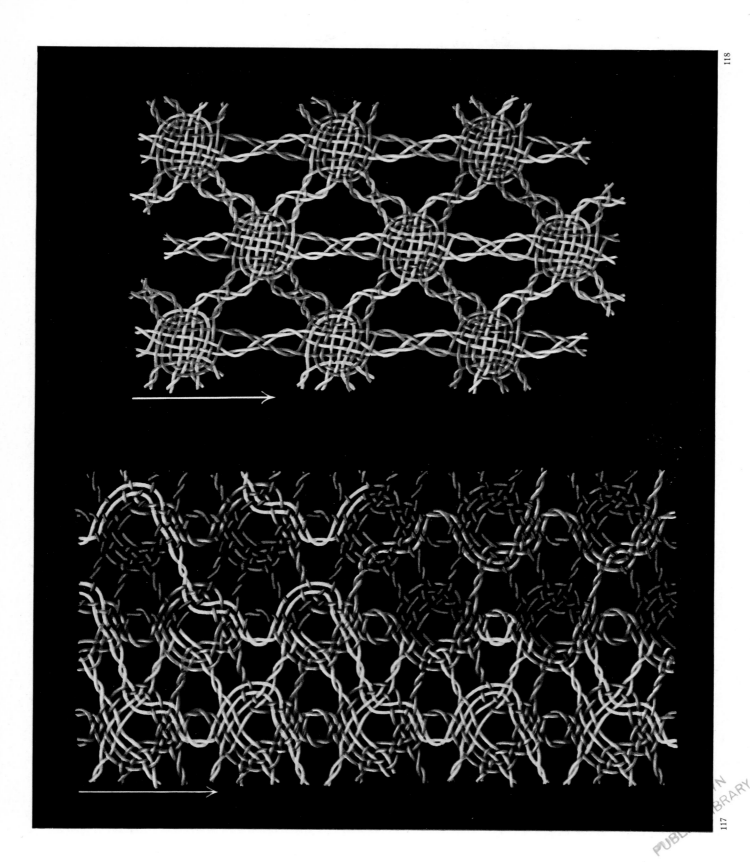

56

Tafel 57

Abb. 119. Leinenschlagsterne b (Tafel 53, Abb. 110) mit erweiterter Stegverbindung. Beschreibung S. 32. — Abb. 120. Leinenschlagsterne d (Tafel 53, Abb. 110) mit erweiterter Stegverbindung. Beschreibung S. 32.

Plate 57

Fig. 119. *Toilé* devices b (Plate 53, fig. 110) connected by expanded *brides*. Description, see p. 32. — Fig. 120. *Toilé* devices d (Plate 53, fig. 110) connected by expanded *brides*. Description see p. 32.

Planche 57

Fig. 119. Etoiles au point de toile b (Planche 53, fig. 110) reliées entre elles par des brides élargies. Description p. 32. — Fig. 120. Etoiles au point de toile d (Planche 53, fig. 110) reliées entre elles par des brides élargies. Description p. 32.

Tavola 57

Fig. 119. Stelle intrecciate b (tavola 53, fig. 110) con collegamento ad orlatura ampliato. Descrizione a pag. 32. — Fig. 120. Stelle intrecciate d (tavola 53, fig. 110) con collegamento ampliato ad orlatura. Descrizione a pag. 32.

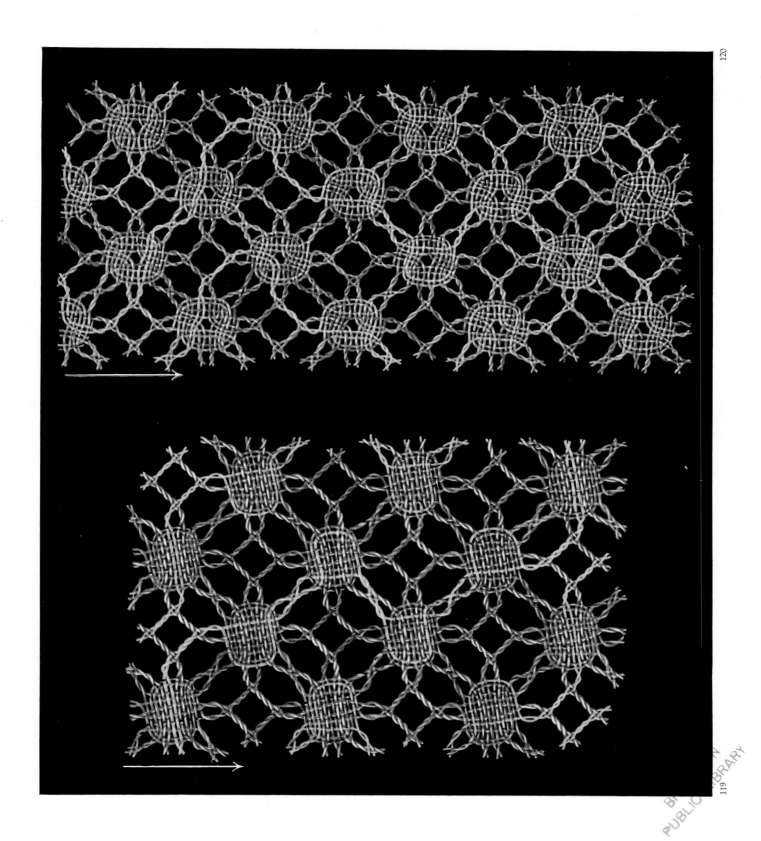

57

Tafel 58

Abb. 121. Leinenschlagsterne a (Tafel 53, Abb. 110) mit erweiterter Stegverbindung. Beschreibung S. 32 — Abb. 122. Leinenschlagsterne c (Tafel 53, Abb 110) mit Stegverbindung und viergliedriger Umrahmung aus selbständigen Fadenpaaren gebildet. Beschreibung S. 32.

Plate 58

Fig. 121. *Toilé* devices a (Plate 53, fig. 110) connected by expanded *brides*. Description see p. 32. — Fig. 122. Toilé devices c (Pl. 53. fig. 110) connected by *brides* and with four-sided framework composed of independent pairs of threads. Description see p. 32.

Planche 58

Fig. 121. Etoiles au point de toille a (Planche 53, fig. 110) reliées entre elles par des brides élargies. Description p. 32. — Fig. 122. Etoiles au point de toile c (Planche 53, fig. 110) reliées entre elles par des brides; encadrement à quatre membres formé de paires de fils indépendantes. Description p. 32.

Tavola 58

Fig. 121. Stelle intrecciate e (tavola 53, fig. 110) con collegamento ampliato ad orlatura. Descrizione a pag. 32. — Fig. 122. Stelle intrecciate e (tavola 53, fig. 110) con collegamento ad orlatura ed incorniciatura a quattro segmenti formata da coppie di fili indipendenti. Descrizione a pag. 32.

Tafel 59

Abb. 123. Leinenschlagsterne a (Tafel 53, Abb. 110) mit Stegverbindung und viergliedriger Umrahmung aus den Fäden der Maschen gebildet. Beschreibung S. 33. — Abb. 124. Muschelsterne e (Tafel 53, Abb. 110) in unregelmäßiger Anordnung. Beschreibung S. 33.

Plate 59

Fig. 123. *Toilé* devices a (Plate 53, fig. 110) connected by *brides* with lozenge-shaped framework made from threads of the mesh. Description see p. 33. — Fig. 124. Shell devices e (Plate 53, fig. 110) irregularly arranged. Description see p. 33.

Planche 59

Fig. 123. Etoiles au point de toile a (Planche 53, fig. 110) reliées entre elles par des brides; encadrement à quatre membres formé des fils des mailles. Description p. 33. — Fig. 124. Etoiles rocaille e (Planche 53, fig. 110) en disposition dissymétrique. Description p. 33.

Tavola 59

Fig. 123. Stelle intrecciate e (tavola 53, fig. 110) con collegamento ad orlatura ed incorniciatura a quattro segmenti formata dai fili delle maglie. Descrizione a pag. 33. — Fig. 124. Stelle a conchiglia e (tavola 53, fig. 110) disposte asimmetricamente. Descrizione a pag. 33.

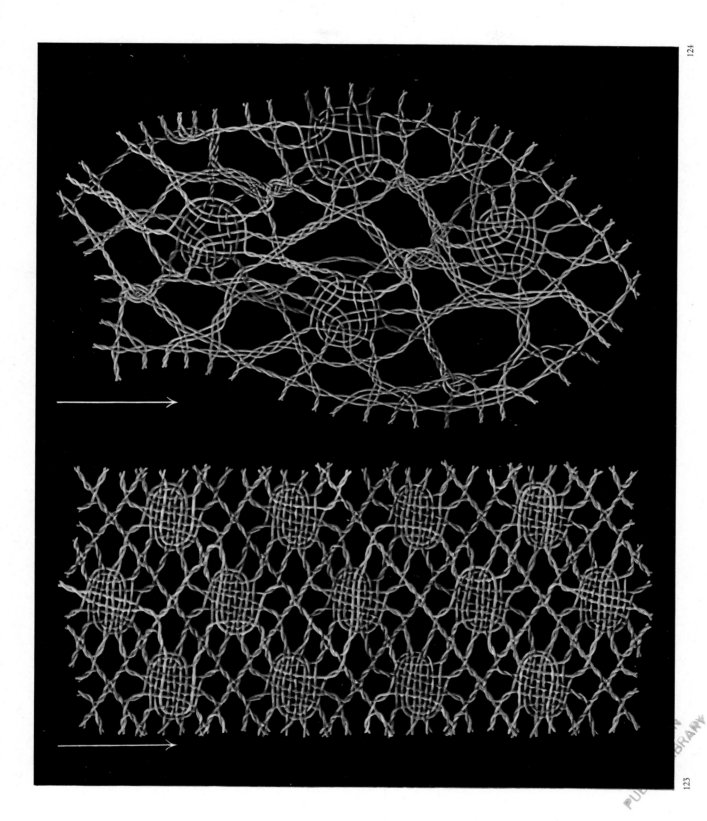

Tafel 60
Abb. 125. Fadenführung im fond de neige der Binche 2061 (Tafel 29, Abb. 55).

Plate 60
Fig. 125. Path of the threads in the *fond de neige* of the Binche 2061 (Plate 29, fig. 55).

Planche 60
Fig. 125. Conduite des fils dans le fond de neige de la Binche 2061 (Planche 29, fig. 55).

Tavola 60
Fig. 125. Direzione del filo nel fond de neige del Binche 2061 (tavola 29, fig. 55).

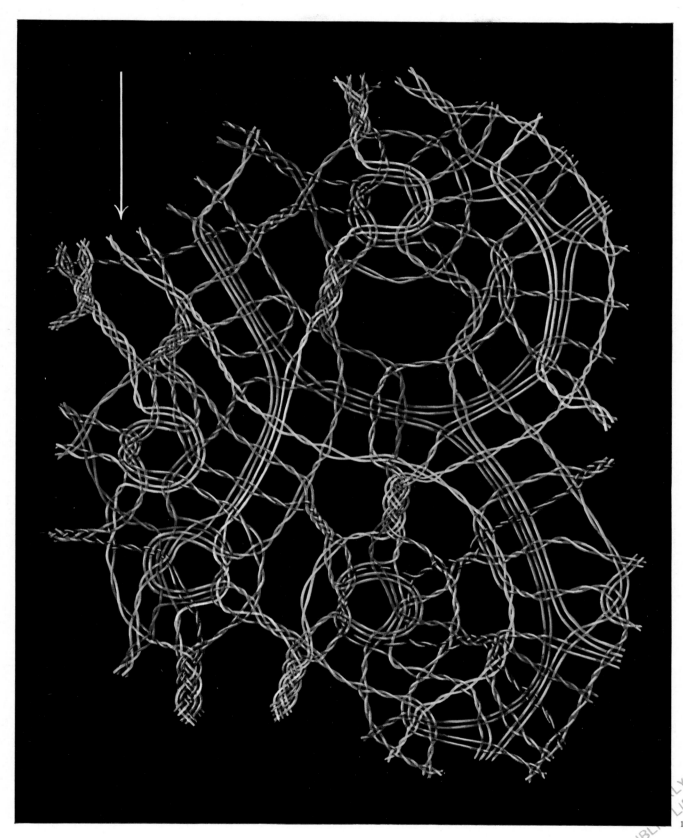

125

Tafel 61
Abb. 126. Geklöppeltes Grundnetz. Nachahmung des Nadelgrundes.

Plate 61
Fig 126. Meshed ground of pillow=work. Imitation of the needlepoint ground.

Planche 61
Fig. 126. Fond de réseau aux fuseaux. Imitation du fond à l'aiguille.

Tavola 61
Fig. 126. Rete di fondo a fuselli. Imitazione del fondo ad aghi.

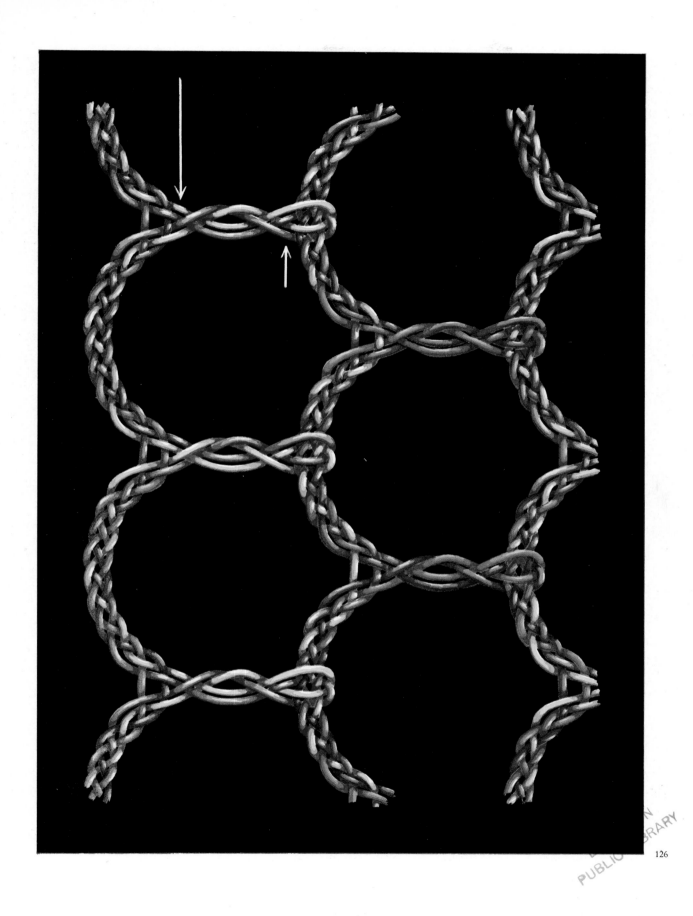

126

Tafel 62
Abb. 127. Armure, 8fädig, in der Binche 2061 (Tafel 29, Abb. 55).

Plate 62
Fig. 127. *Armure*, eight-thread, in the Binche 2061 (Plate 29, fig. 55).

Planche 62
Fig. 127. Armure composée de huit fils dans la Binche 2061 (Planche 29, fig. 55).

Tavola 62
Fig. 127. Armatura ad 8 fili nel Binche 2061 (tavola 29, fig. 55).

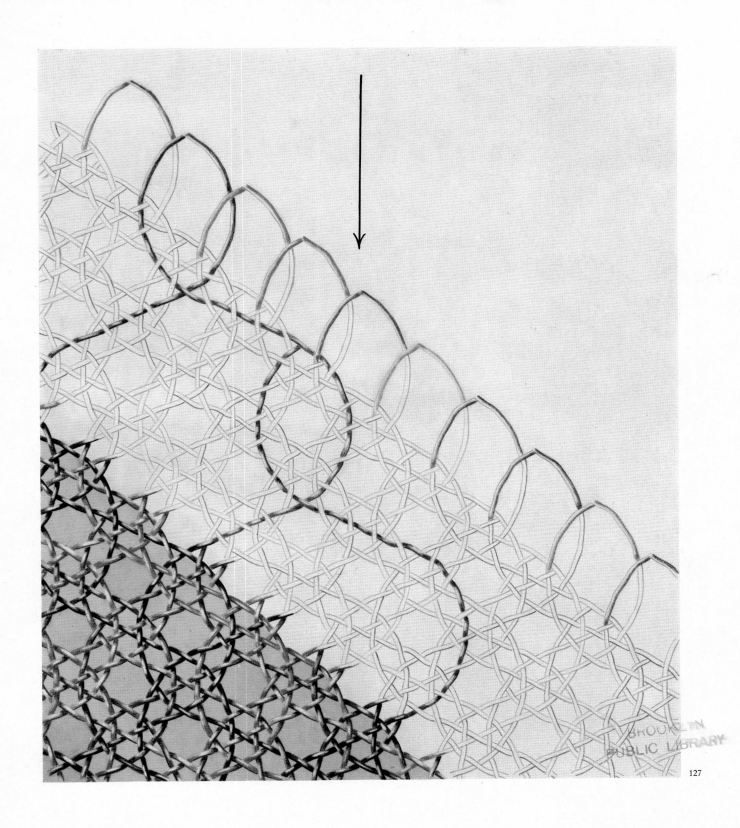

127

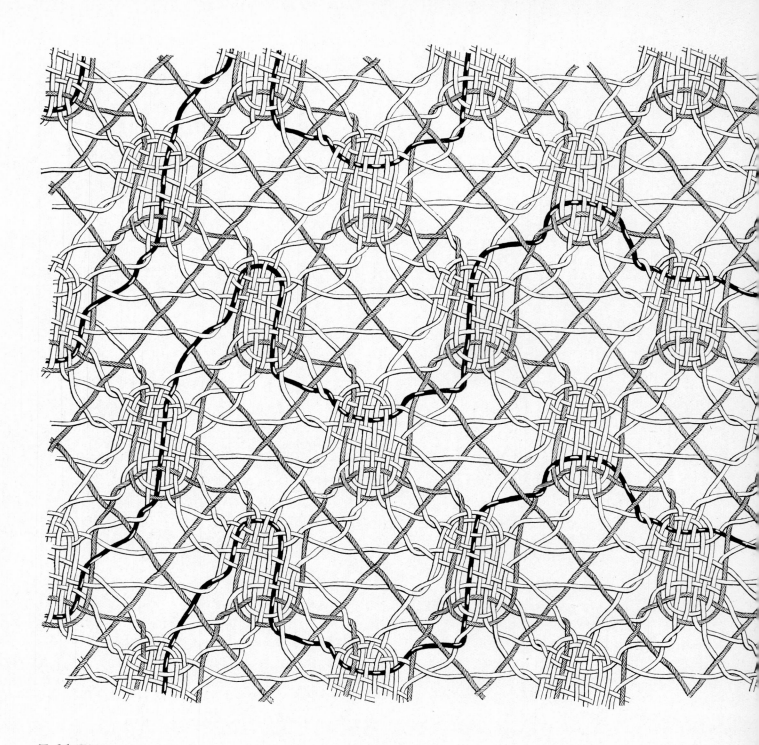

Tafel 63/64

Abb. 128. Leinenschlagsterne a (Tafel 53, Abb. 110) mit Stegverbindung und viergliedriger Umrahmu᷈
aus einzelnen selbständigen Fäden gebildet. Beschreibung S. 32.

Plate 63/64

Fig. 128. *Toilé* devices a (Plate 53, fig. 110) connected by *brides* with lozenge-shaped framework of separate ind᷈
pendent threads. Description see p. 32.

Planche 63/64

Fig. 128. Etoiles au point de toile a (Planche 53, fig. 110) reliées entre elles par des brides; encadrement à quatre memb᷈
formé de quelques fils indépendants. Description p. 32.

Tavola 63/64

Fig. 128. Stelle intrecciate e (tavola 53, fig. 110) con collegamento ad orlaturo ed incorniciatura a quattro segmenti forma᷈
da singoli fili indipendenti. Descrizione a pag. 32.

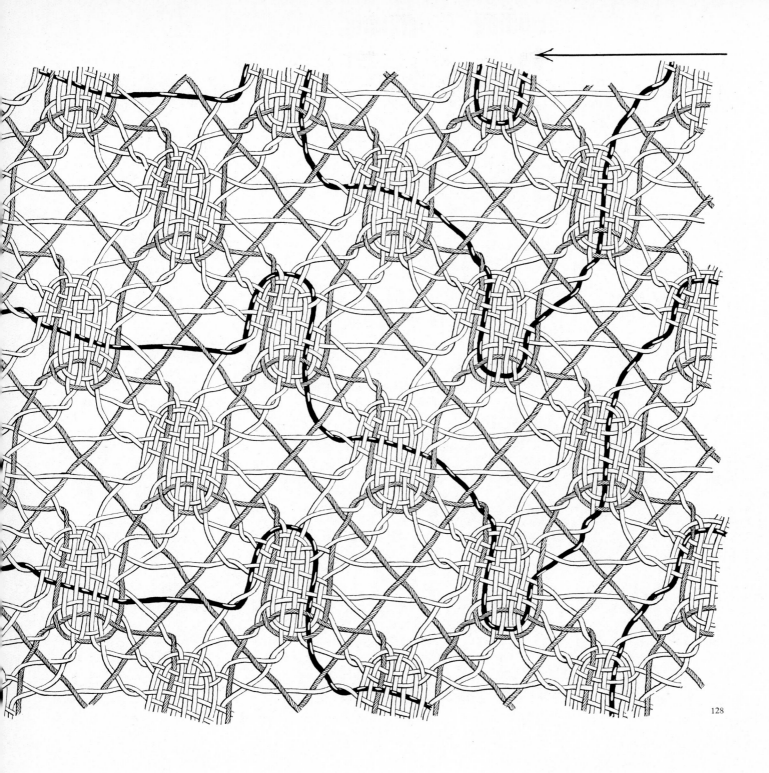

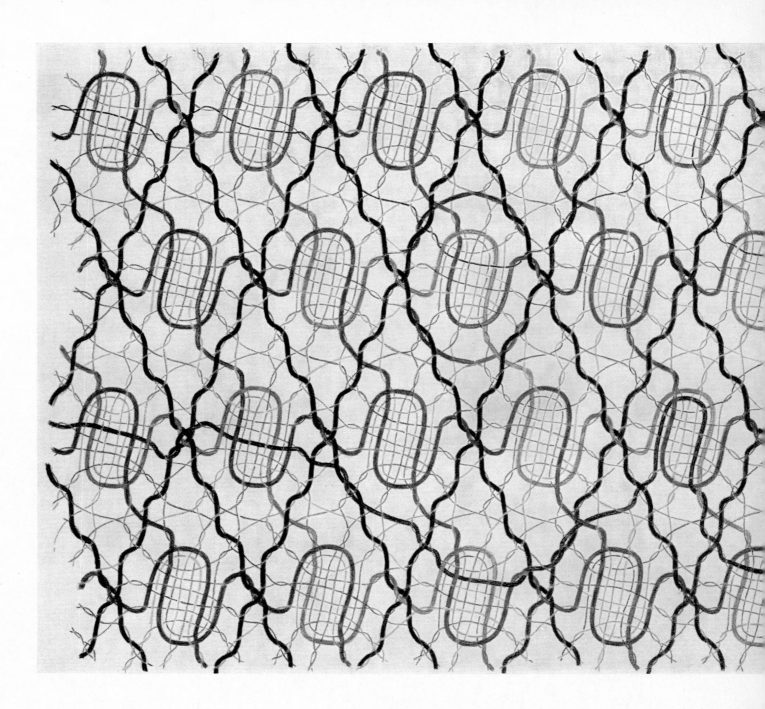

Tafel 65/66
Abb. 129. Leinenschlagsterne a (Tafel 53, Abb. 110) mit rautenförmiger und runder Umrahmung a
Maschenfäden und einzelnen selbständigen Fäden gebildet. Beschreibung S. 33.

Plate 65/66
Fig. 129. *Toilé* devices a (Plate 53, fig. 110) with round and lozenge-shaped framework composed of threads from t
mesh and separate independent threads. Description see p. 33.

Planche 65/66
Fig. 129. Etoiles au point de toile a (Planche 53, fig. 110); encadrement en losange et en rond formé de fils de mailles
de quelques fils indépendants. Description p. 32.

Tavola 65/66
Fig. 129. Stelle intrecciate a (tavola 53, fig. 110) con incorniciatura in forma di tralci rotonda, costituita da fili de
maglie e da singoli fili indipendenti. Descrizione a pag. 33.

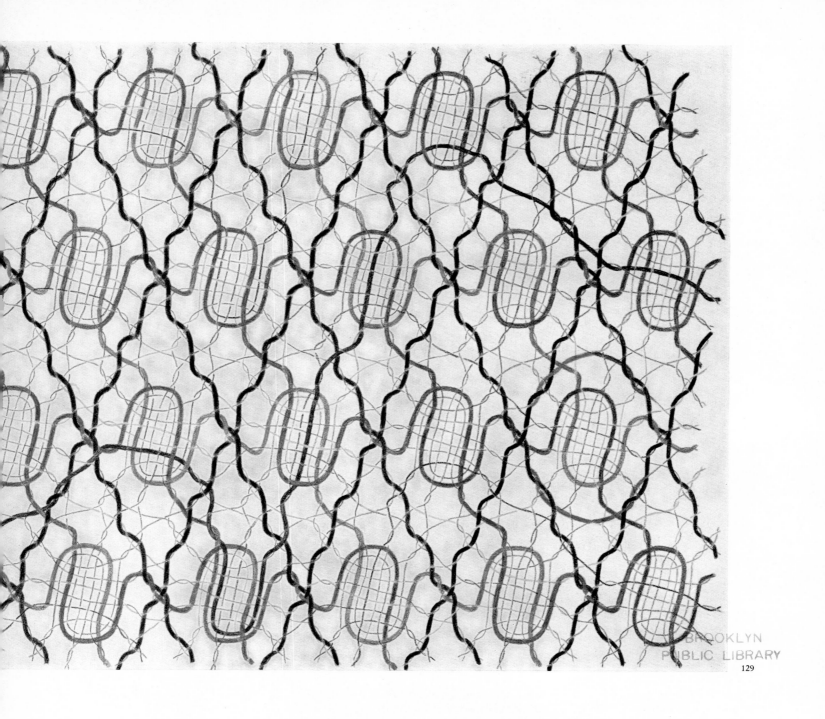

129

Tafel 67
Abb. 130. Ornament der Binche 2061 (Tafel 29, Abb. 55).

Plate 67
Fig. 130. Ornament of the Binche 2061 (Plate 28, fig. 55).

Planche 67
Fig. 130. Ornementation de la Binche 2061 (Planche 29, fig. 55).

Tavola 67
Fig. 130. Ornamento del Binche 2061 (tavola 29, fig. 55).

Tafel 68
Abb. 131. Textur der Binche 2061 (Tafel 29, Abb. 55).

Plate 68
Fig. 131. Texture of the Binche 2061 (Plate 29, fig. 55).

Planche 68
Fig. 131. Texture de la Binche 2061 (Planche 29, fig. 55).

Tavola 68
Fig. 131. Tessitura del Binche 2061 (tavola 29, fig. 55).

131

Tafel 69

Abb. 132. Armure, 8fädig, in der Mechelner Spitze 103 (Tafel 40, Abb. 81). — Abb. 133. Armure, 12fädig.

Plate 69

Fig. 132. *Armure*, eight-thread, in the Mechlin lace 103 (Plate 40, fig. 81). — Fig. 133. *Armure*, twelvethread.

Planche 69

Fig. 132. Armure composée de huits fils dans la dentelle de Malines 103 (Planche 40, fig. 81). — Fig. 133. Armure composée de douze fils.

Tavola 69

Fig. 132. Armatura ad 8 fili nel merletto di Malines 103 (tavola 40, fig. 81). — Fig. 133. Armatura, a 12 fili.

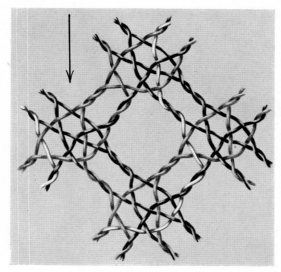

132

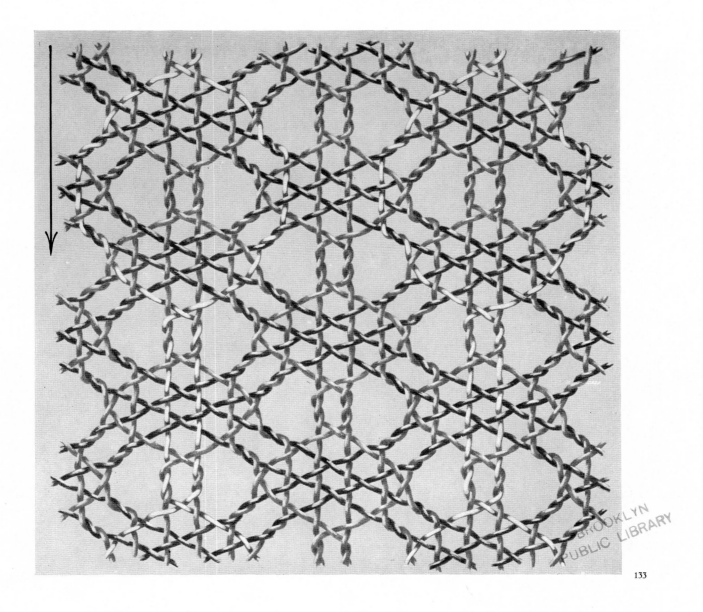

133

Tafel 70

Abb. 135. Fond triangulaire in der Mechelner Spitze 102 (Tafel 40, Abb. 80). — Abb. 134. Fond triangulaire in der Mechelner Spitze 105 (Tafel 38, Abb. 75) und in der Antwerpener Spitze Tafel 74, Abb. 142.

Plate 70

Fig. 135. *Fond triangulaire* in the Mechlin lace 102 (Plate 40, Fig. 80). — Fig. 134. *Fond triangulaire* in the Mechlin lace 105 (Plate 38, fig. 75) and in the Antwerp lace Plate 74, fig 142.

Planche 70

Fig. 135. Fond triangulaire de la dentelle de Malines 102 (Planche 40, fig. 80). — Fig. 134. Fond triangulaire de la dentelle de Malines 105 (Planche 38, Fig. 75) et de la dentelle d'Anvers (Planche 74, fig. 142).

Tavola 70

Fig. 135. Fondo triangolare nel merletto di Malines 102 (tavola 40, fig. 80). Pag. — Fig. 134. Fondo triangolare nel merletto di Malines 105 (tavola 38, fig. 75) e nel merletto di Anversa (tavola 74, fig. 142).

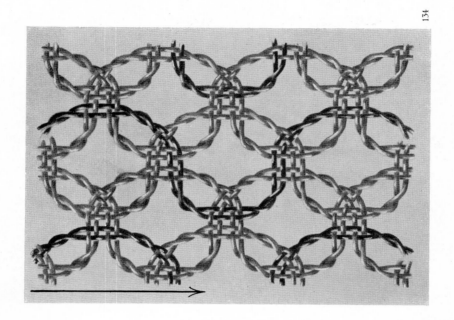

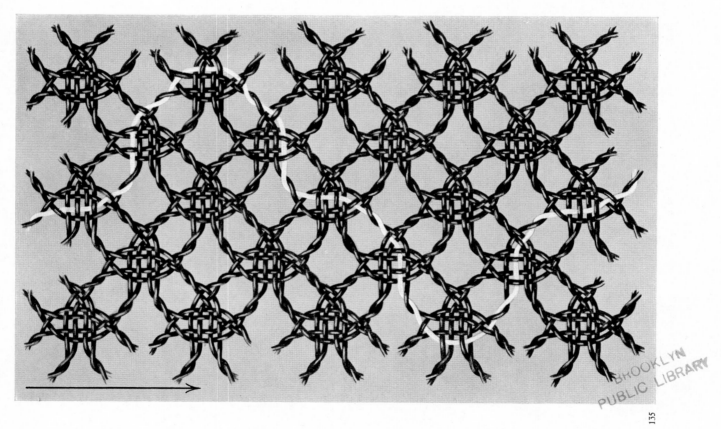

70

Tafel 71
Abb. 136. Viereckige Valenciennes Masche. — Abb. 137. Valenciennesspitze des 19. Jahrhunderts.

Plate 71
Fig. 136. Square Valenciennes mesh. — Fig. 137. 19th Century Valenciennes lace.

Planche 71
Fig. 136. La maille carrée de Valenciennes. — Fig. 137. Dentelle de Valenciennes du XIXe siècle.

Tavola 71
Fig. 136. Maglia Valenciennes quadrangolare. — Merletto Valenciennes del Secolo XIX.

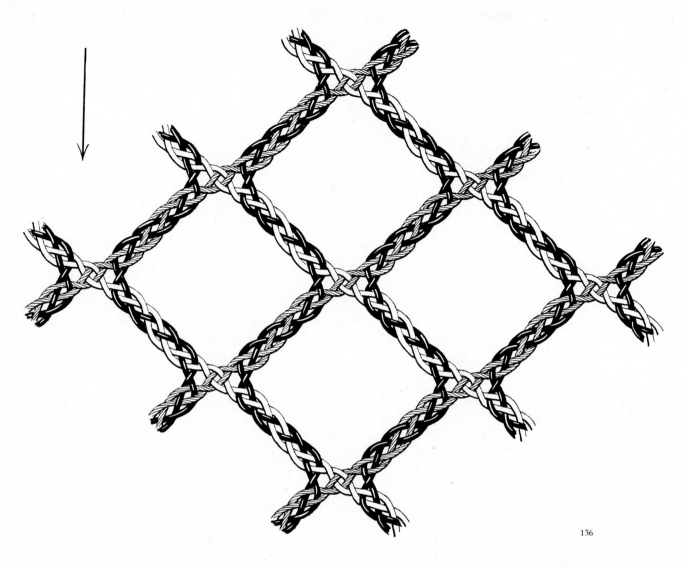

136

137

Tafel 72

Abb. 138. Doppelter Löcherschlag (Le point torchon avec passées tordues 2 fois). — Abb. 139. Doppelter Löcherschlag mit Formenschlagquadraten (Points d'esprit).

Plate 72

Fig. 138. Double *Fond Torchon (Le point torchon avec passies tordues deux fois)*. — Fig. 139. Double *Fond Torchon* with *points d'esprit*.

Planche 72

Fig. 138. Le point torchon avec passées tordues 2 tois. — Fig. 139. Le même réseau avec points d'esprit.

Tavola 72

Fig. 138. Doppio intreccio del foro (le point torchon avec passées tordues 2 fois). — Fig. 139. Doppio intreccio del foro con intrecci foggiati a quadri (points d'esprit).

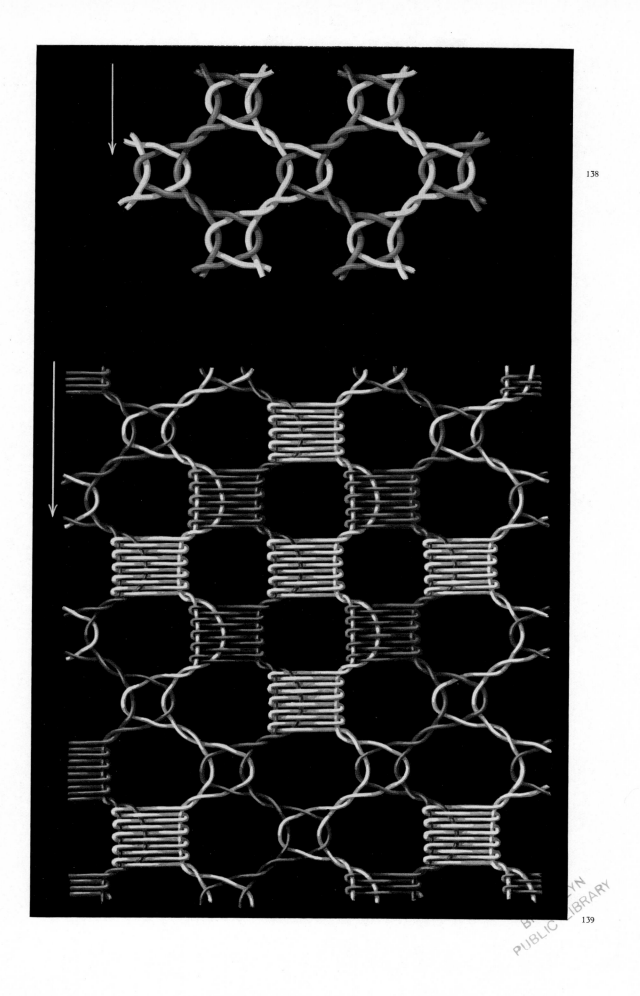

138

139

72

Tafel 73
Abb. 140. Antwerpener Spitze. Netzgrund: Verstärkter Löcherschlag, s. Abb. 141. — Abb. 141.
Verstärkter Löcherschlag. (Point de Paris. Fond Chant. Spelgrond).

Plate 73
Fig. 140. Antwerp lace. *Réseau:* reinforced *point torchon* s. fig. 141. — Fig. 141. Reinforced *point torchon*
(Point de Paris. Fond. Chant. Spelgrond).

Planche 73
Fig. 140. Dentelle anversoise. Fond de réseau: Point de Paris. Cf. fig. 141. — Fig. 141. Le point de Paris,
fond Chant, Spelgrond.

Tavola 73
Fig. 140. Merletto d'Anversa. Fondo della rete: intreccio rafforzato dei fori, cfr. fig. 141. — Fig. 141. Intreccio
rafforzato dei fori (Point de Paris. Fond Chant. Spelgrond).

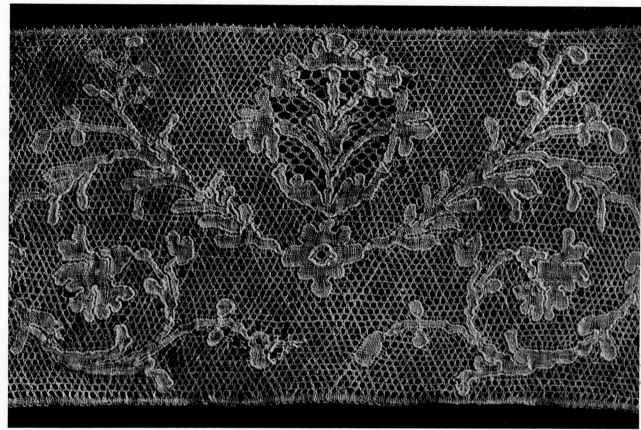

140

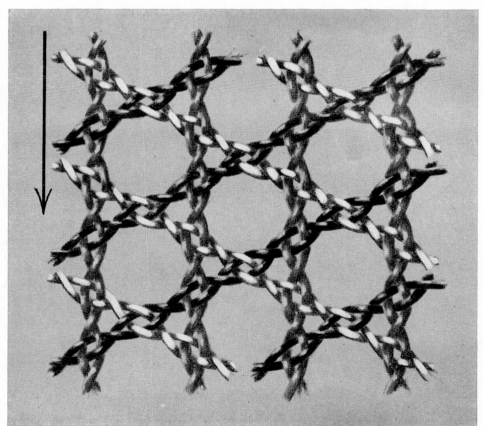

141

Tafel 74
Abb. 142. Antwerpener Spitze. Netzgrund: Fünflöchrige Masche 2. (Tafel 50, Abb. 106.)
Abb. 143. Antwerpener Spitze. Netzgrund: 12 fädige Armure (Tafel 69, Abb. 133).

Plate 74
Fig. 142. Antwerp lace. *Réseau*: five-hole mesh 2 (Plate 50, fig. 106). — Fig. 143. Antwerp lace. *Réseau*: 12-thread *Armure* (Plate 69, fig. 133).

Planche 74
Fig. 142. Dentelle anversoise. Fond de réseau: Maille à cinq trous 2 (Planche 50, fig. 106). — Fig. 143. Dentelle anversoise. Fond de réseau: Armure composée de douze fils (Planche 69, fig. 133).

Tavola 74
Fig. 142. Merletto di Anversa. Fondo della rete: Maglia 2 a cinque fori (tavola 50, fig. 106). — Fig. 143. Merletto di Anversa. Fondo della rete: Armatura a 12 fili (tavola 69, fig. 133).

142

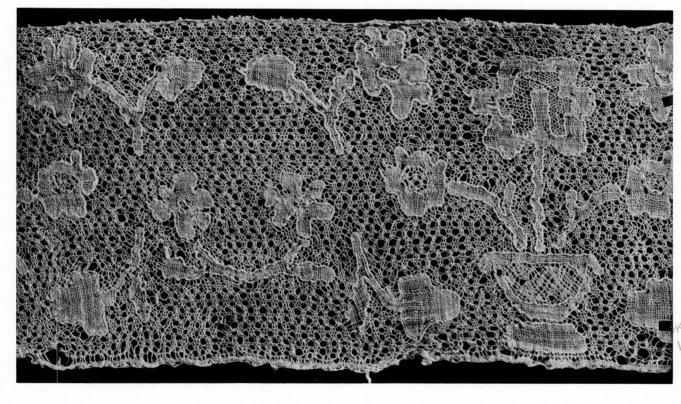

143

Tafel 75

Abb. 144. Sogenannte Holländische Spitze. Verkleinert.— Abb. 145. Teilstück der Spitze Abb. 144 in natürlicher Größe. — Abb. 146. Sogenannte Holländische Spitze, natürliche Größe. — Abb. 147. Sogenannte Holländische Spitze, natürliche Größe.

Plate 75

Fig. 144. So-called Dutch lace Reduced. — Fig. 145. Part of lace shewn in fig. 144, original size. — Fig. 146. So-called Dutch lace, original size. — Fig. 147. So called Dutch lace, original size.

Planche 75

Fig. 144. Dentelle aux fuseaux dite de Hollande. Figure réduite. — Fig. 145. Fragment de la dentelle fig. 144, mais en grandeur naturelle. — Fig. 146. Dentelle aux fuseaux dite de Hollande; en grandeur naturelle. — Fig. 147. Dentelle aux fuseaux dite de Hollande; en grandeur naturelle.

Tavola 75

Fig. 144. Merletto cosiddetto olandese. — Impiccolita. — Fig. 145. Particolare del merletto fig. 144, in grandezza naturale. — Fig. 146. Merletto cosiddetto olandese, grandezza naturale. — Fig. 147. Merletto cosiddetto olandese, grandezza naturale.

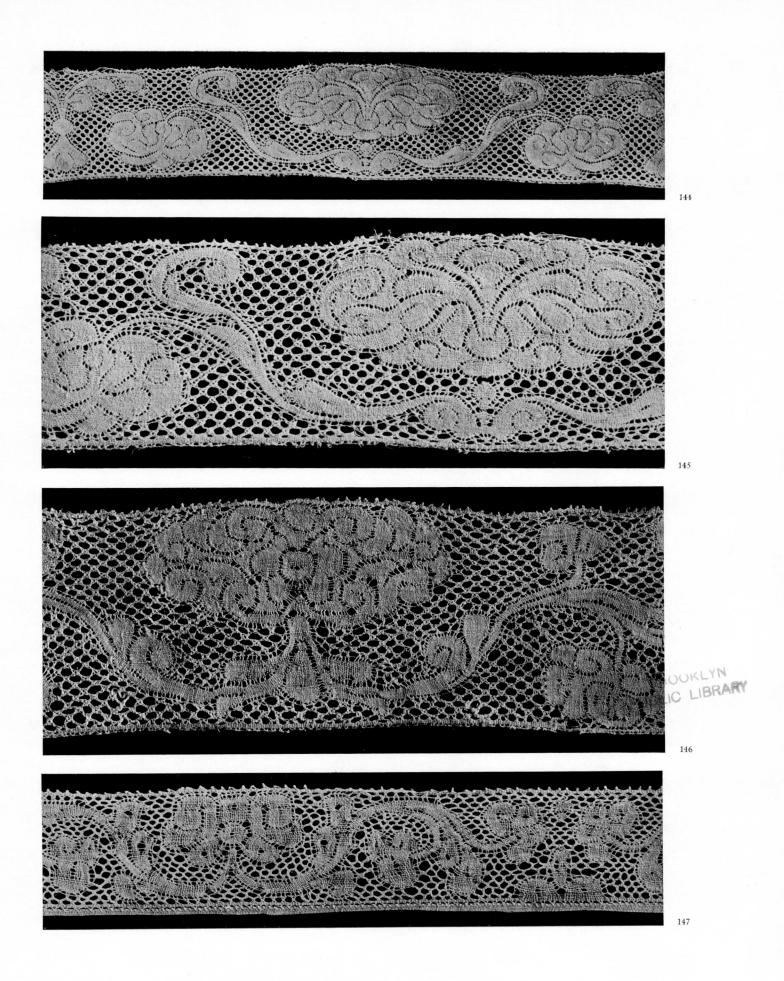

144

145

146

147

75

Tafel 76
Abb. 148. Liller Spitze, natürliche Größe. 19. Jahrhundert. Die Ränder des Musters sind von einem stärkeren Faden umgeben. Auf dem Netzgrund (Abb. 149). Formenschlagquadrate. — Abb. 149. Netzgrund der Liller Spitze.

Plate 76
Fig. 148. Lille lace, original size. 19th Century. The edges of the pattern are surrounded by a stouter thread. On the *réseau* (fig. 149) *points d'esprit*. — Fig. 149. *Réseau* of Lille lace.

Planche 76
Fig. 148. Dentelle de Lille en grandeur naturelle. XIXᵉ siècle. L'ornementation est cernée d'un fil plus fort. Sur le fond de réseau (fig. 149) des points d'esprit. — Fig. 149. Réseau de Lille.

Tavola 76
Fig. 148. Merletto di Lilla, grandezza naturale. XIX. Secolo. I disegni sono circondati da un filo più grosso. Sul fondo della rete (fig. 149) dei quadrati intrecciati. — Fig. 149. Fondo della rete dei merletti di Lilla.

148

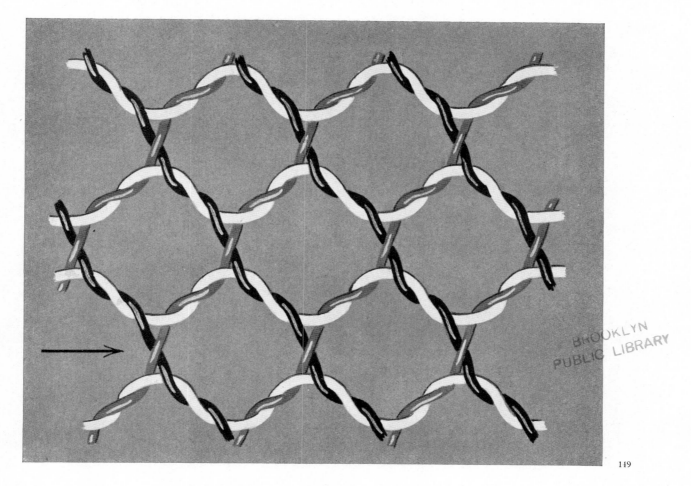

119

METHOD OF CALCULATION FOR THE TABLE OF COMPARISON Shewn in Pl. 76a

The threads may be regarded as cylinders hanging together and each 300 yards long. The relation of volume to weight is constant.

The number of these cylinders of the same volume which, taken together, weigh one English pound is expressed by "count" or number representing the degree of fineness of the thread.

As all the cylinders are the same lenght of 300 yards, the number of cylinders that go to make up one pound must depend on their volume. The greater the volume, the fewer will be the number of cylinders to the pound, and vice versa.

The volume is arrived at by multiplying the circular surface of the cylinder by its height.

The square of half the diameter, r, multiplied by the number π (3.14159), gives the content of the circular surface of the cylinder.

If N is the "count",

      300 the lenght of the cylinder, the constant,

        r half the diameter of the thread,

     1 lb. one English pound,

then we have the following formula:

$$r^2 \times \pi \times N \times 300 = 1 \text{ lb.}$$

If we take the thread a with a "count" of 300 and a width of 90 μ as the basis of comparison, the width of thread b ($2\varkappa$) with a "count" of 210, works out as follows:

$$\text{Thread } a) \quad 45^2 \times \pi \times 300 \times 300 = 1 \text{ lb.,}$$
$$\text{Thread } b) \quad \varkappa^2 \times \pi \times 210 \times 300 = 1 \text{ lb.,}$$
$$\varkappa^2 \times \pi \times 210 \times 300 = 45^2 \times \pi \times 300 \times 300.$$

Equal multiples on either side cancel out and we get:

$$\varkappa^2 \times 210 = 45^2 \times 300,$$
$$\varkappa^2 = \frac{45^2 \times 300}{210} = \frac{607\,500}{210} = 2893,$$
$$\varkappa = \sqrt{2893} = 53.8,$$
$$2\varkappa = 107.6\,\mu.$$

Thus, the width of the thread by calculation is 107.4 μ.

The width of the thread by measurement is   105 μ.

By the same method of calculation:

    The width of thread No. 100 = 156 μ, its measurement was 135 μ,

    The width of thread No.   60 = 201.2 μ, its measurement was 190 μ,

and the "count" of a thread 45 μ wide is 1200.

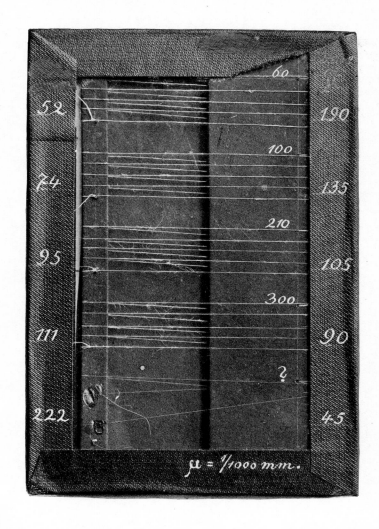

		Count	Measured width μ	Width by calculation μ
	d	60	190	201,2
Machine-made	c	100	135	156
threads	b	210	105	107,6
	a	300	90	
Old hand-made thread	e	1200	45	

76a

Die nachfolgenden Abbildungen sollen die vorhergehende zur Erläuterung des Textes dienende Beispielreihe ergänzen und einen Überblick über den Formenreichtum in den alten Spitzen geben.

The following plates supplement the examples illustrating the text and afford a general survey of the manifold patterns of antique lace.

Les planches suivantes sont destinées à compléter la série d'exemples illustrant le texte et à donner un aperçu de la richesse de formes des vieilles dentelles.

La serie di riproduzioni dell'appendice mira a completare gli esempi intesi ad illustrare il testo e a dare un'idea generale sulla ricchezza delle forme delle antiche trine.

Tafel 77

Durchbruch. Nadelarbeit, Italien. Ende 16. Jahrhundert. Natürliche Größe. Aus dem Bayerischen National=
museum in München.

Plate 77

Punto tagliato. Needlepoint, Italy. End of 16th Century. Original size. From the Bavarian National Museum,
Munich.

Planche 77

Point coupé. Ouvrage à l'aiguille. Italie. Fin du XVIe siècle. En grandeur naturelle. Collections du Musée
National Bavarois de Munich.

Tavola 77

Punto tagliato. Lavoro ad ago, Italia. Fine del XVI. secolo. Grandezza naturale. Dal Museo Nazionale
Bavarese di Monaco.

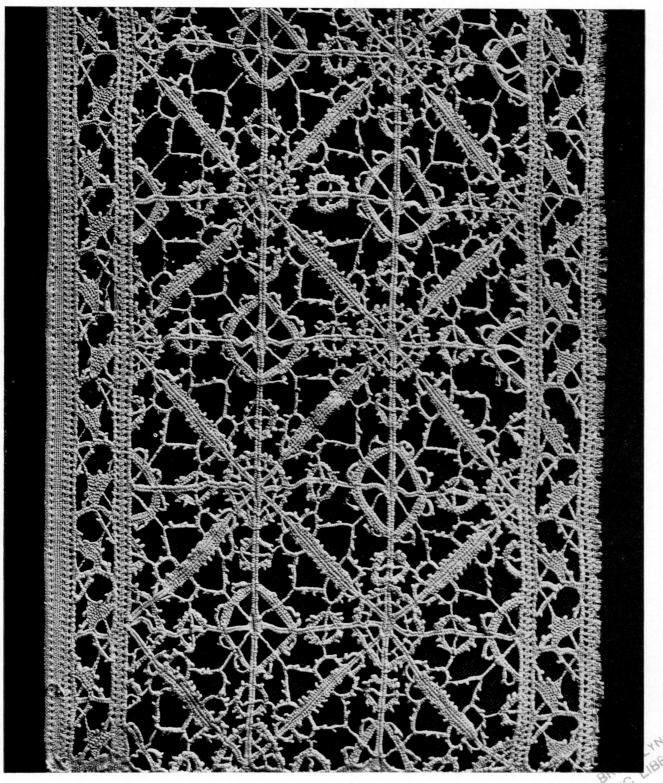

77

Tafel 78
Italienische Klöppelspitze nach der Art von Beispielen aus dem Musterbuch „Le Pompe", Venedig 1557.
Aus Ricci, Antiche Trine Italiane.

Plate 78
Italian pillow lace, in the same style as examples in the pattern-book "Le Pompe", Venice 1557. From
Ricci, Antiche Trine Italiane.

Planche 78
Dentelle italienne aux fuseaux dans le genre des exemples du Livre de modèles «Le Pompe», Venise
1557. D'après Ricci, Antiche Trine Italiane.

Tavola 78
Trine italiane a fuselli simili ai modelli delle «Pompe», Venezia 1557. Riprodotto dal Ricci, Antiche
Trine Italiane.

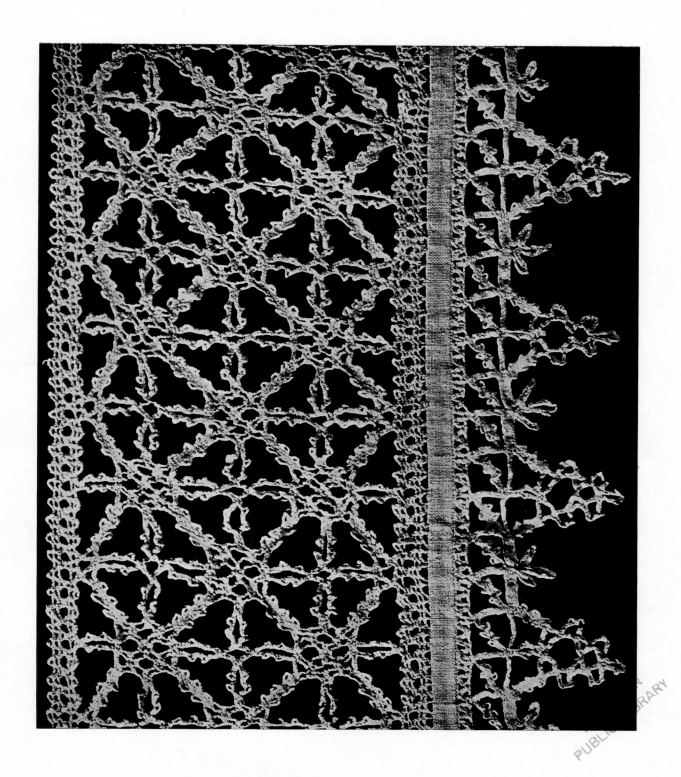

Tafel 79
Italienische Klöppelspitze nach der Art von Beispielen aus dem Musterbuch „Le Pompe", Venedig 1557.
Aus Ricci, Antiche Trine Italiane.

Plate 79
Italian pillow lace, in the same style as examples in the pattern-book "Le Pompe", Venice 1557. From Ricci, Antiche Trine Italiane.

Planche 79
Dentelle italienne aux fuseaux dans le genre des exemples du Livre de modèles «Le Pompe», Venise 1557. D'après Ricci, Antiche Trine Italiane.

Tavola 79
Trine italiane a fuselli simili ai modelli delle «Pompe», Venezia 1557. Riprodotto dal Ricci, Antiche Trine Italiane.

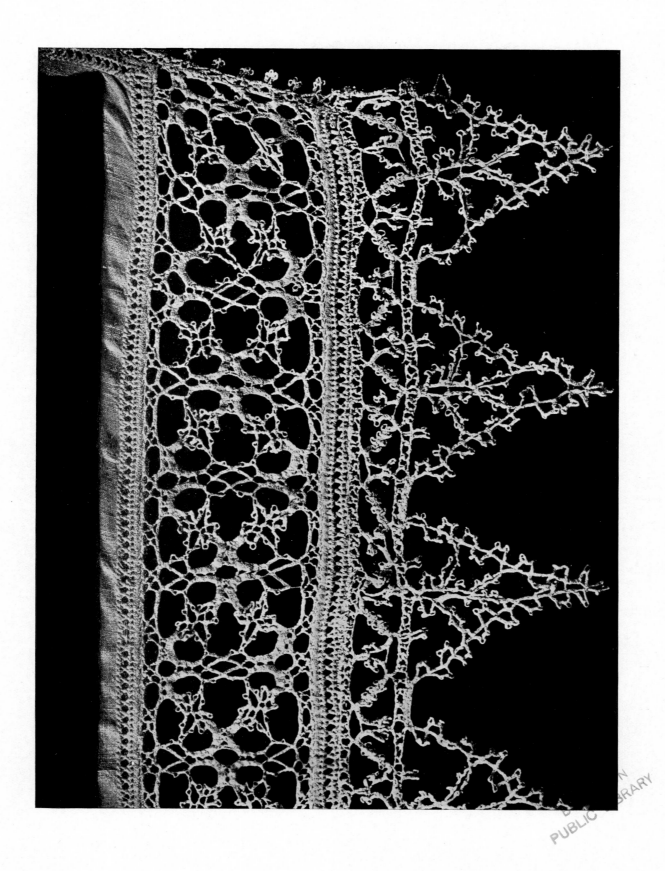

79

Tafel 80
Nadelarbeit. Reticella. Italien. 16. Jahrhundert. Natürliche Größe. Aus Ricci, Antiche Trine Italiane.

Plate 80
Needlepoint. Reticella. Italy. 16th Century. Original size. From Ricci, Antiche Trine Italiane.

Planche 80
Ouvrage à l'aiguille. Reticella. Italie. XVIe siècle. En grandeur naturelle. D'après Ricci, Antiche Trine Italiane.

Tavola 80
Lavoro ad ago. Falsature e punto di reticello. Italia. XVI. secolo. Grandezza naturale. Riprodotto dal Ricci, Antiche Trine Italiane.

83

Tafel 84

a, b, c. Genuesische Klöppelspitzen. Reticellamotiv. 16. Jahrhundert. Aus Ricci, Antiche Trine Italiane.

Plate 84

a, b, c. Genoese pillow lace. Reticella motif. 16th Century. From Ricci, Antiche Trine Italiane.

Planche 84

a, b, c. Dentelles de Gênes aux fuseaux. Imitation du motif du Reticella. XVIe siècle. D'après Ricci, Antiche Trine Italiane.

Tavola 84

a. b. c. Falsature genovesi a fuselli su disegno per reticello. XVI. secolo. Riprodotti dal Ricci, Antiche Trine Italiane.

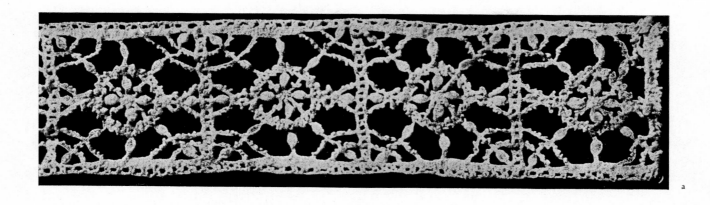

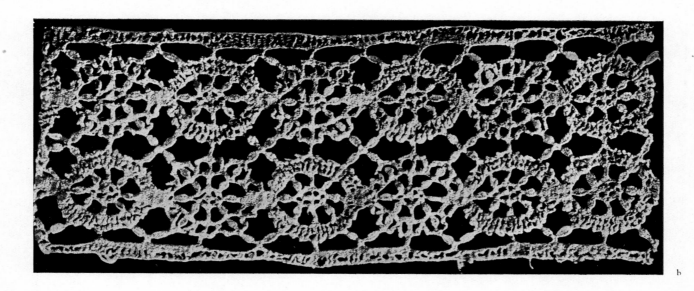

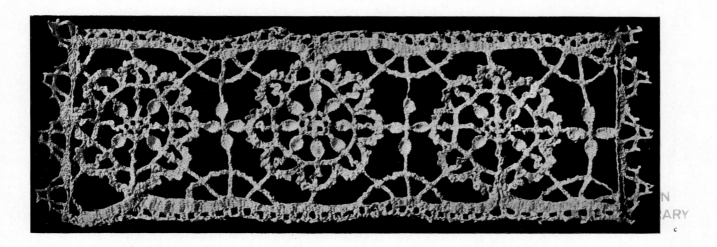

84

Tafel 85
a, b. Genuesische Klöppelspitzen. Rosenmotiv (Rosoni Genovesi). 17. Jahrhundert. Aus Ricci, Antiche Trine Italiane.

Plate 85
a, b. Genoese pillow lace. Rose motif (Rosoni Genovesi). 17th Century. From Ricci, Antiche Trine Italiane.

Planche 85
a, b. Dentelles de Gênes aux fuseaux. Motif: Rosoni Genovesi. XVIIᵉ siècle. D'après Ricci, Antiche Trine Italiane.

Tavola 85
a. b. Trine a fuselli. Rosoni Genovesi. XVII. Secolo. Riprodotte dal Ricci, Antiche Trine Italiane.

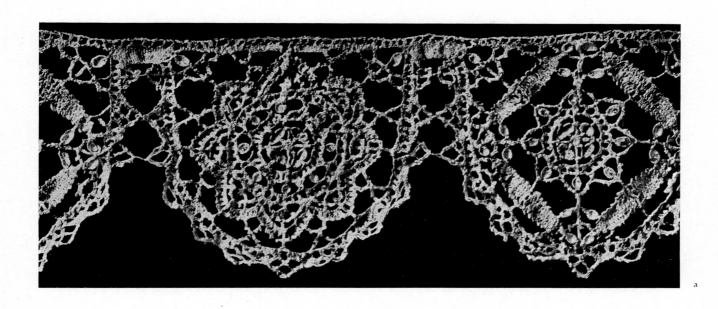

a

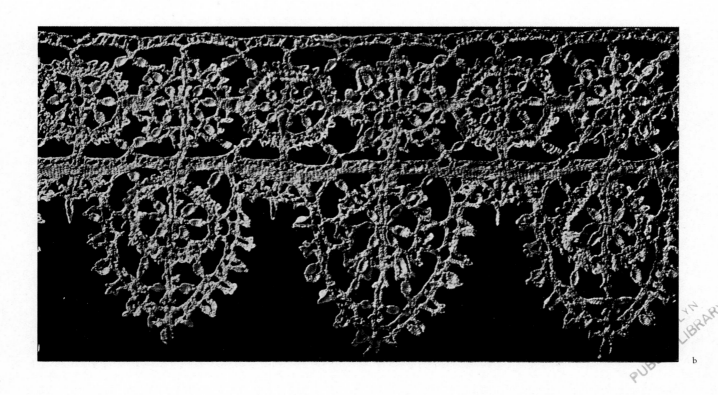

b

Tafel 86
Musterkarte für Reticella. Nadelarbeit. Italien. 16. Jahrhundert. Verkleinert. Aus Ricci, Antiche Trine Italiane.

Plate 86
Sempter. Reticella. Needlework. Italy. 16th Century. Reduced. From Ricci, Antiche Trine Italiane.

Planche 86
Dessin de Reticella. Ouvrage à l'aiguille. Italie. XVIᵉ siècle. Figure réduite. D'après Ricci, Antiche Trine Italiane.

Tavola 86
Campionario di reticello. Lavoro ad ago. Italia. XVI. Secolo. Impiccolita. Riprodotta dal Ricci, Antiche Trine Italiane.

Tafel 87
Nadelarbeit. Reticella. Italien. 16. Jahrhundert. Verkleinert. Aus Ricci, Antiche Trine Italiane.

Plate 87
Needlework. Reticella. Italy. 16th Cent. Reduced. From Ricci, Antiche Trine Italiane.

Planche 87
Ouvrage à l'aiguille. Reticella. Italie. XVIᵉ siècle. Figure réduite. D'après Ricci, Antiche Trine Italiane.

Tavola 87
Lavoro ad ago. Falsatura di reticello. Italia. XVI. Secolo. Impiccolita. Riprodotto dal Ricci, Antiche Trine Italiane.

87

Tafel 88
Nadelspitze. Punto in aria. Spanien? 16. Jahrhundert. Verkleinert. Aus der Sammlung Leopold Iklé, St. Gallen.

Plate 88
Needlepoint lace. *Punto in aria*. Spain? 16th Century. Reduced. From the Leopold Iklé Collection, St. Gall.

Planche 88
Dentelle à l'aiguille. Punto in aria. Espagne? XVIe siècle. Figure réduite. Collection Léopold Iklé, de Saint-Gall.

Tavola 88
Trine ad ago. Punto in aria. Spagna? XVI. Secolo. Impiccolita. Dalla collezione Leopold Iklé, St. Gallen.

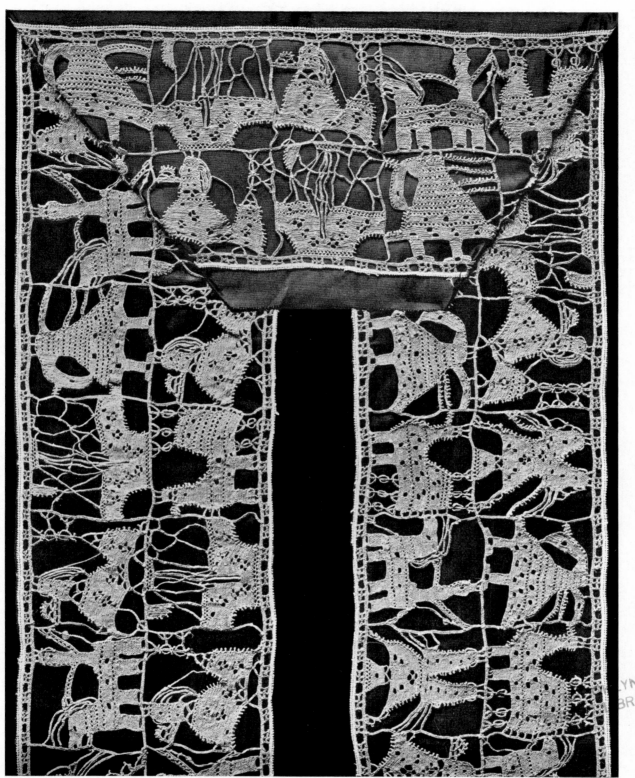

Tafel 89
a, b, c. Nadelspitzen. Punto in aria. Italien. 16.—17. Jahrhundert. Aus der Sammlung Leopold Iklé, St. Gallen.

Plate 89
a, b, c. Needlepoint lace. *Punto in aria*. Italy. 16—17th Cent. From the Leopold Iklé Collection St. Gall.

Planche 89
a, b, c. Dentelles à l'aiguille. Punto in aria. Italie. XVIᵉ —XVIIᵉ s. Collection Léopold Iklé, de Saint-Gall.

Tavola 89
a. b. c. Punte e falsatura ad ago. Punto in aria. Italia. XVI—XVII. Secolo. Dalla Collezione di Leopold Iklé, St. Gallen.

a

c

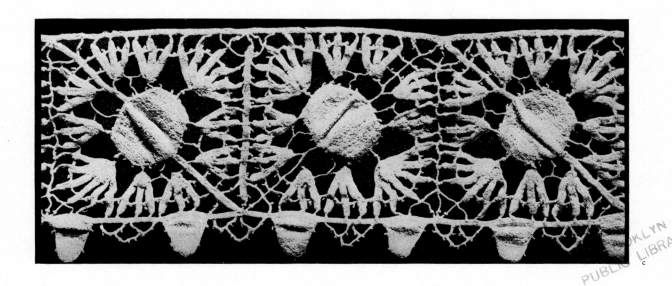

b

Tafel 90
Brüsseler Klöppelspitze von 1599. Verkleinert. Aus dem Kgl. Museum in Brüssel, nach Overloop.

Plate 90
Brussels pillow lace of 1599. Reduced. From the Royal Museum, Brussels, after Overloop.

Planche 90
Dentelle de Bruxelles aux fuseaux. 1599. Figure réduite. Collections du Musée Royal de Bruxelles; d'après van Overloop.

Tavola 90
Trina a fuselli di Brusselles del 1599. Impiccolita. Dal R. Museo di Brusselles, secondo Overloop.

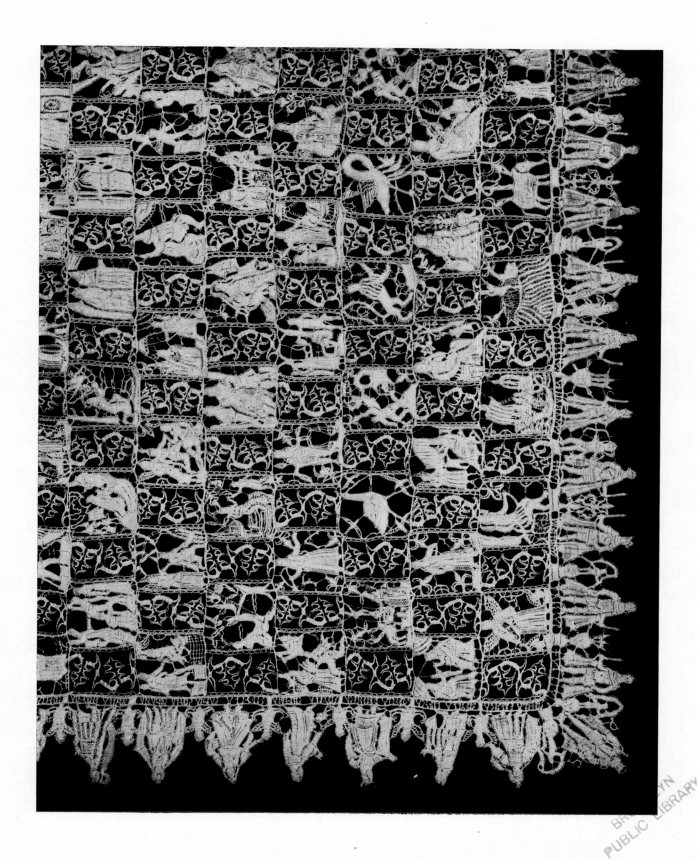

Tafel 91

a, b, c. Nadelarbeiten. Reticella. — d. Nadelspitze. Punto in aria. Zweite Hälfte 16. und Anfang 17. Jahrhundert. Stark verkleinert. Aus dem Bayerischen Nationalmuseum in München. — Die Spitze d in natürlicher Größe s. Tafel 92.

Plate 91

a, b, c. Needlework. Reticella. — d. Needlepoint lace. *Punto in aria.* Second half 16th and beginning 17th Cents. Greatly reduced. From the Bavarian National Museum, Munich. — Specimen d. in original size, see Plate 92.

Planche 91

a, b, c. Ouvrages à l'aiguille Reticella. — d. Dentelle à l'aiguille. Punto in aria. Deuxième moitié du XVIe siècle et commencement du XVIIe siècle. Figures très réduites. Collections du Musée National Bavarois de Munich. — La dentelle d. en grandeur naturelle: Cf. pl. 92.

Tavola 91

a. b. c. Lavori ad ago. Falsature e punte di reticello. — d. Trina ad ago. Punto in aria. Seconda metà del XVI. ed inizio del XVII. Secolo. Fortemente impiccolito. Dal Museo Nazionale Bavarese di Monaco. — La trina d in grandezza naturale, cfr. Tav. 92.

91

Tafel 92
Teilstück der Spitze Tafel 91 d in natürlicher Größe.

Plate 92
Part of lace shewn in Plate 91 d, original size.

Planche 92
Fragment de la dentelle pl. 91, d. mais en grandeur naturelle.

Tavola 92
Particolare della trina. Tav. 91 d in grandezza naturale.

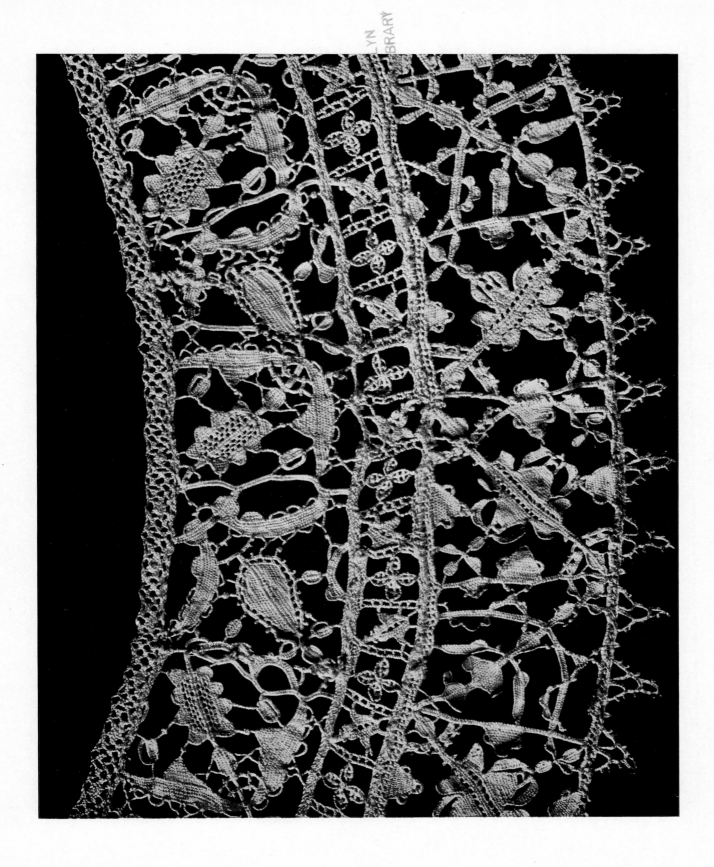

92

Tafel 93
Nadelarbeit. Reticella. Die Knöpfe und Knopfschlingen sind in der Technik der Nadelspitzen ausgeführt.
Italien. 16. Jahrhundert. Verkleinert. Aus Ricci, Antiche Trine Italiane.

Plate 93
Needlework. Reticella. The buttons and button-laces are made in the same technique as needlepoint lace.
Italy, 16th Century. Reduced. From Ricci, Antiche Trine Italiane.

Planche 93
Ouvrage à l'aiguille. Reticella. Les boutons et les boutonnières sont exécutés dans la technique des
dentelles à l'aiguille. Italie. XVIe siècle. Figure réduite. D'après Ricci, Antiche Trine Italiane.

Tavola 93
Lavoro ad ago. Falsature di reticello, bottoncini e allaciatura ad ago. Italia. XVI. Secolo. Impiccolita.
Riprodotto dal Ricci, Antiche Trine Italiane.

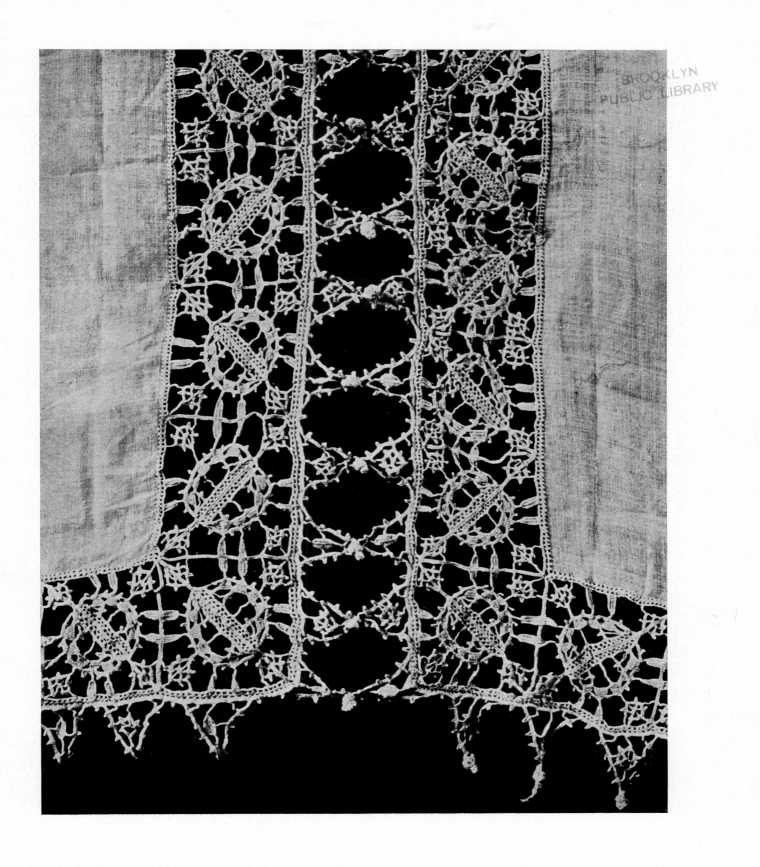

Tafel 94

a. Bestickte Reticella. Nadelarbeit. Italien. 16. Jahrhundert. Verkleinert. Aus Ricci, Antiche Trine Italiane.
— b. Nadelspitze. Punto in aria. Italien 16. Jahrhundert. Verkleinert. Aus Ricci, Antiche Trine Italiane.
Die Längsverstrebungen oben und unten bestehen aus Klöppelleisten.

Plate 94

a. Embroidered Reticella. Needlework. Italy. 16th Century. Reduced. From Ricci, Antiche Trine Italiane.
— b. Needlepoint lace. *Punto in aria.* Italy. 16th Century. Reduced. From Ricci, Antiche Trine Italiane.
The connecting links lengthways, above and below, are bobbin-made.

Planche 94

a. Dentelle reticella brodée. Ouvrage à l'aiguille. Italie. XVIᵉ siècle. Figure réduite. D'après Ricci, Antiche
Trine Italiane. — b. Dentelle à l'aiguille. Punto in aria. Italie. XVIᵉ siècle. Figure réduite. D'après Ricci.
Antiche Trine Italiane. Le soutien dans le sens de la longueur, en haut et en bas: lacets faits aux
fuseaux.

Tavola 94

a. Reticello ricamato. Lavoro ad ago. Italia. XVI. Secolo. Impiccolita. Riprodotta dal Ricci, Antiche
Trine Italiane. — b. Trina ad ago. Punto in aria. Italia. XVI. Secolo. Impiccolita. Riprodotto dal Ricci,
Antiche Trine Italiane. I puntellamenti superiori ed inferiori nel senso della lunghezza sono costituiti di
listelli a fuselli.

a

b

Tafel 95
a, b. Nadelarbeit. Reticella. Italien. 16. Jahrhundert. Verkleinert. Aus Ricci, Antiche Trine Italiane.

Plate 95
a, b. Needlework. Reticella. Italy. 16th Century. Reduced. From Ricci, Antiche Trine Italiane.

Planche 95
a, b. Ouvrage à l'aiguille. Reticella. Italie. XVIe siècle. Figures réduites. D'après Ricci, Antiche Trine Italiane.

Tavola 95
a. b. Lavoro ad ago. Quadrati, falsature e punte di reticello. Italia. XVI. Secolo. Impiccolita. Riprodotto dal Ricci, Antiche Trine Italiane.

a

b

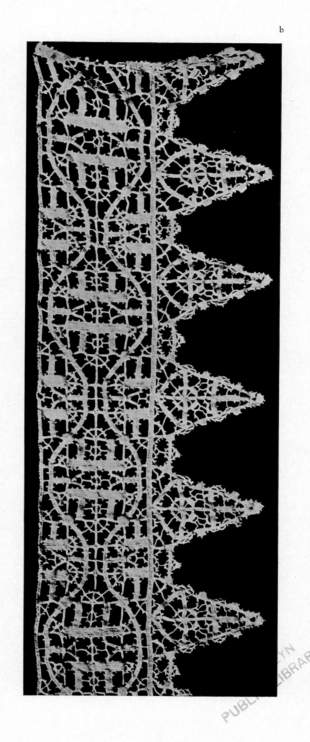

95

Tafel 96
Nadelspitze. Punto in aria. Italien. 17. Jahrhundert. Aus der Sammlung Leopold Iklé, St. Gallen.

Plate 96
Needlepoint lace. Punto in aria. Italy. 17th Century. From the Leopold Iklé Collection, St. Gall.

Planche 96
Dentelle à l'aiguille. Punto in aria. Italie. XVIIᵉ siècle. Collection Léopold Iklé, de Saint-Gall.

Tavola 96
Trina ad ago. Punto in aria. Italia. XVII. Secolo. Dalla collezione di Leopold Iklé, St. Gallen.

Tafel 97
Nadelspitze. Punto in aria. Italien. 16.—17. Jahrhundert. Aus der Sammlung Leopold Iklé, St. Gallen.

Plate 97
Needlepoint lace. Punto in aria. Italy. 16—17th Century. From the Leopold Iklé Collection, St. Gall.

Planche 97
Dentelle à l'aiguille. Punto in aria. Italie. XVIᵉ—XVIIᵉ siècles. Collection Léopold Iklé, de Saint-Gall.

Tavola 97
Trina ad ago. Punto in aria. Italia. XVI.—XVII. Secolo. Dalla collezione di Leopold Iklé, St. Gallen.

Tafel 98

a, b, c. Nadelarbeiten. Reticella. Italien. Zweite Hälfte 16. und Anfang 17. Jahrhundert. Stark verkleinert. Aus dem Bayerischen Nationalmuseum in München. — Die Durchbrucharbeit a in natürlicher Größe s. Tafel 99.

Plate 98

a, b, c. Specimen of needlework. Reticella. Italy. Second half 16th and beginning 17th Cents. Greatly reduced. From the Bavarian National Museum, Munich. — Specimen a, in original size, see Plate 99.

Planche 98

a, b, c. Ouvrages à l'aiguille. Reticella. Italie. Deuxième moitié du XVIe et commencement du XVIIe siècle. Figures très réduites. Collections du Musée National Bavarois de Munich. — Le point coupé a. en grandeur naturelle: Cf. pl. 99.

Tavola 98

a. b. c. Lavori ad ago. Falsature e punte a reticello. Italia. Secondo metà del XVI. ed inizio del XVII. Secolo. Fortemente impiccoliti. Dal Museo Nazionale Bavarese di Monaco. — La trina a, in grandezza naturale, cfr. Tav. 99.

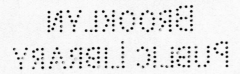

a b c

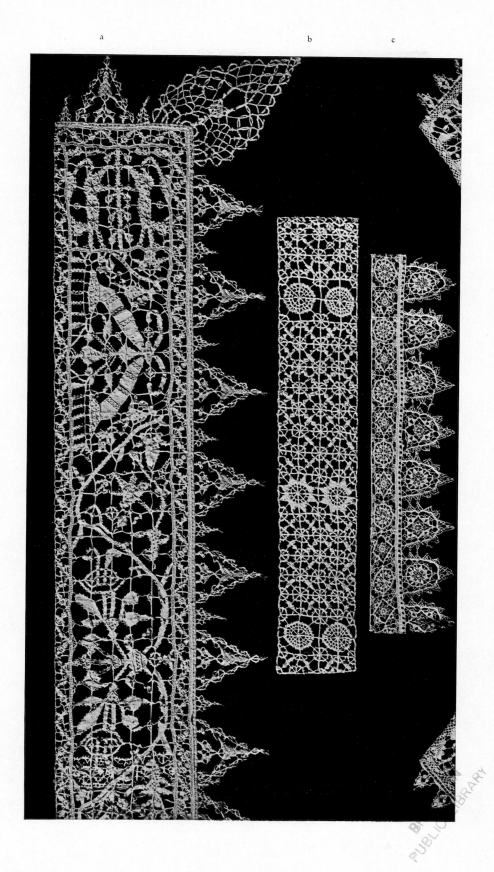

98

Tafel 99
Teilstück der Reticella Tafel 98a in natürlicher Größe. Die Randzacken Nadelspitze, Punto in aria.

Plate 99
Part of the Reticella shewn in Plate 98a, original size. The scallops round the edge are needlepoint lace. *Punto in aria.*

Planche 99
Fragment de l'ouvage pl. 98a, mais en grandeur naturelle. Les dents du bord: Dentelle à l'aiguille Punto in aria.

Tavola 99
Particolare della trina Tav. 98a in grandezza naturale. I denti dell'orlatura sono eseguiti a punto in aria.

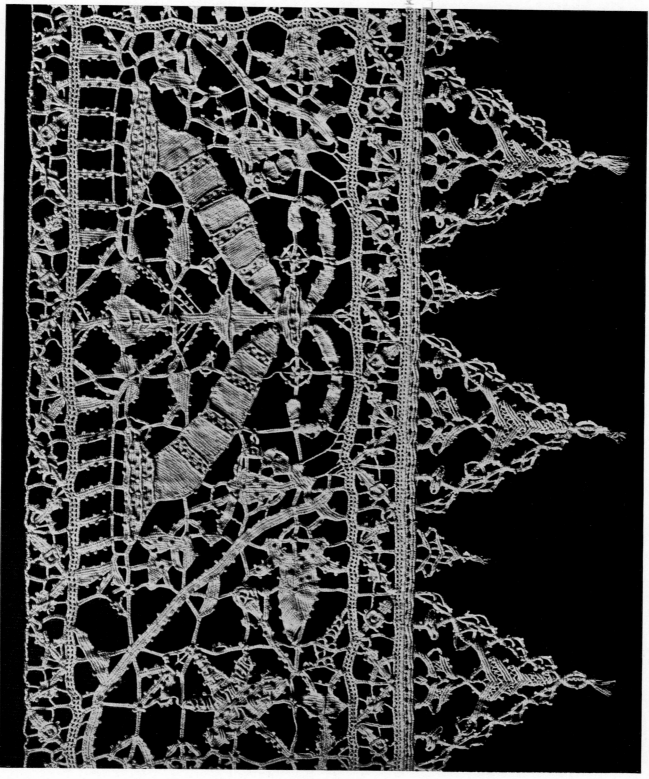

Tafel 100
a, b. Italienische Klöppelspitzen nach der Art von Beispielen aus dem Musterbuch von Isabetta Catanea Parasole, Venedig 1615. Aus Ricci, Antiche Trine Italiane.

Plate 100
a, b. Italian pillow lace in the same style as examples in the pattern=book of Isabetta Catanea Parasole, Venice 1615. From Ricci, Antiche Trine Italiane.

Planche 100
a, b. Dentelles italiennes aux fuseaux dans le genre d'exemples du Livre de modèles de Mme Isabetta Catanea Parasole, Venise, 1615. D'après Ricci, Antiche Trine Italiane.

Tavola 100
a. b. Falsature e punte simili ai modelli di Isabetta Catanea Parasole, Venezia 1615. Riprodotte dal Ricci, Antiche Trine Italiane.

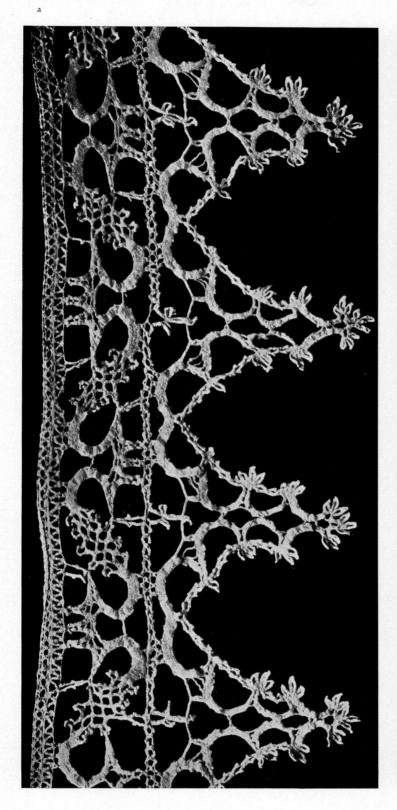
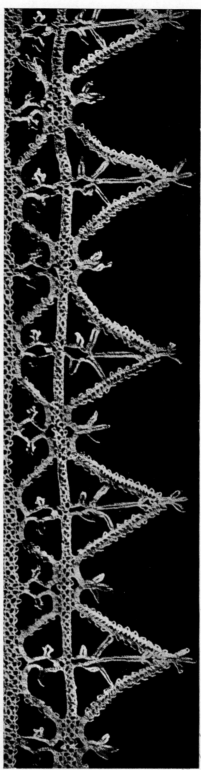

Tafel 101

a, b. Italienische Klöppelspitzen nach der Art von Beispielen aus dem Musterbuch von Isabetta Catanea Parasole, Venedig 1615. Aus Ricci, Antiche Trine Italiane. — Die Spitze b, aus der Sammlung Signora Ida Schiff, Florenz, die Spitze Tafel 102 aus München und die Spitze Tafel 103, b aus Brüssel sind nach demselben Muster angefertigt. Die Ausführungen zeigen Verschiedenheiten. Die Spitzen Tafel 101, b und Tafel 102 in ihrer gedrungeneren Art lassen den Ursprung in Italien vermuten. Die mehr lockere Spitze Tafel 103, b weist eher nach Flandern.

Plate 101

a, b. Italian pillow lace in the same style as examples in the pattern-book of Isabella Catanea Parasole, Venice 1615. From Ricci, Antiche Trine Italiane. — Lace b, from the collection of Signora Ida Schiff, Florence, the lace in Plate 102 from Munich and the lace in Plate 103b from Brussels were made from the same pattern. Differences occur in the execution. The more closely worked style of the laces shewn in Plate 101b and Plate 102 tends to indicate Italian origin. The more losely worked lace in Plate 103 b points rather to Flanders.

Planche 101

a, b. Dentelles italiennes aux fuseaux dans le genre d'exemples du Livre de modèles de Mme Isabetta Catanea Parasole, Venise, 1615. D'après Ricci, Antiche Trine Italiane. — La dentelle b, qui fait partie de la collection de Mme Ida Schiff, de Florence, ainsi que la dentelle reproduite à la planche 102 (Collections du Musée National Bavarois de Munich) et la dentelle reproduite à la planche 103, b (Collections du Musée Royal de Bruxelles), ont été exécutées d'après le même dessin. Ces dentelles présentent des différences. Les dentelles reproduites à la planche 101, b et à la planche 102 font, par leur genre serré, supposer une origine italienne. La dentelle reproduite à la planche 103, b, qui est plus relâchée, fait plutôt supposer une origine flamande.

Tavola 101

a. b. Trine italiane a fuselli. Falsature e punte simili ai modelli di Isabetta Catanea Parasole, Venezia 1615. Riprodotti dal Ricci, Antiche Trine Italiane. La trina b, dalla collezione della signora Ida Schiff, Firenze, la trina Tav. 102 di Monaco e la trina Tav. 103 b. di Brusselles sono eseguite secondo lo stesso modello. Le esecuzioni mostrano delle variazioni. Le trine della Tav. 101 b e della Tav. 102, data la loro maggiore compattezza, sembrano d'origine italiana. La trina più leggera della Tav. 103 b, sembra provenire invece dalla Fiandra.

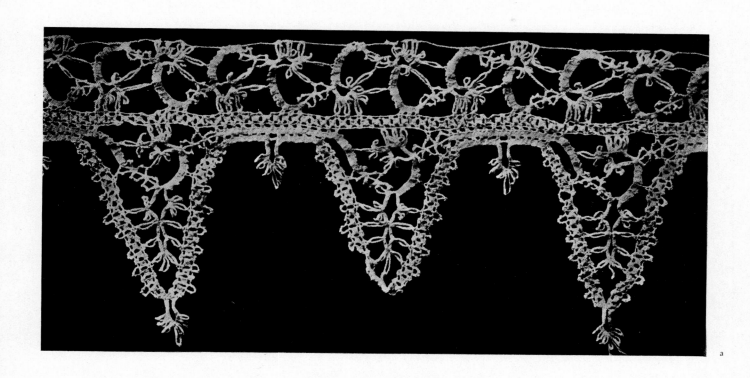

a

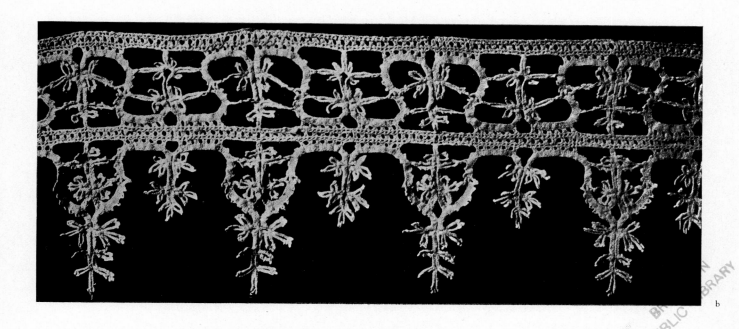

b

Tafel 102
Italienische Klöppelspitze. Anfang 17. Jahrhundert. Natürliche Größe. Aus dem Bayerischen National=
museum in München. — Vgl. Bemerkung zu Tafel 101, b.

Plate 102
Italian pillow lace. Beginning of 17th Century. Original size. From the Bavarian National Museum, Mu=
nich. Cp. note to Plate 101b.

Planche 102
Dentelle italienne aux fuseaux. Commencement du XVIIe siècle. En grandeur naturelle. Collections du
Musée National Bavarois de Munich. Cf. la remarque se rapportant à la planche 101, b.

Tavola 102
Trine italiane a fuselli. Inizio del XVII. Secolo. Grandezza naturale. Dal Museo Nazionale Bavarese
di Monaco. Cfr. l'osservazione alla Tav. 101 b.

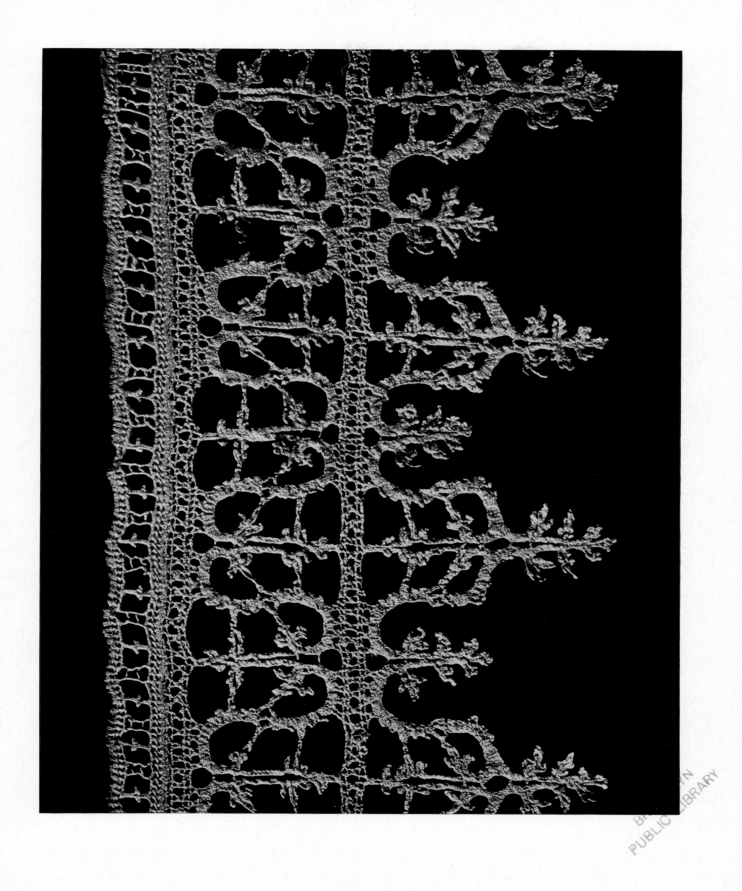

102

Tafel 103

a, b. Flandrische Klöppelspitzen. Anfang 17. Jahrhundert. Aus dem Kgl. Museum in Brüssel, nach Overloop. — Vgl. Bemerkung zu Tafel 101, b.

Plate 103

a, b. Flemish pillow lace. Beginning of 17th Century. From the Royal Museum, Brussels, after Overloop. — Cp. note to Plate 101 b.

Planche 103

a. b. Dentelles flamandes aux fuseaux. Commencement du XVIIe siècle. Collections du Musée Royal de Bruxelles; d'après van Overloop. — Cf. la remarque se rapportant à la planche 101, b.

Tavola 103

a. b. Trine a fuselli di Fiandra. Inizio del XVII. Secolo. Dal R. Museo di Brusselles, secondo Overloop Cfr. l'osservazione alla Tav. 101 b.

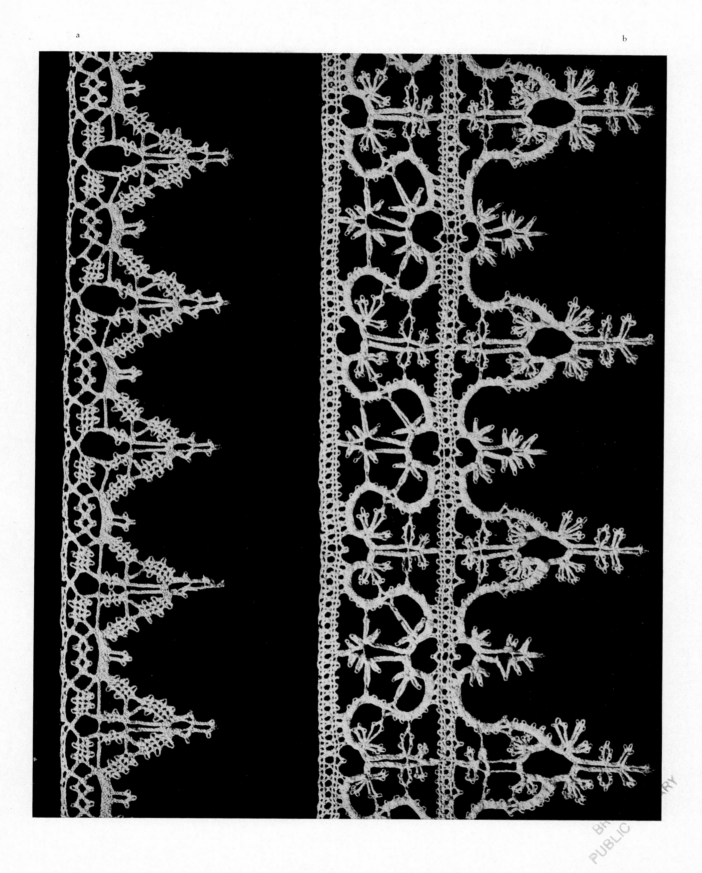

103

Tafel 104
Nadelspitze. Punto in aria. Italien. Anfang 17. Jahrhundert. Natürliche Größe. Aus Ricci, Antiche Trine Italiane.

Plate 104
Needlepoint lace. Punto in aria. Italy. Beginning of 17th Century. Original size. From Ricci, Antiche Trine Italiane.

Planche 104
Dentelle à l'aiguille. Punto in aria. Italie. Commencement du XVIIe siècle. En grandeur naturelle. D'après Ricci, Antiche Trine Italiane.

Tavola 104
Trine ad ago. Punto in aria. Italia. Inizio del XVII. Secolo. Grandezza naturale. Riprodotto dal Ricci, Antiche Trine Italiane.

104

Tafel 105
Nadelspitze. Punto in aria. Italien. Anfang 17. Jahrhundert. Verkleinert. Aus Ricci, Antiche Trine Italiane.

Plate 105
Needlepoint lace. Punto in aria. Italy. Beginning of 17th Century. Reduced. From Ricci, Antiche Trine Italiane.

Planche 105
Dentelle à l'aiguille. Punto in aria. Italie. Commencement du XVIIe siècle. Figure réduite. D'après Ricci, Antiche Trine Italiane.

Tavola 105
Trina ad ago. Punto in aria. Italia. Inizio del XVII. Secolo. Impiccolita. Riprodotto dal Ricci, Antiche Trine Italiane.

105

Tafel 106

Genuesische Klöppelspitzen. Nachahmung gleichzeitiger Nadelspitze (Punto in aria). Anfang 17. Jahrhundert. Aus Ricci, Antiche Trine Italiane.

Plate 106

Genoese pillow lace. Imitation of contemporary needlepoint lace (Punto in aria). Beginning of 17th Century. From Ricci, Antiche Trine Italiane.

Planche 106

Dentelles de Gênes aux fuseaux. Imitation de la dentelle à l'aiguille de l'époque (Punto in aria). Commencemeut du XVIIᵉ siècle. D'après Ricci, Antiche Trine Italiane.

Tavola 106

Trine a fuselli. Falsature e punte su disegno di punto in aria. Genova. Inizio del XVII. Secolo. Riprodotte dal Ricci, Antiche Trine Italiane.

106

Tafel 107
Genuesische Klöppelspitze. Nachahmung gleichzeitiger Nadelspitze (Punto in aria). Anfang 17. Jahrhundert. Aus Ricci, Antiche Trine Italiane.

Plate 107
Genoese pillow lace. Imitation of contemporary needlepoint lace (Punto in aria). Beginning of 17th Century. From Ricci, Antiche Trine Italiane.

Planche 107
Dentelle de Gênes aux fuseaux. Imitation de la dentelle à l'aiguille de l'époque (Punto in aria). Commencement du XVIIᵉ siècle. D'après Ricci, Antiche Trine Italiane.

Tavola 107
Trine a fuselli. Punte eseguite su disegno per punto in aria. Genova. Inizio del XVII. Secolo. Riprodotte dal Ricci, Antiche Trine Italiane.

Tafel 108
Nadelspitze. Punto in aria. Italien. Anfang 17. Jahrhundert. Aus Ricci, Antiche Trine Italiane.

Plate 108
Needlepoint lace. Punto in aria. Italy. Beginning of 17th Century. From Ricci, Antiche Trine Italiane.

Planche 108
Dentelle à l'aiguille. Punto in aria. Italie. Commencement du XVIIe siècle. D'après Ricci, Antiche Trine Italiane.

Tavola 108
Trine ad ago. Punto in aria. Italia. Inizio del XVII. Secolo. Riprodotte dal Ricci, Antiche Trine Italiane.

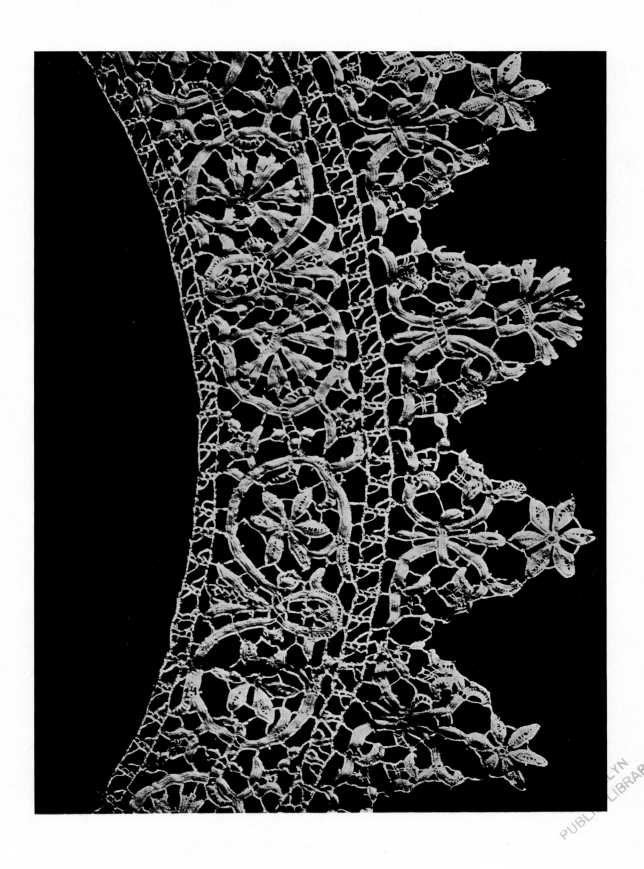

108

Tafel 109

Nadelspitze. Punto in aria. Italien. Erste Hälfte 17. Jahrhundert. Verkleinert. Aus Ricci, Antiche Trine Italiane.

Plate 109

Needlepoint lace. Punto in aria. Italy. First half 17th Century. Reduced. From Ricci, Antiche Trine Italiane.

Planche 109

Dentelle à l'aiguille. Punto in aria. Italie. Première moitié du XVIIᵉ siècle. Figure réduite. D'après Ricci, Antiche Trine Italiane.

Tavola 109

Trina ad ago. Punto in aria. Italia. Prima metà del XVII. Secolo. Impiccolita. Riprodotto dal Ricci, Antiche Trine Italiane.

109

Tafel 110
Nadelspitze. Punto in aria. Italien. Erste Hälfte 17. Jahrhundert. Verkleinert. Aus Ricci, Antiche Trine Italiane.

Plate 110
Needlepoint lace. Punto in aria. Italy. First half 17th Century. Reduced. From Ricci, Antiche Trine Italiane.

Planche 110
Dentelle à l'aiguille. Punto in aria. Italie. Première moitié du XVIIe siècle. Figure réduite. D'après Ricci, Antiche Trine Italiane.

Tavola 110
Trina ad ago. Punto in aria. Italia. Prima metà del XVII. Secolo. Impiccolita. Riprodotto dal Ricci, Antiche Trine Italiane.

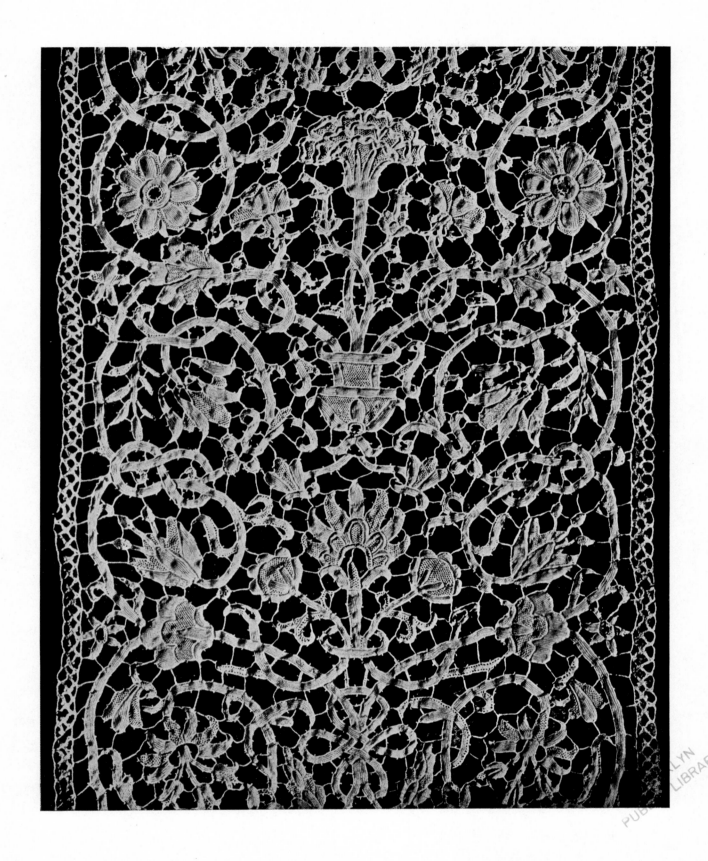

110

Tafel 111
Nadelspitze. Punto in aria. Italien. Erste Hälfte 17. Jahrhundert. Verkleinert. Aus Ricci, Antiche Trine Italiane.

Plate 111
Needlepoint lace. Punto in aria. Italy. First half 17th Century. Reduced. From Ricci, Antiche Trine Italiane.

Planche 111
Dentelle à l'aiguille. Punto in aria. Italie. Première moitié du XVIIe siècle. Figure réduite. D'après Ricci, Antiche Trine Italiane.

Tavola 111
Trina ad ago. Punto in aria. Italia. Prima metà del XVII. Secolo. Impiccolita. Riprodotto dal Ricci, Antiche Trine Italiane.

111

Tafel 112
Nadelspitze. Punto in aria. Italien. Erste Hälfte 17. Jahrhundert. Verkleinert. Aus Ricci, Antiche Trine Italiane.

Plate 112
Needlepoint lace. Punto in aria. Italy. First half 17th Century. Reduced. From Ricci, Antiche Trine Italiane.

Planche 112
Dentelle à l'aiguille. Punto in aria. Italie. Première moitié du XVIIe siècle. Figure réduite. D'après Ricci, Antiche Trine Italiane.

Tavola 112
Trina ad ago. Punto in aria. Italia. Prima metà del XVII. Secolo. Impiccolita. Riprodotto dal Ricci, Antiche Trine Italiane.

112

Tafel 113

a. Italienische Klöppelspitze. Erste Hälfte 17. Jahrhundert. Verkleinert. — b. Nadelspitze. Punto in aria.
Italien. Erste Hälfte 17. Jahrhundert. Verkleinert. — Aus der Sammlung Leopold Iklé, St. Gallen.

Plate 113

a. Italian pillow lace. First half 17th Century. Reduced. — b. Needlepoint lace. Punto in aria. Italy. First
half 17th Century. Reduced. — From the Leopold Iklé Collection, St. Gall.

Planche 113

a. Dentelle italienne aux fuseaux. Première moitié du XVIIe siècle. Figure réduite. — b. Dentelle à l'aiguille.
Punto in aria. Italie. Première moitié du XVIIe siècle. Figure réduite. — Collection Léopold Iklé, de Saint-Gall.

Tavola 113

a. Trina a fuselli italiana. Prima metà del XVII. Secolo. Impiccolita. — b. Trina ad ago. Punto in aria. Italia.
Prima metà del XVII. Secolo. Impiccolita. — Dalla collezione di Leopold Iklé, St. Gallen.

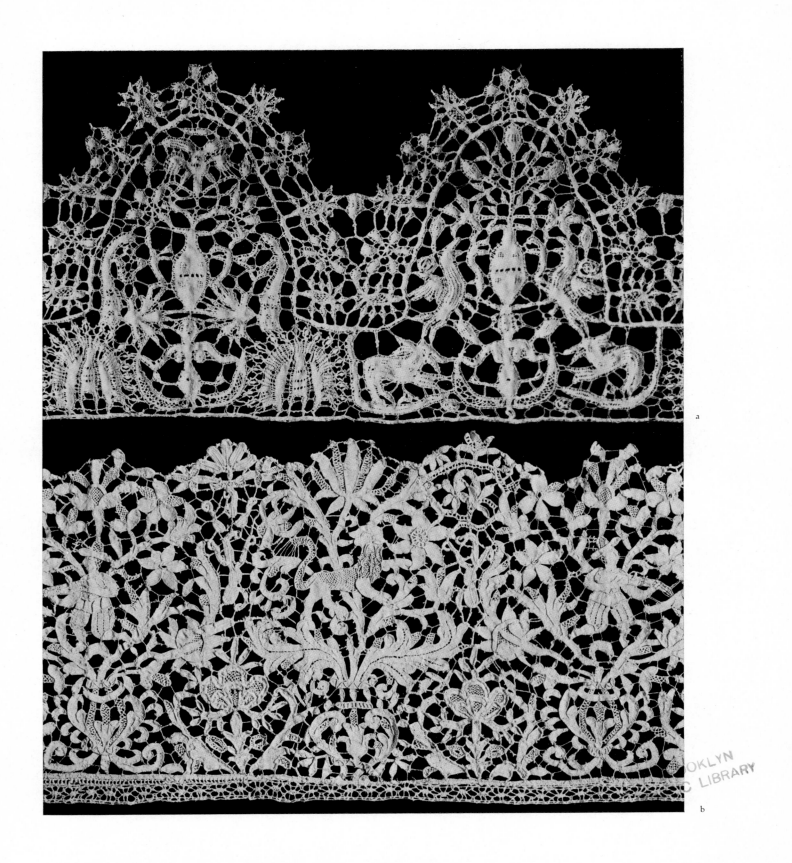

a

b

113

Tafel 114

a, b. Flandrische Klöppelspitzen. Erste Hälfte 17. Jahrhundert. Natürliche Größe. Aus dem Bayerischen Nationalmuseum in München.

Plate 114

a, b. Flemish pillow lace. First half 17th Century. Original size. From the Bavarian National Museum, Munich.

Planche 114

a, b. Dentelles flamandes aux fuseaux. Première moitié du XVIIe siècle. En grandeur naturelle. Collections du Musée National Bavarois de Munich.

Tavola 114

a, b. Trine a fuselli di Fiandra. Prima metà del XVII. Secolo. Grandezza naturale. Dal Museo Nazionale Bavarese di Monaco.

a

b

114

Tafel 115

a, b, c, d. Geklöppelte Gold= und Silberborten. 17. Jahrhundert. Natürliche Größe. Aus dem Baye=
rischen Nationalmuseum in München.

Plate 115

a, b, c, d. Bobbin=made gold and silver lace. 17th Century. Original size. From the Bavarian National
Museum, Munich.

Planche 115

a, b, c, d. Galons d'or et d'argent faits aux fuseaux. XVIIᵉ siècle. En grandeur naturelle. Collections du
Musée National Bavarois de Munich.

Tavola 115

a, b, c, d. Galloni a fuselli in oro ed argento. XVII. Secolo. Grandezza naturale. Dal Museo Nazionale
Bavarese di Monaco.

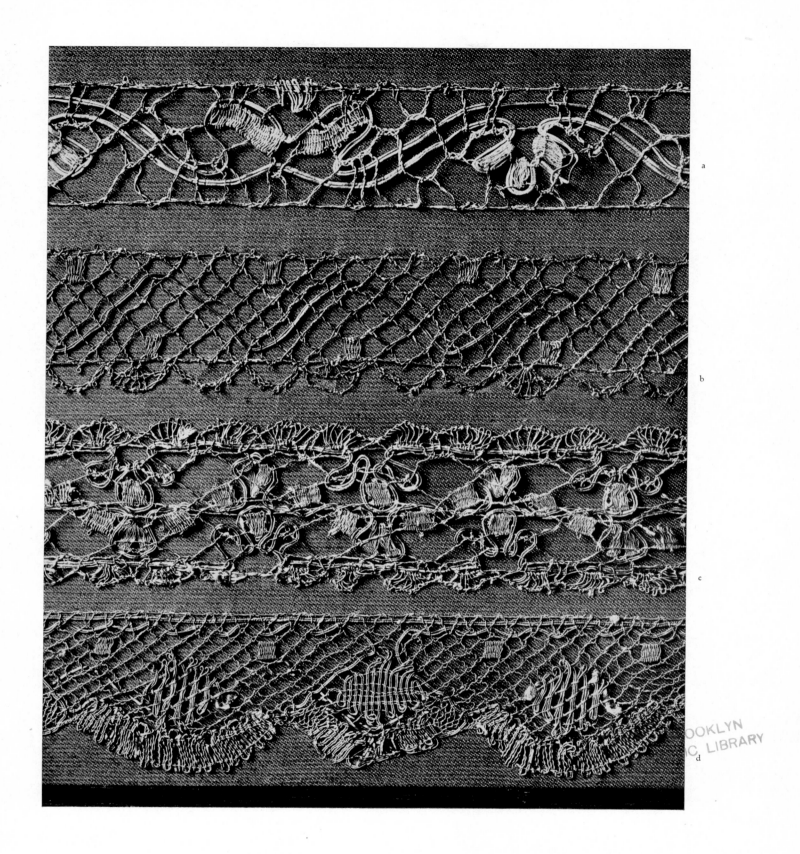

a

b

c

d

115

Tafel 116
Nadelspitze. Punto tagliato a fogliami. Italien. Mitte 17. Jahrhundert. Aus der Sammlung Leopold Iklé, St. Gallen.

Plate 116
Needlepoint lace. Punto tagliato a fogliami. Italy. Middle of 17th Century. From the Leopold Iklé Collection, St. Gall.

Planche 116
Dentelle à l'aiguille. Point gros de Venise. Punto tagliato a fogliami. Italie. Milieu du XVIIe siècle. Collection Léopold Iklé de Saint-Gall.

Tavola 116
Trina ad ago. Punto tagliato a fogliami. Italia. Metà del XVII. Secolo. Dalla collezione di Leopold Iklé, St. Gallen.

116

Tafel 117
Nadelspitze. Punto tagliato a fogliami. Italien. Mitte 17. Jahrhundert. Verkleinert. Aus dem South Kensington Museum, London, nach Alan S. Cole.

Plate 117
Needlepoint lace. Punto tagliato a fogliami. Italy. Middle of 17th Century. From the South Kensington Museum, London, after Alan S. Cole.

Planche 117
Dentelle à l'aiguille. Point gros de Venise. Punto tagliato a fogliami. Italie. Milieu du XVIIe siècle. Figure réduite. Collections du South Kensington Museum de Londres; d'après Alan S. Cole.

Tavola 117
Trina ad ago. Punto tagliato a fogliami. Italia. Metà del XVII. Secolo. Impiccolita. Dal South Kensington Museum, Londra, secondo Alan S. Cole.

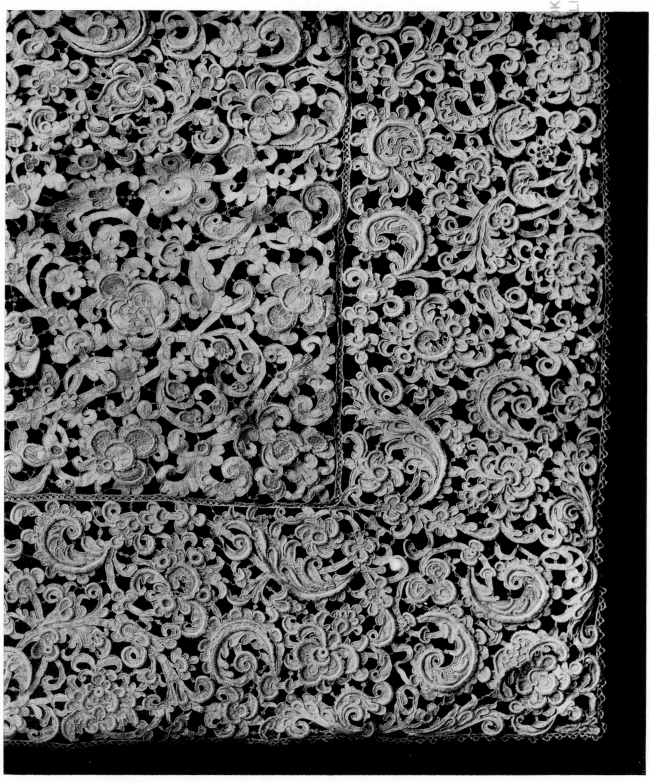

117

Tafel 118

a, b. Nadelspitzen. Punto tagliato a fogliami. Italien Mitte 17. Jahrhundert. Verkleinert. Aus dem South Kensington Museum, London, nach Alan S. Cole.

Plate 118

a, b. Needlepoint lace. Punto tagliato a fogliami. Italy. Middle of 17th Century. Reduced. From the South Kensington Museum, London, after Alan S. Cole.

Planche 118

a, b. Dentelles à l'aiguille. Point gros de Venise. Punto tagliato a fogliami. Italie. Milieu du XVIIe siècle. Figures réduites. Collections du South Kensington Museum de Londres; d'après Alan S. Cole.

Tavola 118

a, b. Trine ad ago. Punto tagliato a fogliami. Italia. Metà del XVII. Secolo. Impiccolita. Dal South Kensington Museum, Londra, secondo Alan S. Cole.

a

b

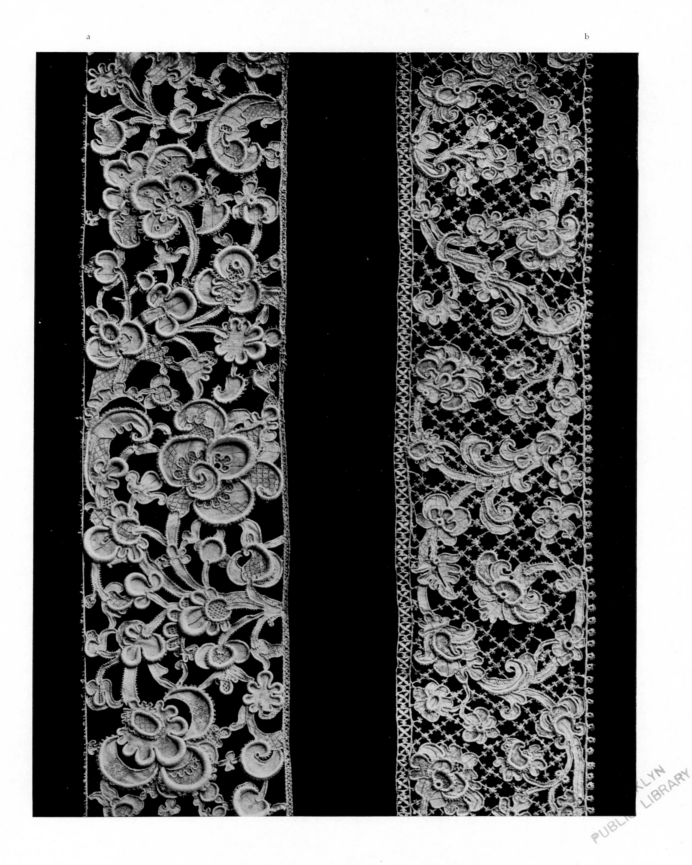

118

Tafel 119
Nadelspitze. Punto tagliato a fogliami. Italien. Mitte 17. Jahrhundert. Verkleinert. Aus Ricci, Antiche Trine Italiane.

Plate 119
Needlepoint lace. Punto tagliato a fogliami. Italy. Middle of 17th Century. Reduced. From Ricci, Antiche. Trine Italiane.

Planche 119
Dentelle à l'aiguille. Point gros de Venise. Punto tagliato a fogliami. Italie. Milieu du XVIIᶜ siècle. Figure réduite. D'après Ricci, Antiche Trine Italiane.

Tavola 119
Trina ad ago. Punto tagliato a fogliami. Italia. Metà del XVII. Secolo. Impiccolita. Riprodotta dal Ricci, Antiche Trine Italiane.

119

Tafel 120
Nadelspitze. Punto tagliato a fogliami. Italien. Mitte 17. Jahrhundert. Verkleinert. Aus der Sammlung Leopold Iklé, St. Gallen.

Plate 120
Needlepoint lace. Punto tagliato a fogliami. Italy. Middle of 17th Century. Reduced. From the Leopold Iklé Collection, St. Gall.

Planche 120
Dentelle à l'aiguille. Point gros de Venise. Punto tagliato a fogliami. Italie. Milieu du XVIIᵉ siècle. Figure réduite. Collection Léopold Iklé, de Saint-Gall.

Tavola 120
Trina ad ago. Punto tagliato a fogliami. Italia. Metà del XVII. Secolo. Impiccolita. Dalla collezione di Leopold Iklé, St. Gallen.

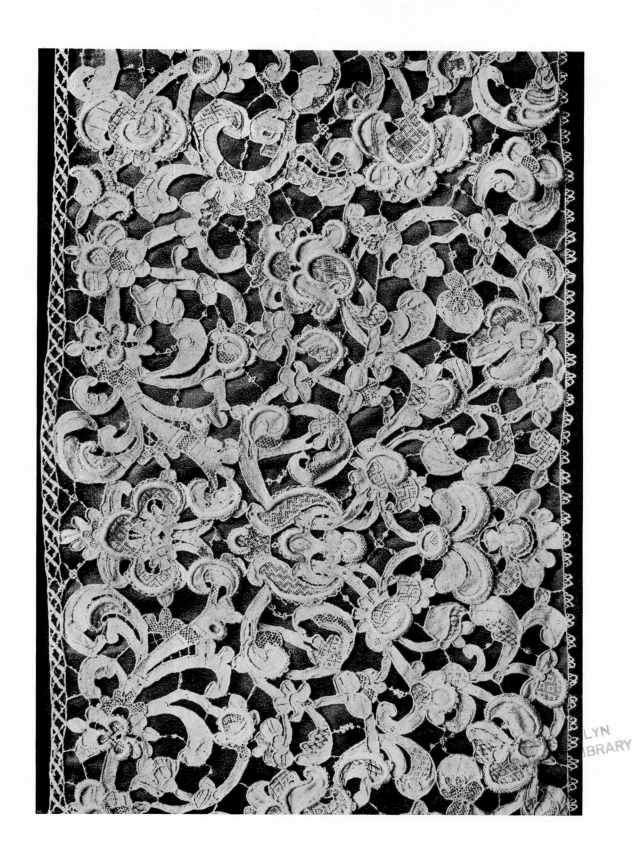

120

Tafel 121

a. Nadelspitze. Punto tagliato a fogliami. Italien. Mitte 17. Jahrhundert. — b. Nadelspitze. Roselline. Italien. Zweite Hälfte 17. Jahrhundert. — Aus der Sammlung Leopold Iklé, St. Gallen.

Plate 121

a. Needlepoint lace. Punto tagliato a fogliami. Italy. Middle of 17th Century. — b. Needlepoint lace. Rose point. Italy. Second half 17th Century. — From the Leopold Iklé Collection, St. Gall.

Planche 121

a. Dentelle à l'aiguille. — Point gros de Venise. — Punto tagliato a fogliami. Italie. Milieu du XVIIe siècle. — b. Dentelle à l'aiguille. Rosellino. Italie. Deuxième moitié du XVIIe siècle. — Collection Léopold Iklé, de Saint-Gall.

Tavola 121

a. Trina ad ago. Punto tagliato a fogliami. Italia. Metà del XVII. Secolo. — b. Trina ad ago. Roselline. Italia. Seconda metà del XVII. Secolo. — Dalla collezione di Leopold Iklé, St. Gallen.

a

b

121

Tafel 122
Nadelspitze, Punto tagliato a fogliami. Italien. Zweite Hälfte 17. Jahrhundert. Verkleinert. Aus dem Nordböhmischen Gewerbemuseum, Reichenberg.

Plate 122
Needlepoint lace. Punto tagliato a fogliami. Italy. Second half 17th Century. Reduced. From the North Bohemian Arts and Crafts Museum, Reichenberg.

Planche 122
Dentelle à l'aiguille. Point gros de Venise. Punto tagliato a fogliami. Italie. Deuxième moitié du XVIIe siècle. Figure réduite. Collections du Musée des Arts industriels du Nord de la Bohême, Reichenberg.

Tavola 122
Trina ad ago. Punto tagliato a fogliami. Seconda metà del XVII. Secolo. Impiccolita. Dal Nordböhmisches Gewerbemuseum (Museo Industriale della Boemia Settentrionale) di Reichenberg.

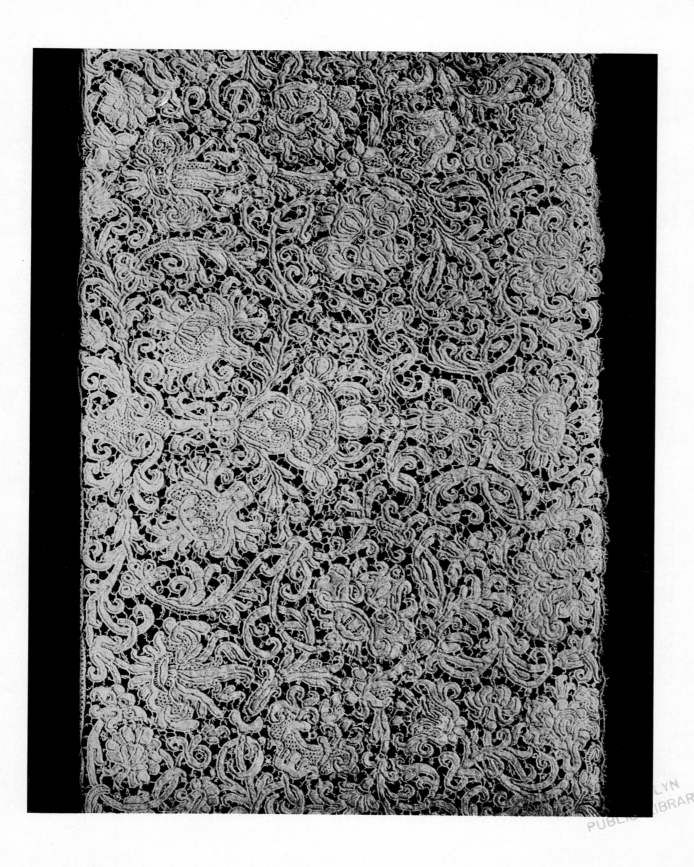

122

Tafel 123
Nadelspitze. Punto tagliato a fogliami. Italien. Zweite Hälfte 17. Jahrhundert. Natürliche Größe. Aus Ricci, Antiche Trine Italiane.

Plate 123
Needlepoint lace. Punto tagliato a fogliami. Italy. Second half 17th Century. Original size. From Ricci. Antiche Trine Italiane.

Planche 123
Dentelle à l'aiguille. Punto tagliato a fogliami. Italie. Deuxième moitié du XVIIe siècle. En grandeur naturelle. D'après Ricci, Antiche Trine Italiane.

Tavola 123
Trina ad ago. Punto tagliato a fogliami. Italia. Seconda metà del XVII. Secolo. Grandezza naturale. Riprodotta dal Ricci, Antiche Trine Italiane.

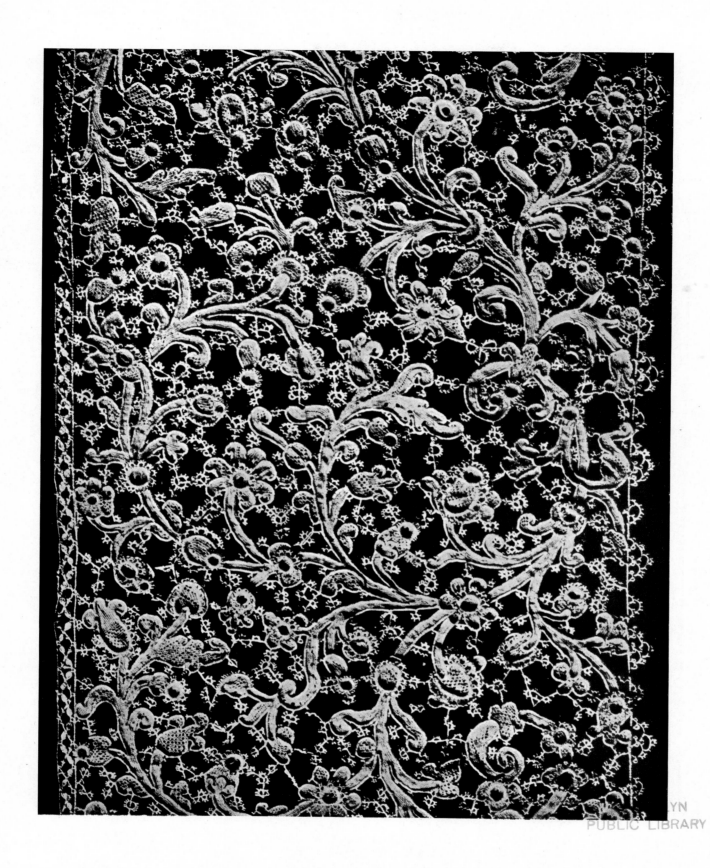

123

Tafel 124
Nadelspitze. Roselline, Italien. Zweite Hälfte 17. Jahrhundert. Verkleinert. Aus Ricci, Antiche Trine Italiane.

Plate 124
Needlepoint lace. Rose point. Italy. Second half 17th Century. Reduced. From Ricci, Antiche Trine Italiane.

Planche 124
Dentelle à l'aiguille. Rosellino. Italie. Deuxième moitié du XVIIe siècle. Figure réduite. D'après Ricci, Antiche Trine Italiane.

Tavola 124
Trina ad ago. Roselline. Italia. Seconda metà del XVII. Secolo. Impiccolita. Riprodotte dal Ricci, Antiche Trine Italiane.

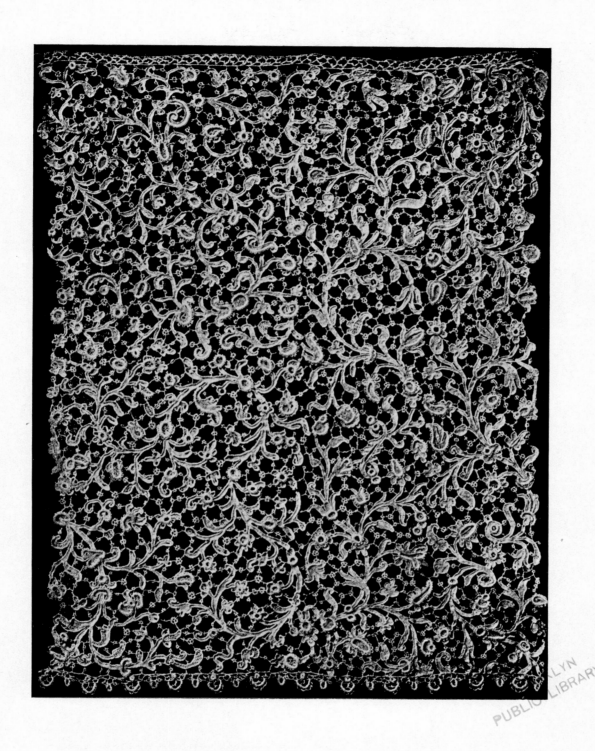

124

Tafel 125
Nadelspitze. Punto tagliato a fogliami. Italien. Zweite Hälfte 17. Jahrhundert. Verkleinert. Aus Ricci, Antiche Trine Italiane.

Plate 125
Needlepoint lace. Punto tagliato a fogliami. Italy. Second half 17th Century. Reduced. From Ricci, Antiche Trine Italiane.

Planche 125
Dentelle à l'aiguille. Punto tagliato a fogliami. Italie. Deuxième moitié du XVIIe siècle. Figure réduite. D'après Ricci, Antiche Trine Italiane.

Tavola 125
Trina ad ago. Punto tagliato a fogliami. Italia. Seconda metà del Secolo XVII. Impiccolita. Riprodotta dal Ricci, Antiche Trine Italiane.

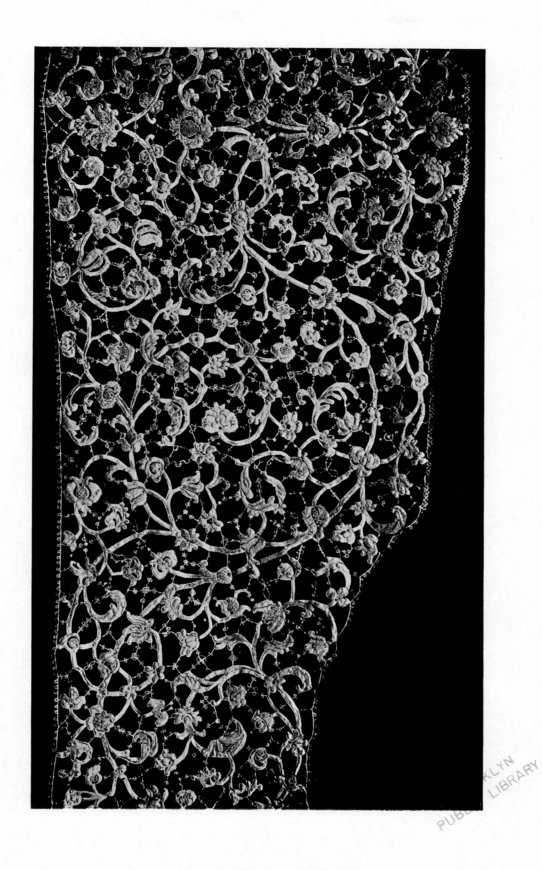

Tafel 126
a, b. Nadelspitzen. Punto di Venezia. Italien. Zweite Hälfte 17. Jahrhundert. Verkleinert. Aus Ricci,
Antiche Trine Italiane.

Plate 126
a, b. Needlepoint laces. Punto di Venezia. Italy. Second half 17th Century. Reduced. From Ricci,
Antiche Trine Italiane.

Planche 126
a, b. Dentelles à l'aiguille. Punto di Venezia. Italie. Deuxième moitié du XVIIe siècle. Figures réduites.
D'après Ricci, Antiche Trine Italiane.

Tavola 126
a, b. Trine ad ago. Punto di Venezia. Italia. Seconda metà del XVII. Secolo. Impiccolita. Riprodotte dal
Ricci, Antiche Trine Italiane.

a

b

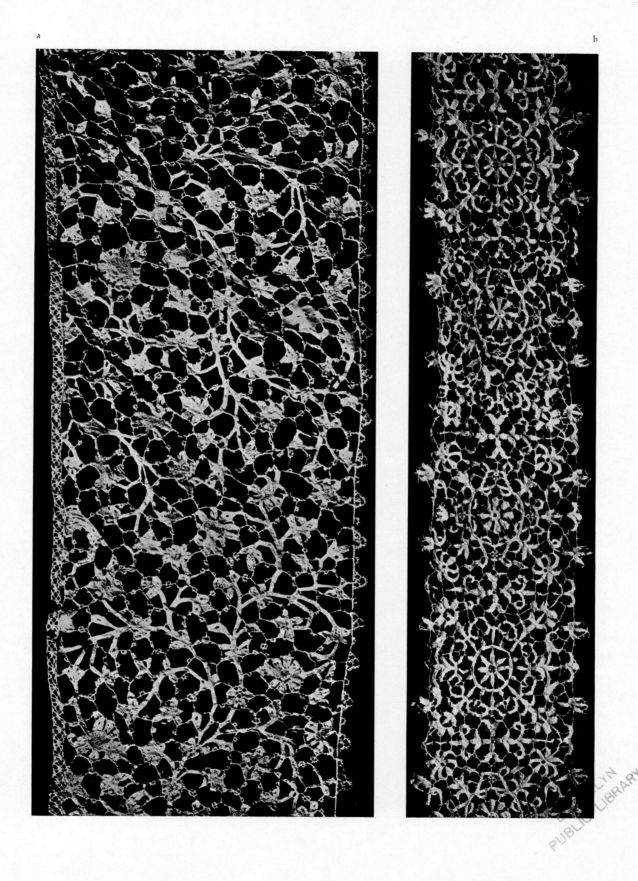

126

Tafel 127
Nadelspitze. Punto di Venezia. Italien. Zweite Hälfte 17. Jahrhundert. Verkleinert. Aus Ricci, Antiche Trine Italiane.

Plate 127
Needlepoint lace. Punto di Venezia. Italy. Second half 17th Century. Reduced. From Ricci, Antiche Trine Italiane.

Planche 127
Dentelle à l'aiguille. Punto di Venezia. Italie. Deuxième moitié du XVIIe siècle. Figure réduite. D'après Ricci, Antiche Trine Italiane.

Tavola 127
Trina ad ago. Punto di Venezia. Italia. Seconda metà del XVII. Secolo. Impiccolita. Riprodotta dal Ricci, Antiche Trine Italiane.

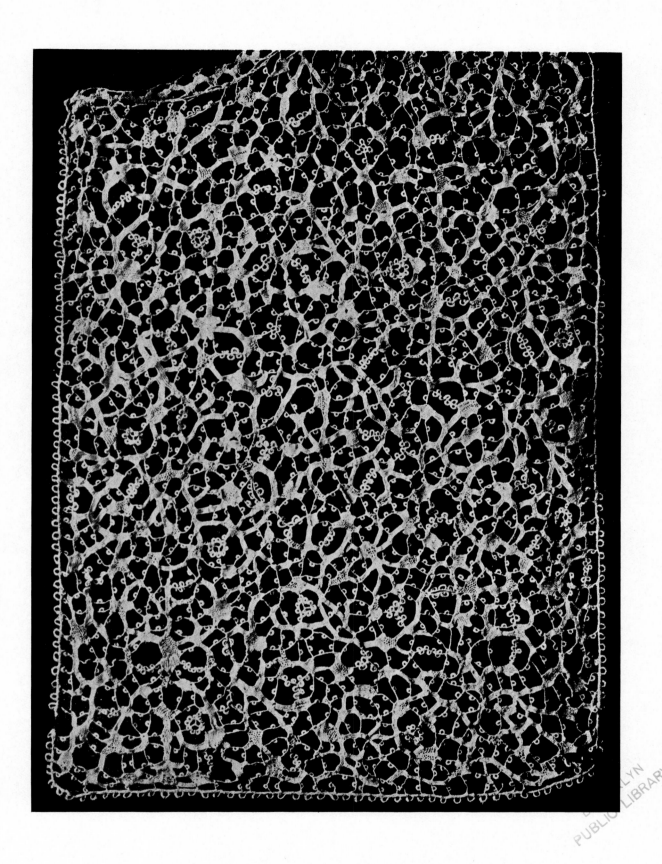

127

Tafel 128
Nadelspitze. Punto di Venezia. Italien. Zweite Hälfte 17. Jahrhundert. Natürliche Größe. Aus dem Bayerischen Nationalmuseum, München.

Plate 128
Needlepoint lace. Punto di Venezia. Italy. Second half 17th Century. Original size. From the Bavarian National Museum, Munich.

Planche 128
Dentelle à l' aiguille. Punto di Venezia. Italie. Deuxième moitié du XVIIᵉ siècle. En grandeur naturelle Collections du Musée National Bavarois de Munich.

Tavola 128
Trina ad ago. Punto di Venezia. Italia. Seconda metà del XVII. Secolo. Grandezza naturale. Dal Museo Nazionale Bavarese, Monaco.

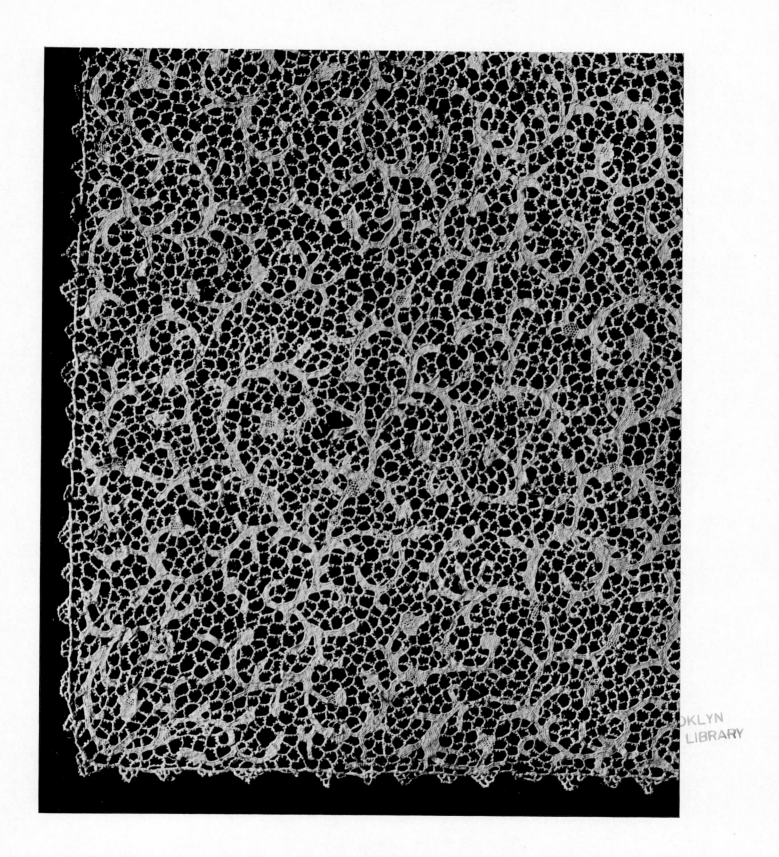

128

Tafel 129

a, b, c. Nadelspitzen. Punto di Venezia. Italien. Zweite Hälfte 17. Jahrhundert. Verkleinert. Aus Ricci, Antiche Trine Italiane.

Plate 129

a, b, c. Needlepoint lace. Punto di Venezia. Italy. Second half 17th Century. Reduced. From Ricci, Antiche Trine Italiane.

Planche 129

a, b, c. Dentelles à l'aiguille. Punto di Venezia. Italie. Deuxième moitié du XVIIe siècle. Figures réduites. D'après Ricci, Antiche Trine Italiane.

Tavola 129

a, b, c. Trine ad ago. Punto di Venezia. Italia. Seconda metà del XVII. Secolo. Impiccolita. Riprodotte dal Ricci, Antiche Trine Italiane.

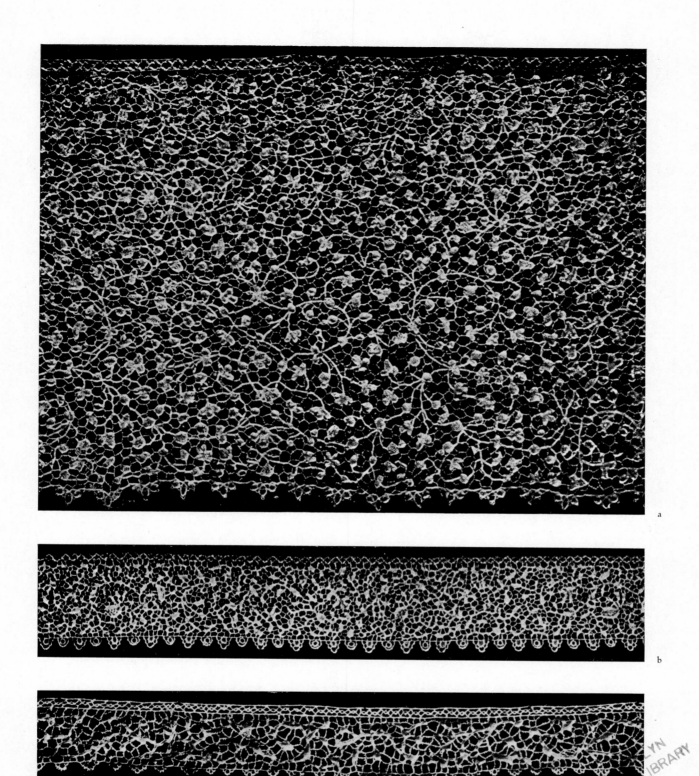

a

b

c

129

Tafel 130
a, b. Nadelspitzen. Roselline. Italien. Zweite Hälfte 17. Jahrhundert. Aus dem South Kensington Museum, London, nach Alan S. Cole.

Plate 130
a, b. Needlepoint lace. Rose point. Italy. Second half 17th Century. From the South Kensington Museum, London, after Alan S. Cole.

Planche 130
a, b. Dentelles à l'aiguille. Rosellino. Italie. Deuxième moitié du XVIIe siècle. Collections du South Kensington Museum de Londres; d'après Alan S. Cole.

Tavola 130
a. b. Trine ad ago. Roselline. Italia. Seconda metà del XVII. Secolo. Dal South Kensington Museum, Londra, secondo Alan S. Cole.

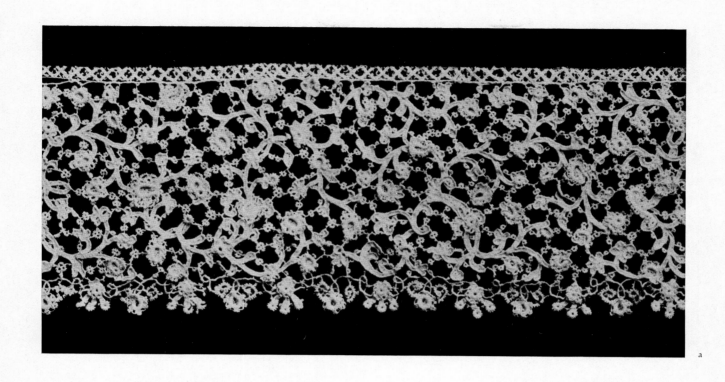

a

b

130

Tafel 131
Nadelspitze. Roselline. Italien. Zweite Hälfte 17. Jahrhundert. Verkleinert. Aus Ricci, Antiche Trine Italiane.

Plate 131
Needlepoint lace. Rose point. Italy. Second half 17th Century. Reduced. From Ricci, Antiche Trine Italiane.

Planche 131
Dentelle à l'aiguille. Rosellino. Italie. Deuxième moitiè du XVIIe siècle. Figure réduite. D'après Ricci, Antiche Trine Italiane.

Tavola 131
Trina ad ago. Roselline. Italia. Seconda metà del XVII. Secolo. Impiccolita. Riprodotta dal Ricci, Antiche Trine Italiane.

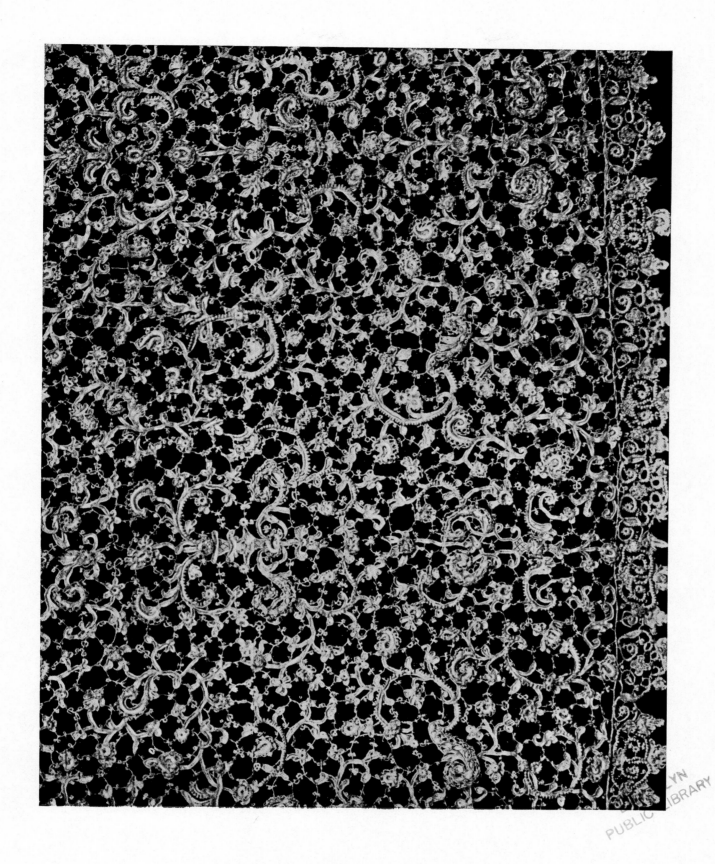

131

Tafel 132

Nadelspitze. Roselline. Italien. Zweite Hälfte 17. Jahrhundert. Aus dem South Kensington Museum, London, nach Alan S. Cole.

Plate 132

Needlepoint lace. Rose point. Italy. Second half 17th Century. From the South Kensington Museum, London, after Alan S. Cole.

Planche 132

Dentelle à l'aiguille. Rosellino. Italie. Deuxième moitié du XVIIe siècle. Collections du South Kensington Museum de Londres; d'après Alan S. Cole.

Tavola 132

Trina ad ago. Roselline. Italia. Seconda metà del XVII. Secolo. Dal South Kensington Museum, Londra, secondo Alan S. Cole.

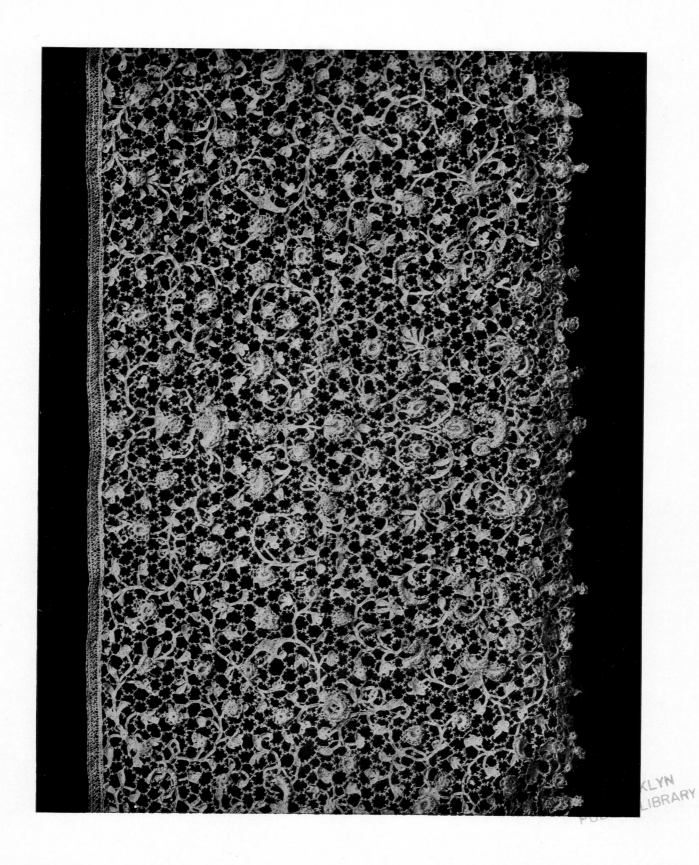

132

Tafel 133

a, b. Mailänder Klöppelspitzen. Zweite Hälfte 17. Jahrhundert. Verkleinert. Die Randzacken Nadelspitzen.
Punto in aria. Aus der Sammlung Leopold Iklé, St. Gallen.

Plate 133

a, b. Milan pillow lace. Second half 17th Century. Reduced. The scalloped border needlepoint lace.
Punto in aria. From the Leopold Iklé Collection, St. Gall.

Planche 133

a, b. Dentelles milanaises aux fuseaux. Deuxième moitié du XVIIᵉ siècle. Figures réduites. Les dents
du bord: Dentelle à l'aiguille. Punto in aria. Collection Léopold Iklé de Saint-Gall.

Tavola 133

a, b. Trine a fuselli. Milano. Seconda metà del XVII. Secolo. Impiccolita. I denti dell'orlatura sono eseguiti
a punto in aria. Dalla collezione di Leopold Iklé, St. Gallen.

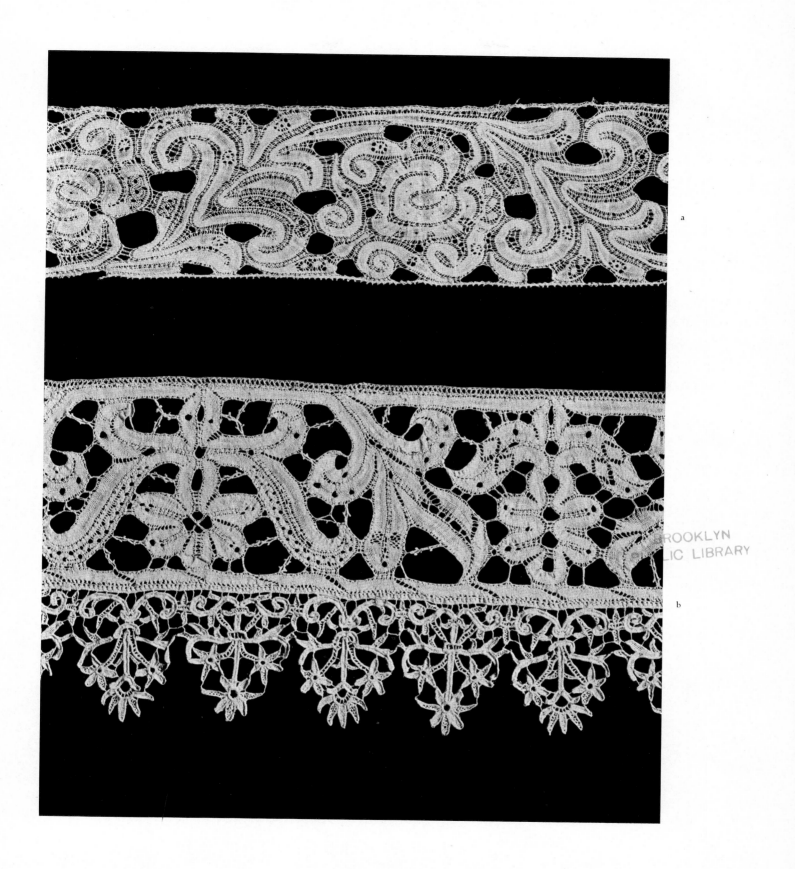

a

b

133

Tafel 134

a, b, c. Mailänder Klöppelspitzen. 17. Jahrhundert. Verkleinert. Aus Ricci, Antiche Trine Italiane.

Plate 134

a, b, c. Milan pillow lace. 17th Century. Reduced. From Ricci, Antiche Trine Italiane.

Planche 134

a, b, c. Dentelles milanaises aux fuseaux. XVIIe siècle. Figures réduites. D'après Ricci, Antiche Trine Italiane.

Tavola 134

a, b, c. Trine a fuselli. Milano. XVII. Secolo. Impiccolita. Riprodotti dal Ricci, Antiche Trine Italiane.

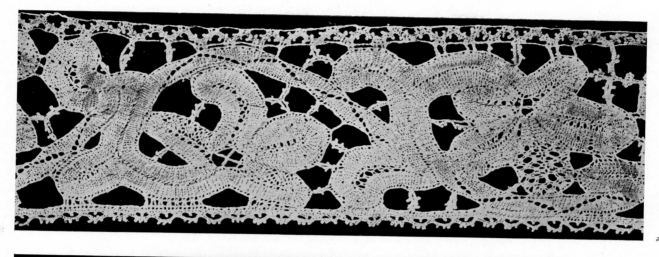

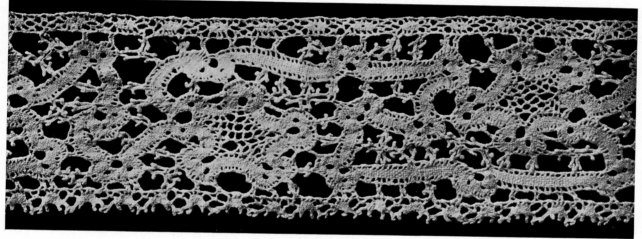

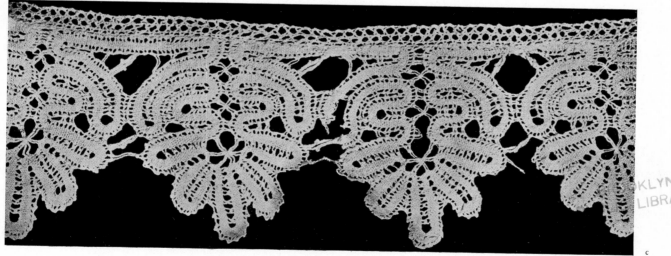

a

b

c

134

Tafel 135
a, b. Mailänder Klöppelspitzen. 17. Jahrhundert. Verkleinert. Aus Ricci, Antiche Trine Italiane.

Plate 135
a, b. Milan pillow lace. 17th Century. Reduced. From Ricci, Antiche Trine Italiane.

Planche 135
a, b. Dentelles milanaises aux fuseaux. XVIIe siècle. Figures réduites. D'après Ricci, Antiche Trine Italiane.

Tavola 135
a, b. Trine a fuselli. Milano. XVII. Secolo. Impiccolita. Riprodotti dal Ricci, Antiche Trine Italiane.

a

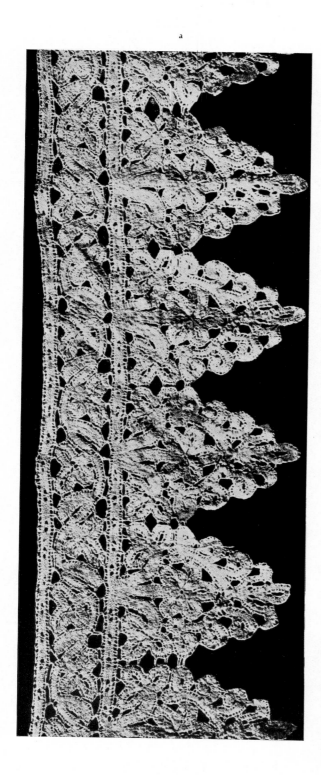

b

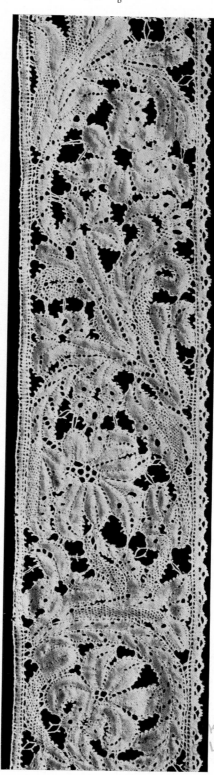

135

Tafel 136
Mailänder Klöppelspitze. 17. Jahrhundert. Verkleinert. Aus Ricci, Antiche Trine Italiane.

Plate 136
Milan pillow lace. 17th Century. Reduced. From Ricci, Antiche Trine Italiane.

Planche 136
Dentelle milanaise aux fuseaux. XVIIᵉ siècle. Figure réduite. D'après Ricci, Antiche Trine Italiane.

Tavola 136
Trina a fuselli. Milano. XVII. Secolo. Impiccolita. Riprodotta dal Ricci, Antiche Trine Italiane.

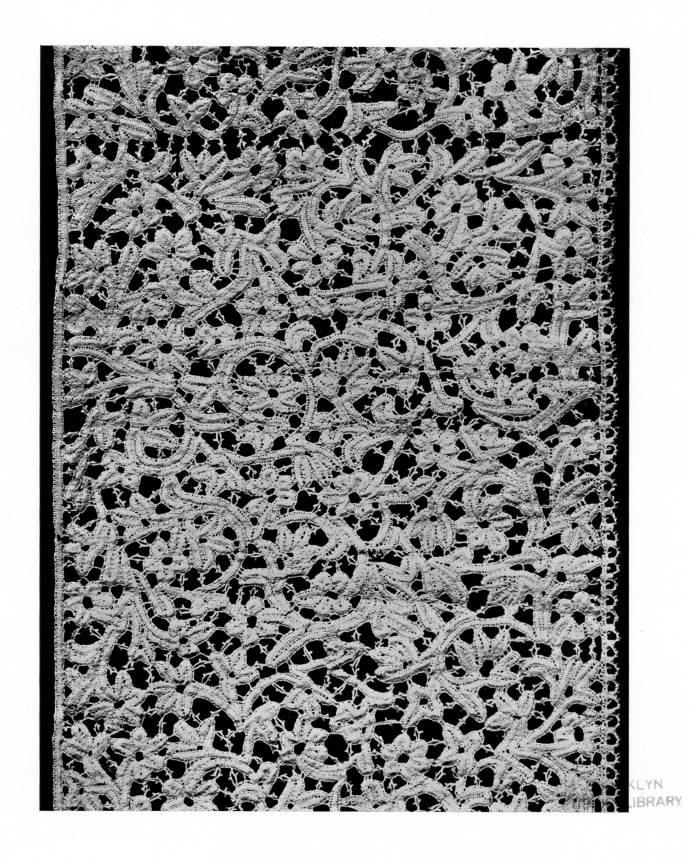

136

Tafel 137
Mailänder Klöppelspitze. 17. Jahrhundert. Verkleinert. Aus Ricci, Antiche Trine Italiane.

Plate 137
Milan pillow lace. 17th Century. Reduced. From Ricci, Antiche Trine Italiane.

Planche 137
Dentelle milanaise aux fuseaux. XVIIᵉ siècle. Figure réduite. D'après Ricci, Antiche Trine Italiane.

Tavola 137
Trina a fuselli. Milano. XVII. Secolo. Impiccolita. Riprodotta dal Ricci, Antiche Trine Italiane.

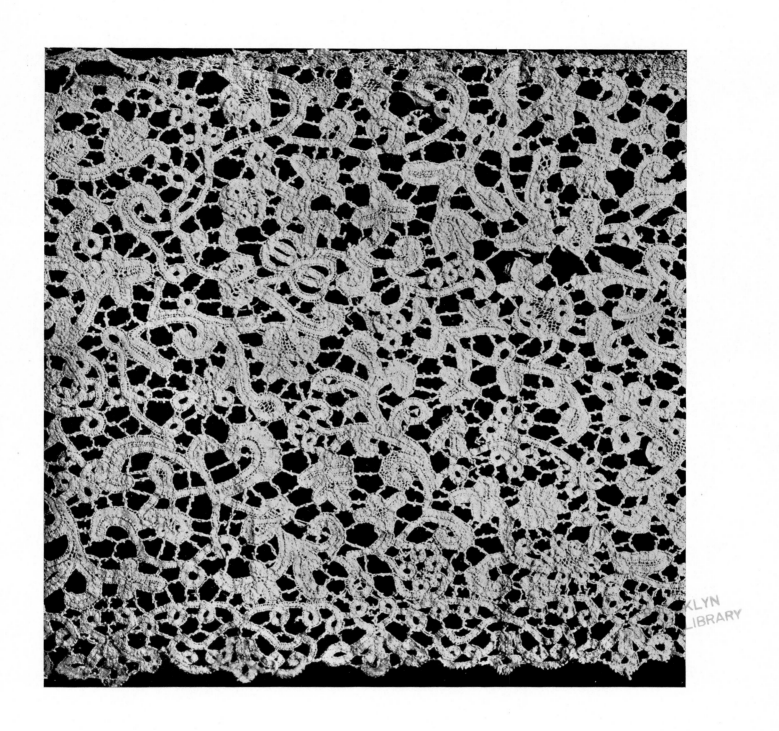

137

Tafel 138
Mailänder Klöppelspitze. Zweite Hälfte 17. Jahrhundert. Verkleinert. Aus Ricci, Antiche Trine Italiane.

Plate 138
Milan pillow lace. Second half 17th Century. Reduced. From Ricci, Antiche Trine Italiane.

Planche 138
Dentelle milanaise aux fuseaux. Deuxième moitié du XVIIe siècle. Figure réduite. D'après Ricci, Antiche Trine Italiane.

Tavola 138
Trina a fuselli. Milano. Seconda metà del XVII. Secolo. Impiccolita. Riprodotta dal Ricci, Antiche Trine Italiane.

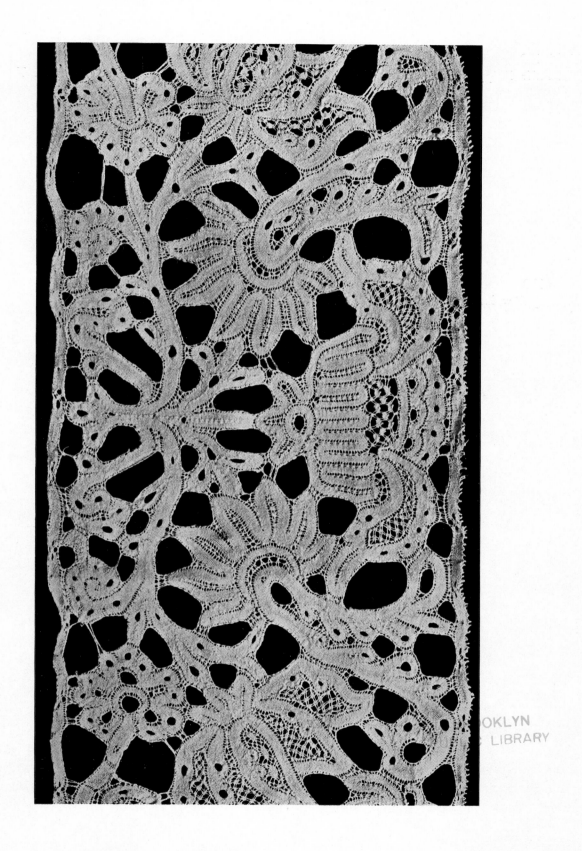

138

Tafel 139
Mailänder Klöppelspitze. Zweite Hälfte 17. Jahrhundert. Verkleinert. Aus Ricci, Antiche Trine Italiane.

Plate 139
Milan pillow lace. Second half 17th Century. Reduced. From Ricci, Antiche Trine Italiane.

Planche 139
Dentelle milanaise aux fuseaux. Deuxième moitié du XVIIe siècle. Figure réduite. D'après Ricci, Antiche Trine Italiane.

Tavola 139
Trina a fuselli. Milano. Seconda metà del XVII. Secolo. Impiccolita. Riprodotta dal Ricci, Antiche Trine Italiane.

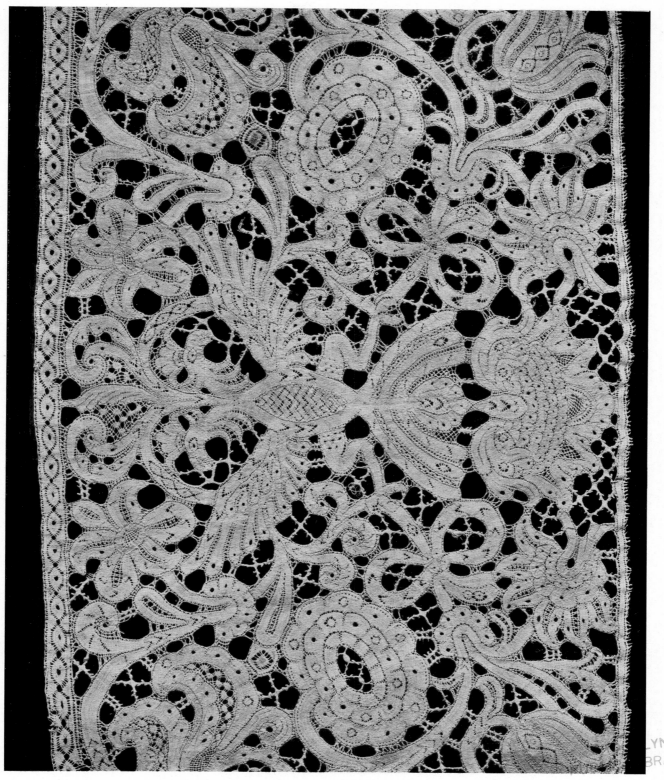

139

Tafel 140

a, b. Flandrische Klöppelspitzen. Aus einzelnen Teilen zusammengesetzt. Zweite Hälfte 17. Jahrhundert. Verkleinert. Aus dem Kgl. Museum in Brüssel, nach Overloop.

Plate 140

a, b. Flemish pillow lace. Made up of separate parts. Second half of 17th Century. Reduced. From the Royal Museum, Brussels, after Overloop.

Planche 140

a, b. Dentelles flamandes aux fuseaux faites de plusieurs parties juxtaposées. Deuxième moitié du XVIIe siècle. Figures réduites. Collections du Musée Royal de Bruxelles; d'après van Overloop.

Tavola 140

a, b. Trine a fuselli di Fiandra. Composti da singole parti. Seconda metà del XVII. Secolo. Impiccolita Dal R. Museo di Brusselles, secondo Overloop.

140

Tafel 141

a, b. Klöppelspitzen. Valenciennes. Zweite Hälfte 17. Jahrhundert. Natürliche Größe. Aus dem Bayerischen Nationalmuseum in München.

Plate 141

a, b. Bobbin lace. Valenciennes. Second half 17th Century. Original size. From the Bavarian National Museum, Munich.

Planche 141

a, b. Dentelles aux fusseaux. Valenciennes. Deuxième moitié du XVIIe siècle. En grandeur naturelle. Collections du Musée National Bavarois de Munich.

Tavola 141

a, b. Trine a fuselli. Valenciennes. Seconda metà del XVII. Secolo. Grandezza naturale. Dal Museo Nazionale Bavarese, Monaco.

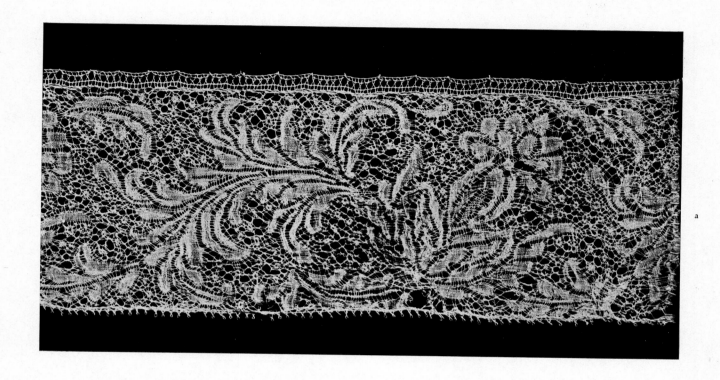

a

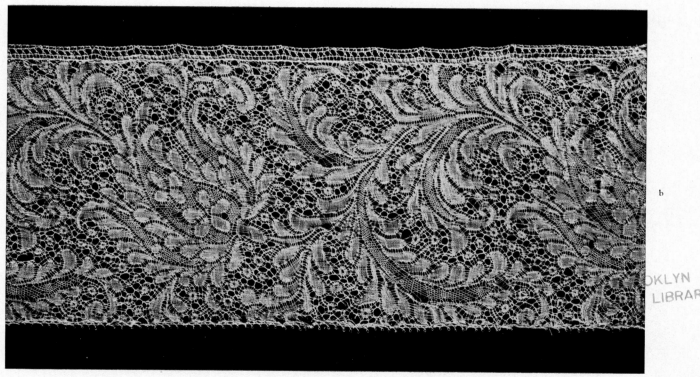

b

141

Tafel 142
Mailänder Klöppelspitze. Zweite Hälfte 17. Jahrhundert. Verkleinert. Aus Ricci, Antiche Trine Italiane.

Plate 142
Milanese bobbin lace. Second half 17th Century. Reduced. From Ricci, Antiche Trine Italiane.

Planche 142
Dentelle de Milan aux fuseaux. Deuxième moitié du XVIIe siècle. Figure réduite. D'après Ricci, Antiche Trine Italiane.

Tavola 142
Trina a fuselli. Milano. Seconda metà del XVII. Secolo. Impiccolita. Riprodotta dal Ricci, Antiche Trine Italiane.

142

Tafel 143
a, b. Mailänder Klöppelspitzen. Zweite Hälfte 17. Jahrhundert. Verkleinert. Aus Ricci, Antiche Trine Italiane.

Plate 143
a, b. Milanese bobbin lace. Second half 17th Century. Reduced. From Ricci, Antiche Trine Italiane.

Planche 143
a, b. Dentelles de Milan aux fuseaux. Deuxième moitié du XVIIᵉ siècle. Figures réduites. D'après Ricci. Antiche Trine Italiane.

Tavola 143
a, b. Trine a fuselli. Milano. Seconda metà del XVII. Secolo. Impiccolita. Riprodotti dal Ricci, Antiche Trine Italiane.

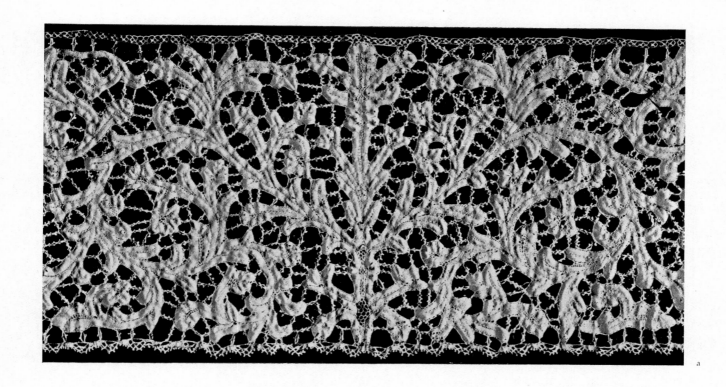

a

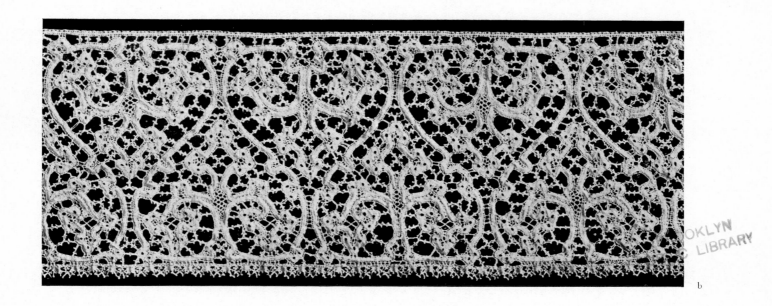

b

143

Tafel 144

Mailänder Klöppelspitze. Zweite Hälfte 17. Jahrhundert. Die mit einem Netzgrund versehenen Ranken=
streifen ahmen in ihrer Verschlingung das Bild einer vierfädigen Flechte nach. Aus Ricci, Antiche Trine
Italiane.

Plate 144

Milanese bobbin lace. Second half 17th Century. The interlacing of the sprays, which are worked on a
réseau gives the impression of a four=threaded plait. From Ricci, Antiche Trine Italiane.

Planche 144

Dentelle de Milan aux fuseaux. Deuxième moitié du XVIIᵉ siècle. Les guirlandes à fond de réseau
ressemblent dans leur entrelacement à des nattes à quatre fils. D'après Ricci, Antiche Trine Italiane.

Tavola 144

Trina a fuselli. Milano. Seconda metà del XVII. Secolo. Le striscie di tralci provviste di un fondo,
imitano nel loro intreccio la figura di una treccia a quattro fili. Riprodotta dal Ricci, Antiche Trine Italiane.

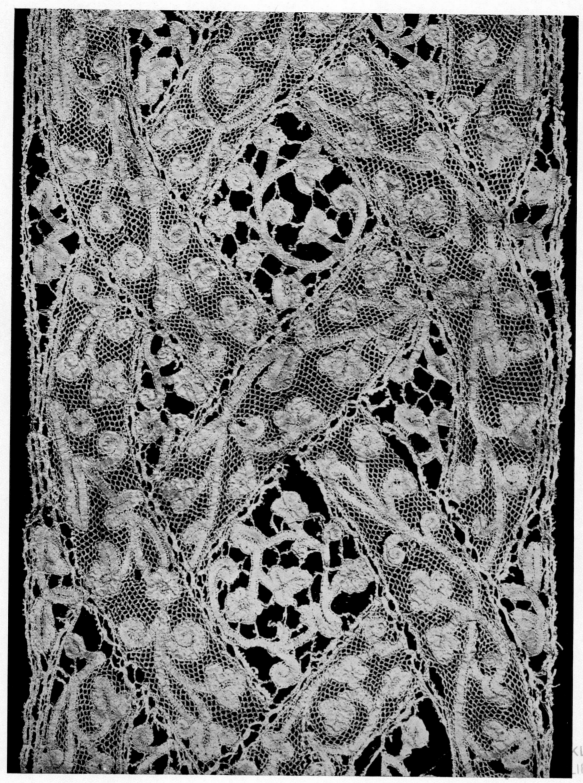

144

Tafel 145

a, b, c. Flandrische Klöppelspitzen. Ende 17. Jahrhundert. Verkleinert. Aus dem Kgl. Museum in Brüssel, nach Overloop.

Plate 145

a, b, c. Flemish pillow lace. End of 17th Century. Reduced. From the Royal Museum, Brussels, after Overloop.

Planche 145

a, b, c. Dentelles de Flandre aux fuseaux. Fin du XVIIe siècle. Figures réduites. Collections du Musée Royal de Bruxelles; d'après van Overloop.

Tavola 145

a, b, c. Trine a fuselli di Fiandra. Fine del XVII. Secolo. Impiccolita. Dal R. Museo di Brusselles, secondo Overloop.

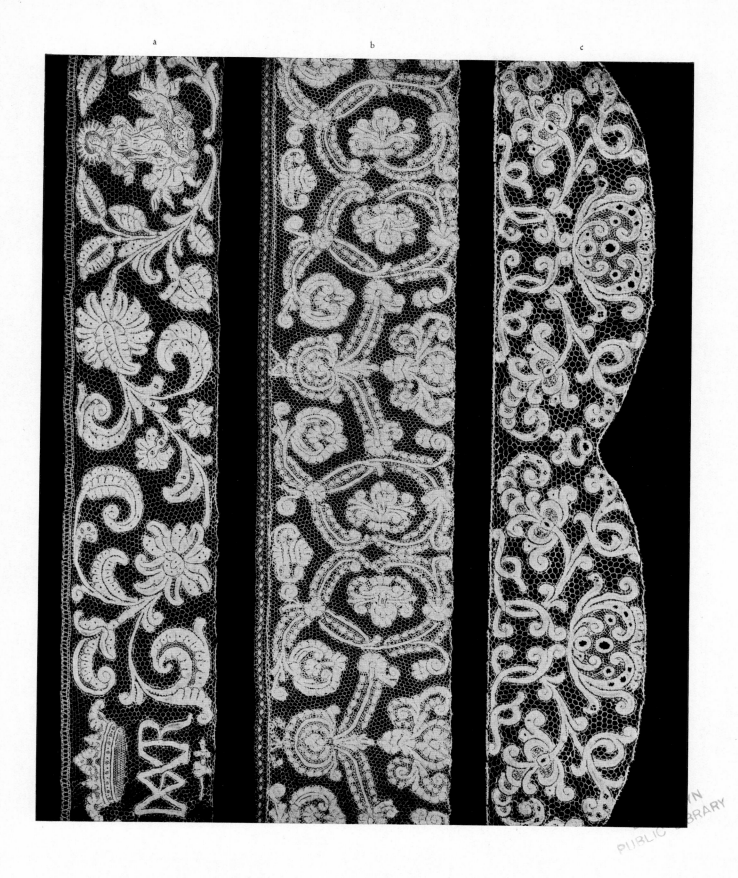

a   b   c

145

Tafel 146

Mailänder Klöppelspitze. Letztes Drittel 17. Jahrhundert. Verkleinert. Aus der Sammlung Leopold Iklé, St. Gallen.

Plate 146

Milanese bobbin lace. Last third of 17th Century. Reduced. From the Leopold Iklé Collection, St. Gall.

Planche 146

Dentelle de Milan aux fuseaux. Dernier tiers du XVIIe siècle. Figure réduite. Collection Léopold Iklé, de Saint Gall.

Tavola 146

Trina a fuselli. Milano. Ultimo terzo del XVII. Secolo. Impiccolita. Dalla collezione di Leopold Iklé, St. Gallen.

146

Tafel 147
Mailänder Klöppelspitze. Letztes Drittel 17. Jahrhundert. Verkleinert. Aus der Sammlung Leopold Iklé,
St. Gallen.

Plate 147
Milanese bobbin lace. Last third of 17th Century. Reduced. From the Leopold Iklé Collection, St. Gall.

Planche 147
Dentelle de Milan aux fuseaux. Dernier tiers du XVIIᵉ siècle. Figure réduite. Collection Léopold Iklé,
de Saint-Gall.

Tavola 147
Trina a fuselli. Milano. Ultimo terzo del XVII. Secolo. Impiccolita. Dalla collezione di Leopold Iklé,
St. Gallen.

147

Tafel 148
Mailänder Klöppelspitze. Ende 17. Jahrhundert. Verkleinert. Aus der Sammlung Leopold Iklé, St. Gallen.

Plate 148
Milanese bobbin lace. End of 17th Century. Reduced. From the Leopold Iklé Collection, St. Gall.

Planche 148
Dentelle de Milan aux fuseaux. Fin du XVIIe siècle. Figure réduite. Collection Léopold Iklé, de Saint-Gall.

Tavola 148
Trina a fuselli. Milano. Fine del XVII. Secolo. Impiccolita. Dalla collezione di Leopold Iklé, St. Gallen.

148

Tafel 149
a. Antwerpener Klöppelspitze mit dem Kurbayerischen Wappen. Ende 17. Jahrhundert. Natürliche Größe.
— b. Antwerpener Klöppelspitze. Pottenkant. Natürliche Größe. Ende 17. Jahrhundert. — Aus dem
Bayerischen Nationalmuseum in München.

Plate 149
a. Antwerp pillow lace with the coat of arms of the Electorate of Bavaria. End of 17th Century. Original
size. — b. Antwerp pillow lace, Pottenkant. Original size. End of 17th Century. — From the Bavarian
National Museum, Munich.

Planche 149
a. Dentelle anversoise aux fuseaux. Dessin: Les armoiries de l'Electorat de Bavière. Fin du XVIIe siècle.
En grandeur naturelle. — b. Dentelle anversoise aux fuseaux. Pottenkant. En grandeur naturelle. Fin du
XVIIe siècle. — Collections du Musée National Bavarois de Munich.

Tavola 149
a. Trina a fuselli di Anversa con lo stemma della Baviera Elettorale. Fine del XVII. Secolo. Grandezza
naturale. — b. Trina a fuselli Pottenkant di Anversa. Grandezza naturale. Fine del XVII. Secolo. — Dal
Museo Nazionale Bavarese di Monaco.

a

b

149

Tafel 150
Französische Nadelspitze. Points de France. Ende 17. Jahrhundert. Verkleinert. Aus der Sammlung Leopold Iklé, St. Gallen.

Plate 150
French needlepoint lace. Points de France. End of 17th Century. Reduced. From the Leopold Iklé Collection, St. Gall.

Planche 150
Dentelle française à l'aiguille. Points de France. Fin du XVIIe siècle. Figure réduite. Collection Léopold Iklé, de Saint-Gall.

Tavola 150
Trina ad ago francese. Points de France. Fine del XVII. Secolo. Impiccolita. Dalla collezione di Leopold Iklé, St. Gallen.

150

Tafel 151
Brüsseler Klöppelspitze. 1708. Verkleinert. Aus dem Kgl. Museum in Brüssel, nach Overloop.

Plate 151
Brussels pillow lace. 1708. Reduced. From the Royal Museum in Brussels, after Overloop.

Planche 151
Dentelle de Bruxelles aux fuseaux. 1708. Figure réduite. Collections du Musée Royal de Bruxelles; d'après van Overloop.

Tavola 151
Trina a fuselli di Brusselles del 1708. Impiccolita. Dal R. Museo di Brusselles, secondo Overloop.

151

Tafel 152
Brüsseler Klöppelspitze. Anfang 18. Jahrhundert. Verkleinert. Aus der Michaelskirche in München. —
Natürliche Größe s. Tafel 153.

Plate 152
Brussels pillow lace. Beginning of 18th Century. Reduced. From St. Michael's Church, Munich. — Original
size, see Plate 153.

Planche 152
Dentelle de Bruxelles aux fuseaux. Commencement du XVIIIᵉ siècle. Figure réduite. Eglise Saint-Michel,
Munich. — Grandeur naturelle: Cf. pl. 153.

Tavola 152
Trina a fuselli di Brusselles. Inizio del XVIII. Secolo. Impiccolita. Dalla chiesa di S. Michele in Monaco.
Grandezza naturale cfr. Tav. 153.

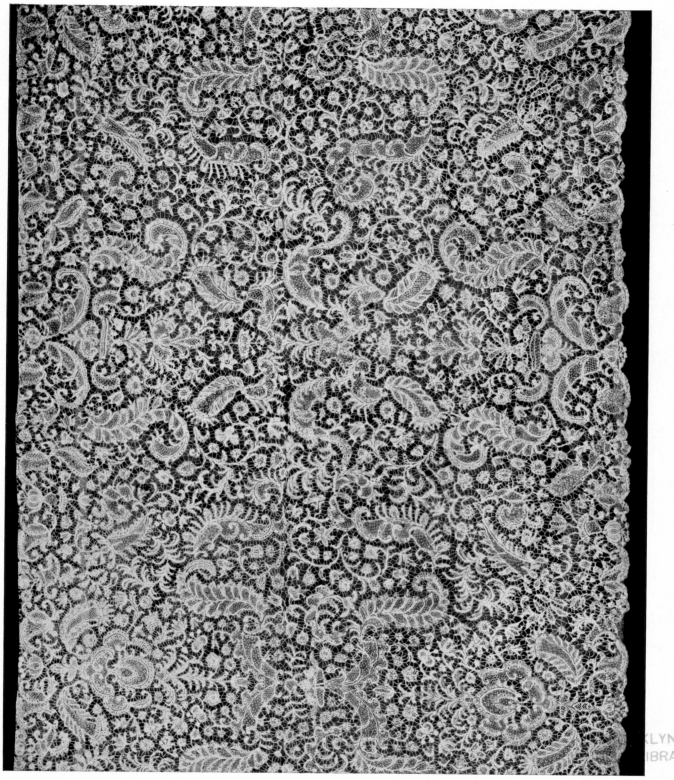

152

Tafel 153
Teilstück der Brüsseler Klöppelspitze Tafel 152 in natürlicher Größe.

Plate 153
Part of Brussels pillow lace shewn in Plate 152, original size.

Planche 153
Fragment de la dentelle de Bruxelles aux fuseaux reproduite à la planche 152, mais en grandeur naturelle.

Tavola 153
Particolare della trina a fuselli di Brusselles Tav. 152 in grandezza naturale.

153

Tafel 154

Brüsseler Klöppelspitze. Erstes Drittel 18. Jahrhundert. Verkleinert. Aus der Michaelskirche in München. — Natürliche Größe s. Tafel 155.

Plate 154

Brussels pillow lace. First third of 18th Century. Reduced. From St. Michael's Church. Munich. — Original size, see Plate 155.

Planche 154

Dentelle de Bruxelles aux fuseaux. Premier tiers du XVIIIᵉ siècle. Figure réduite. Eglise Saint-Michel, Munich. — Grandeur naturelle: Cf. pl. 155.

Tavola 154

Trina a fuselli di Brusselles. Primo terzo del XVIII. Secolo. Impiccolita. Dalla Chiesa di S. Michele in Monaco. — Grandezza naturale cfr. Tav. 155.

154

Tafel 155
Teilstück der Brüsseler Klöppelspitze Tafel 154 in natürlicher Größe.

Plate 155
Part of Brussels pillow lace shewn in Plate 154, original size.

Planche 155
Fragment de la dentelle de Bruxelles aux fuseaux reproduite à la planche 154, mais en grandeur naturelle.

Tavola 155
Particolare della trina a fuselli di Brusselles della Tav. 154 in grandezza naturale.

155

Tafel 156

Brüsseler Klöppelspitze datiert 1720. Stark verkleinert. Aus dem Kgl. Museum in Brüssel, nach Overloop.

Plate 156

Brussels pillow lace dated 1720. Greatly reduced. From the Royal Museum in Brussels, after Overloop.

Planche 156

Dentelle de Bruxelles aux fuseaux, datée de 1720. Figure très réduite. Collections du Musée Royal de Bruxelles; d'après van Overloop.

Tavola 156

Trina a fuselli di Brusselles colla data del 1720. Fortemente rimpiccolita. Dal R. Museo di Brusselles, secondo Overloop.

156

Tafel 157

Brüsseler Klöppelspitze. Erste Hälfte 18. Jahrhundert. Verkleinert. Aus der Allerheiligen=Hofkirche in München. — Natürliche Größe s. Tafel 158.

Plate 157

Brussels pillow lace. First half 18th Century. Reduced. From the Court Church of All Saints, Munich. Original size, see Plate 158.

Planche 157

Dentelle de Bruxelles aux fuseaux. Première moitié du XVIIIᵉ siècle. Figure réduite. Eglise de Tous=Les=Saints, Munich. — Grandeur naturelle: Cf. pl. 158.

Tavola 157

Trina a fuselli di Brusselles. Prima metà del XVIII. Secolo. Impiccolita. Dalla Allerheiligenhofkirche in Monaco. — Grandezza naturale cfr. la Tav. 158.

157

Tafel 158
Teilstück der Brüsseler Klöppelspitze Tafel 157 in natürlicher Größe.

Plate 158
Part of Brussels pillow lace shewn in Plate 157, original size.

Planche 158
Fragment de la dentelle de Bruxelles aux fuseaux reproduite à la planche 157, mais en grandeur naturelle.

Tavola 158
Particolare della trina a fuselli di Brusselles della Tav. 157 in grandezza naturale.

158

Tafel 159

Brabanter Klöppelspitze. Erste Hälfte 18. Jahrhundert. Verkleinert. Aus der Allerheiligen-Hofkirche in München. — Natürliche Größe s. Tafel 160.

Plate 159

Brabant pillow lace. First half 18th Century. Reduced. From the Court Church of All Saints, Munich. — Original size, see Plate 160.

Planche 159

Dentelle de Brabant aux fuseaux. Première moitié du XVIIIe siècle. Figure réduite. Eglise de Tous-Les-Saints, Munich. — Grandeur naturelle: Cf. pl. 160.

Tavola 159

Trina a fuselli del Brabante. Prima metà del XVIII. Secolo. Impiccolita. Dalla chiesa «Allerheiligen-hofkirche» in Monaco. — Grandezza naturale: cfr. la Tav. 160.

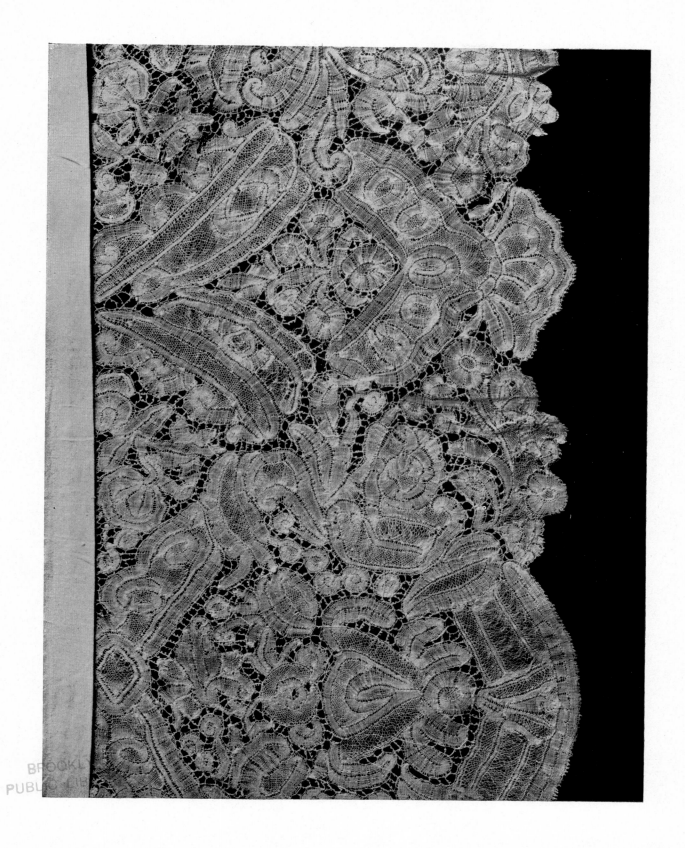

159

Tafel 160
Teilstück der Brabanter Klöppelspitze Tafel 159 in natürlicher Größe.

Plate 160
Part of Brabant pillow lace shewn in Plate 159, original size.

Planche 160
Fragment de la dentelle de brabant aux fuseaux reproduite à la planche 159, mais en grandeur naturelle

Tavola 160
Particolare della trina fuselli del Brabante della Tav. 159 in grandezza naturale.

160

Tafel 161

Brabanter Klöppelspitze. Erste Hälfte 18. Jahrhundert. Verkleinert. Aus der Allerheiligen=Hofkirche in München. — Natürliche Größe s. Tafel 162.

Plate 161

Brabant pillow lace. First half 18th Century. Reduced. From the Court Church of all Saints, Munich. — Original size, see Plate 162.

Planche 161

Dentelle de Brabant aux fuseaux. Première moitié du XVIIIᵉ siècle. Figure réduite. Eglise de Tous=Les=Saints, Munich. — Grandeur naturelle: Cf. pl. 162.

Tavola 161

Trina a fuselli del Brabante. Prima metà del XVIII. Secolo. Impiccolita. Dalla chiesa «Allerheiligen=hofkirche» in Monaco. — Grandezza naturale: cfr. la Tav. 162.

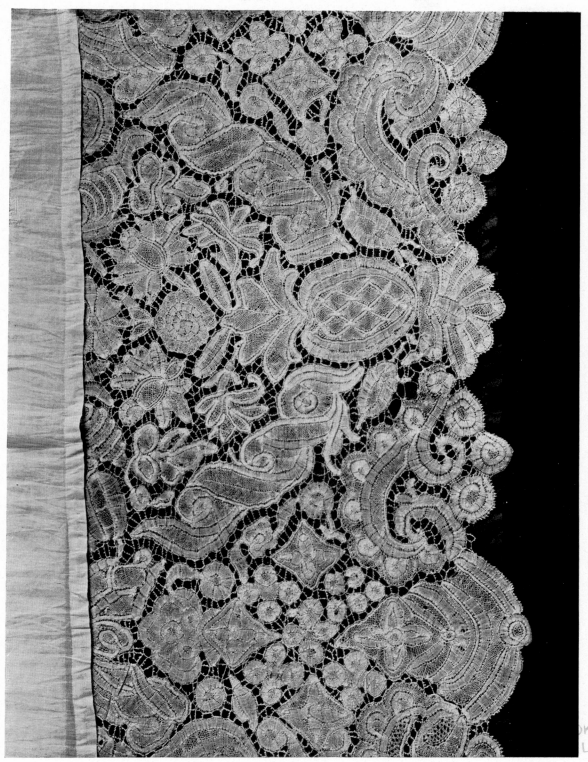

161

Tafel 162
Teilstück der Brabanter Klöppelspitze Tafel 161 in natürlicher Größe.

Plate 162
Part of Brabant pillow lace shewn in Plate 161, original size.

Planche 162
Fragment de la dentelle de Brabant aux fuseaux reproduite à la planche 161, mais en grandeur naturelle.

Tavola 162
Particolare della trina a fuselli del Brabante della Tav. 161 in grandezza naturale.

162

Tafel 163

Brabanter Klöppelspitze. Erste Hälfte 18. Jahrhundert. Stark verkleinert. Aus dem Kgl. Museum in Brüssel, nach Overloop.

Plate 163

Brabant pillow lace. First half 18th Century. Greatly reduced. From the Royal Museum, Brussels, after Overloop.

Planche 163

Dentelle de Brabant aux fuseaux. Première moitié du XVIIIe siècle. Figure très réduite. Collections du Musée Royal de Bruxelles; d'après van Overloop.

Tavola 163

Trina a fuselli del Brabante. Prima metà del XVIII. Secolo. Fortemente impiccolita. Dal R. Museo di Brusselles, secondo Overloop.

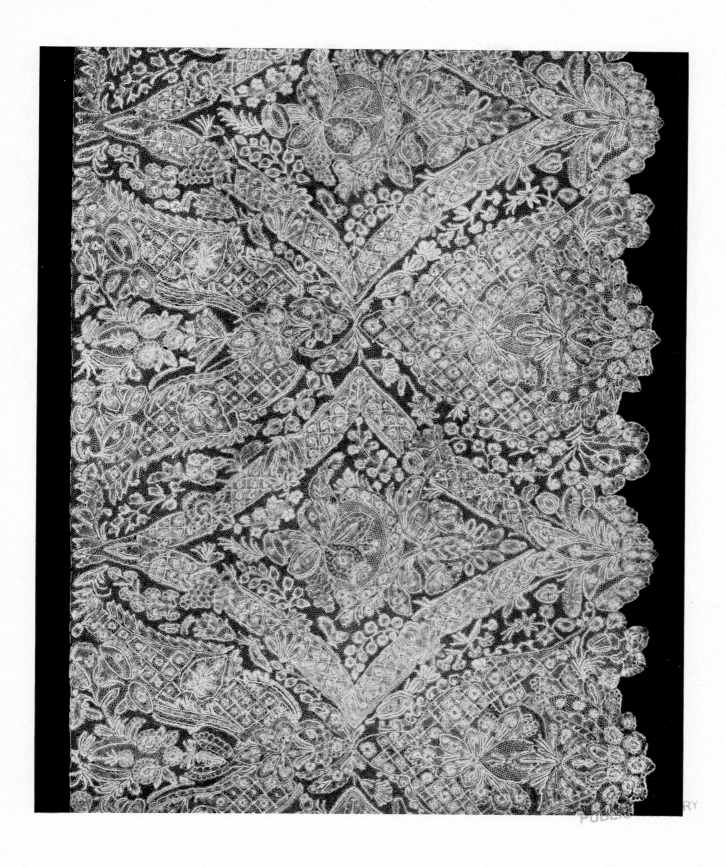

Tafel 164

Französische Nadelspitze. Erste Hälfte 18. Jahrhundert. Verkleinert. Aus der Sammlung Leopold Iklé, St. Gallen.

Plate 164

French needlepoint lace. First half 18th Century. Reduced. From the Leopold Iklé Collection, St. Gall

Planche 164

Dentelle française à l'aiguille. Première moitié du XVIIIe siècle. Figure réduite. Collection Léopold Iklé, de Saint-Gall.

Tavola 164

Trina ad ago francese. Prima metà del XVIII. Secolo. Impiccolita. Dalla collezione di Leopold Iklé, St. Gallen.

Tafel 165

Brüsseler Klöppelspitze. Erste Hälfte 18. Jahrhundert. Verkleinert. Aus dem Kgl. Museum in Brüssel, nach Overloop.

Plate 165

Brussels pillow lace. First half 18th Century. Reduced. From the Royal Museum, Brussels, after Overloop.

Planche 165

Dentelle de Bruxelles aux fuseaux. Première moitié du XVIIIe siècle. Figure réduite. Collections du Musée Royal de Bruxelles; d'après van Overloop.

Tavola 165

Trina a fuselli di Brusselles. Prima metà del XVIII. Secolo. Impiccolita. Dal R. Museo di Brusselles, secondo Overloop.

165

Tafel 166

Brüsseler Klöppelspitze. Erste Hälfte 18. Jahrhundert. Verkleinert. Aus der Allerheiligen=Hofkirche in München. — Natürliche Größe s. Tafel 167.

Plate 166

Brussels pillow lace. First half 18th Century. Reduced. From the Court Church of All Saints, Munich. — Original size, see Plate 167.

Planche 166

Dentelle de Bruxelles aux fuseaux. Première moitié du XVIIIᵉ siècle. Figure réduite. Eglise de Tous=Les=Saints, Munich. — Grandeur naturelle: Cf. pl. 167.

Tavola 166

Trina a fuselli di Brusselles. Prima metà del XVIII. Secolo. Dalla chiesa «Allerheiligenhofkirche» in Monaco. — Grandezza naturale: cfr. la Tav. 167.

166

Tafel 167
Teilstück der Brüsseler Klöppelspitze Tafel 166 in natürlicher Größe.

Plate 167
Part of Brussels pillow lace shewn in Plate 166, original size.

Planche 167
Fragment de la dentelle de Bruxelles aux fuseaux reproduite à la planche 166, mais en grandeur naturelle.

Tavola 167
Particolare della trina a fuselli di Brusselles della Tav. 166 in grandezza naturale.

Tafel 168
Brabanter Klöppelspitze. Erste Hälfte 18. Jahrhundert. Aus dem Kgl. Museum in Brüssel, nach Overloop.

Plate 168
Brabant pillow lace. First half 18th Century. From the Royal Museum, Brussels, after Overloop.

Planche 168
Dentelle de Brabant aux fuseaux. Première moitié du XVIIIe siècle. Collections du Musée Royal de Bruxelles; d'après van Overloop.

Tavola 168
Trina a fuselli del Brabante. Prima metà del XVIII. Secolo. Dal R. Museo di Brusselles, secondo Overloop.

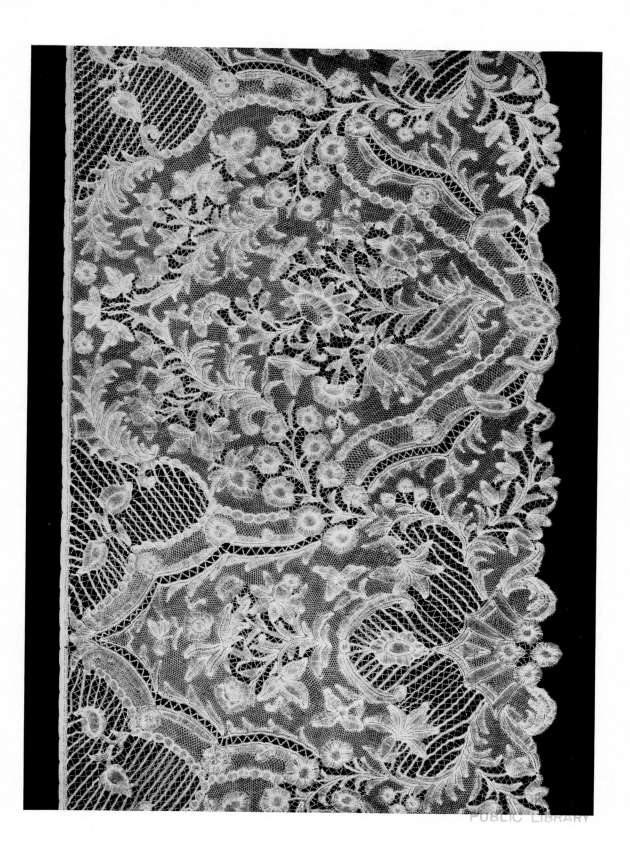

168

Tafel 169

Brüsseler Klöppelspitze. Gegen Mitte 18. Jahrhundert. Verkleinert. Aus der Allerheiligen=Hofkirche in München. — Natürliche Größe s. Tafel 170.

Plate 169

Brussels pillow lace. Towards the middle of the 18th Century. Reduced. From the Court Church of All Saints, Munich. — Original size, see Plate 170.

Planche 169

Dentelle de Bruxelles aux fuseaux. Vers le milieu du XVIIIe siècle. Figure réduite. Eglise de Tous=Les= Saints, Munich. — Grandeur naturelle: Cf. pl. 170.

Tavola 169

Trina a fuselli di Brusselles. Verso la metà del XVIII. Secolo. Impiccolita. Dalla chiesa «Allerheiligen= hofkirche» in Monaco. — Grandezza naturale: cfr. la Tav. 170.

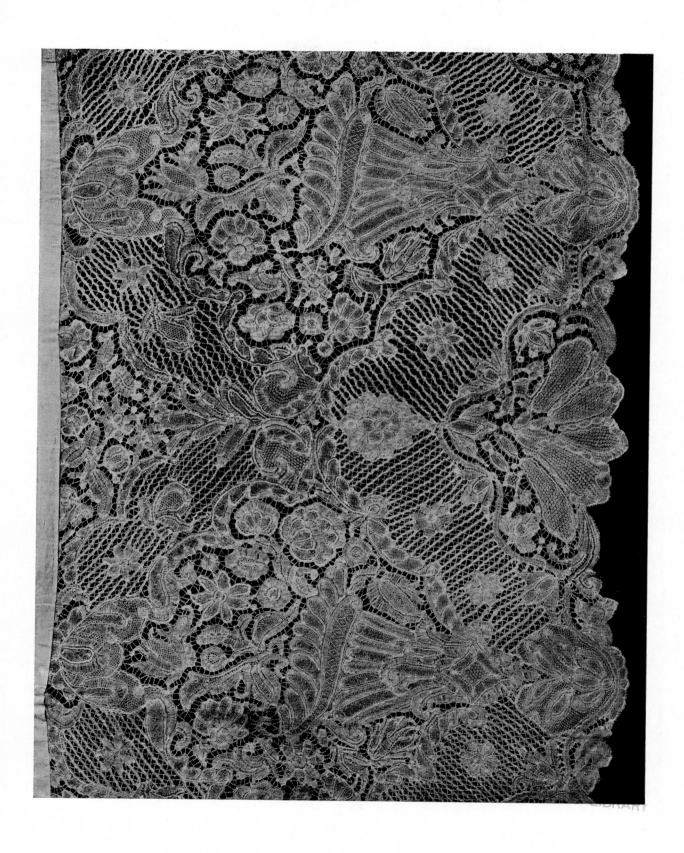

169

Tafel 170
Teilstück der Brüsseler Klöppelspitze Tafel 169 in natürlicher Größe.

Plate 170
Part of the Brussels pillow lace shewn in Plate 169, original size.

Planche 170
Fragment de la dentelle de Bruxelles aux fuseaux reproduite à la planche 169, mais en grandeur naturelle.

Tavola 170
Particolare della trina a fuselli di Brusselles della Tav. 169 in grandezza naturale.

170

Tafel 171

Brüsseler Klöppelspitze. Mitte 18. Jahrhundert. Verkleinert. Aus der Allerheiligen=Hofkirche in München. — Natürliche Größe s. Tafel 172.

Plate 171

Brussels pillow lace. Middle of 18th Century. Reduced. From the Court Church of All Saints, Munich. — Original size, see Plate 172.

Planche 171

Dentelle de Bruxelles aux fuseaux. Milieu du XVIIIᵉ siècle. Figure réduite. Eglise de Tous=Les=Saints, Munich. — Grandeur naturelle: Cf. pl. 172.

Tavola 171

Trina a fuselli di Brusselles. Metà del XVIII. Secolo. Impiccolita. Dalla «Allerheiligenhofkirche» in Mo=naco. — Grandezza naturale: cfr. la Tav. 172.

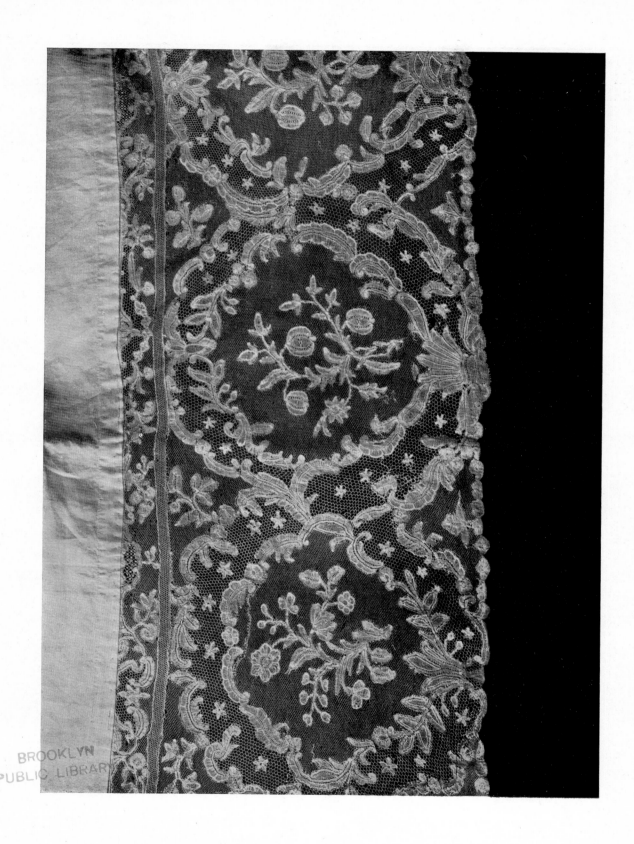

Tafel 172
Teilstück der Brüsseler Klöppelspitze Tafel 171 in natürlicher Größe.

Plate 172
Part of Brussels pillow lace shewn in Plate 171, original size.

Planche 172
Fragment de la dentelle de Bruxelles aux fuseaux reproduite à la planche 171, mais en grandeur naturelle.

Tavola 172
Particolare della trina a fuselli di Brusselles della Tav. 171 in grandezza naturale.

172

Tafel 173
Brabanter Klöppelspitze. Mitte 18. Jahrhundert. Verkleinert. Aus dem Kgl. Museum in Brüssel, nach Overloop.

Plate 173
Brabant pillow lace. Middle of 18th Century. Reduced. From the Royal Museum, Brussels, after Overloop.

Planche 173
Dentelle de Brabant aux fuseaux. Milieu du XVIIIᵉ siècle. Figure réduite. Collections du Musée Royal de Bruxelles; d'après van Overloop.

Tavola 173
Trina a fuselli del Brabante. Metà del XVIII. Secolo. Impiccolita. Dal R. Museo di Brusselles, secondo Overloop.

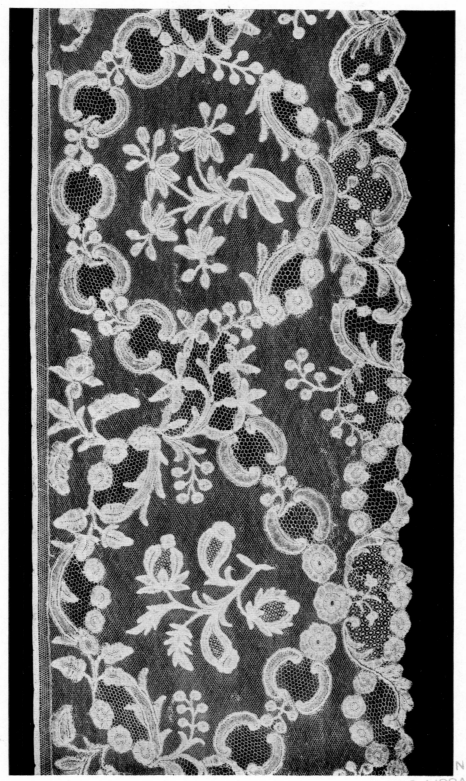

173

Tafel 174

a, b, c. Mechelner Spitzen. Mitte 18. Jahrhundert. Verkleinert. Die Spitzen b und c datiert 1751. Aus dem Kgl. Museum in Brüssel, nach Overloop.

Plate 174

a, b, c. Mechlin lace. Middle of 18th Century. Reduced. Laces b and c dated 1751. From the Royal Museum, Brussels, after Overloop.

Planche 174

a, b, c. Dentelles de Malines. Milieu du XVIIIᵉ siècle. Figures réduites. Les dentelles b et c sont datées de 1751. Collections du Musée royal de Bruxelles; d'après van Overloop.

Tavola 174

a, b, c. Trine di Malines. Metà del XVIII. Secolo. Impiccolita. I trine b. e c. portano la data del 1751. Dal R. Museo di Brusselles, secondo Overloop.

a   b   c

174

Tafel 175

a, b. Brüsseler Klöppelspitzen von 1751 und 1757. Verkleinert. Aus dem Kgl. Museum in Brüssel, nach Overloop.

Plate 175

a, b. Brussels pillow lace of 1751 and 1757. Reduced. From the Royal Museum, Brussels, after Overloop.

Planche 175

a, b. Dentelles de Bruxelles aux fuseaux datées de 1751 et de 1757. Figures réduites. Collections du Musée Royal de Bruxelles; d'après van Overloop.

Tavola 175

a, b. Trine a fuselli di Brusselles del 1751 e del 1757. Impiccolita. Dal R. Museo di Brusselles, secondo Overloop.

175

Tafel 176

a. Mechelner Spitze. Mitte 18. Jahrhundert. Verkleinert. — b. Valenciennesspitze. Zweite Hälfte 18. Jahrhundert. Verkleinert. — Aus der Sammlung Leopold Iklé, St. Gallen.

Plate 176

a. Mechlin lace. Middle of 18th Century. Reduced. — b. Valenciennes lace. Second half 18th Century. Reduced. — From the Leopold Iklé Collection, St. Gall.

Planche 176

a. Dentelle de Malines. Milieu du XVIIIe siècle. Figure réduite. — b. Dentelle de Valenciennes. Deuxième moitié du XVIIIe siècle. Figure réduite. — Collection Léopold Iklé, de Saint-Gall.

Tavola 176

a. Trina di Malines. Metà del XVIII. Secolo. Impiccolita. b. Trina di Valenciennes. Seconda metà del XVIII. Secolo. Impiccolita. Dalla collezione di Leopold Iklé, St. Gallen.

a   b

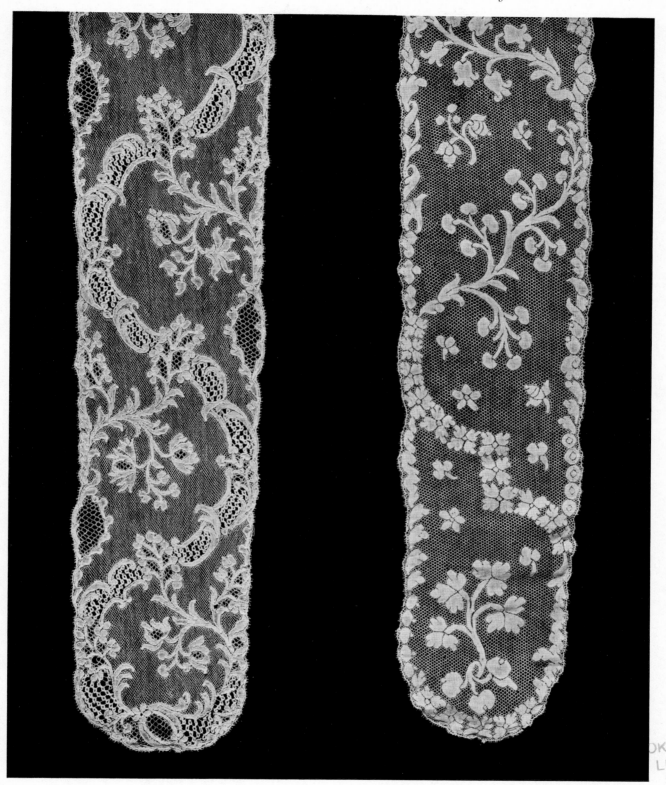

176

Tafel 177

Brüsseler Klöppelspitze datiert 1759. Stark verkleinert. Aus dem Kgl. Museum in Brüssel, nach Overloop.

Plate 177

Brussels pillow lace dated 1759. Greatly reduced. From the Royal Museum, Brussels, after Overloop.

Planche 177

Dentelle de Bruxelles aux fuseaux datée de 1759. Figure très réduite. Collections du Musée Royal de Bruxelles; d'après van Overloop.

Tavola 177

Trina a fuselli di Brusselles portante la data del 1759. Fortemente impiccolita. Dal R. Museo di Brusselles, secondo Overloop.

177

Tafel 178

a, b, c. Valenciennesspitzen. Letztes Drittel 18. Jahrhundert. Verkleinert. Aus der Sammlung Alfred Lescure, nach Overloop.

Plate 178

a, b, c. Valenciennes lace. Last third of 18th Century. Reduced. From the Alfred Lescure Collection, after Overloop.

Planche 178

a, b, c. Dentelles de Valenciennes. Dernier tiers du XVIIIe siècle. Figures réduites. Collection Alfred Lescure; d'après van Overloop.

Tavola 178

a, b, c. Trine di Valenciennes. Ultimo terzo del XVIII. Secolo. Impiccolita. Dalla collezione di Alfred Lescure, secondo Overloop.

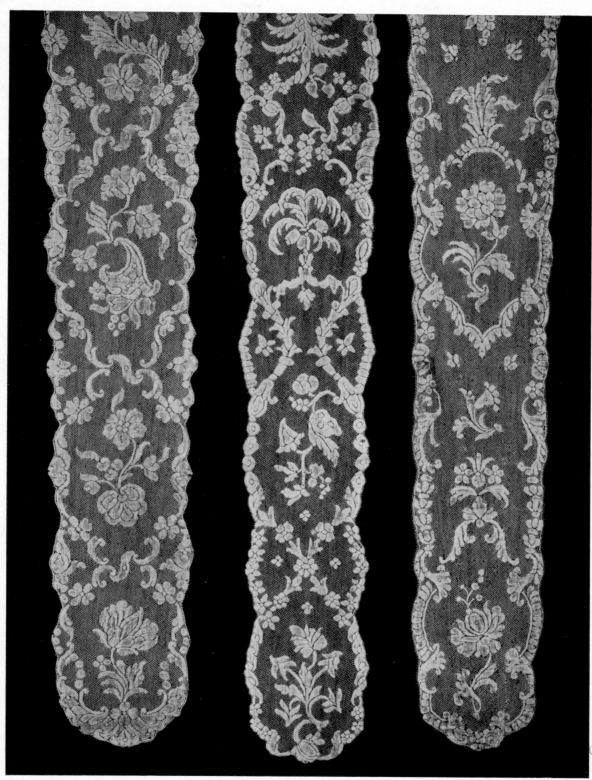

Tafel 179
Brüsseler Klöppelspitze. Letztes Drittel 18. Jahrhundert. Verkleinert. Aus dem Kgl. Museum in Brüssel, nach Overloop.

Plate 179
Brussels pillow lace. Last third of 18th Century. Reduced. From the Royal Museum, Brussels, after Overloop.

Planche 179
Dentelle de Bruxelles aux fuseaux. Dernier tiers du XVIIIe siècle. Figure réduite. Collection du Musée royal de Bruxelles; d'après van Overloop.

Tavola 179
Trina a fuselli di Brusselles. Ultimo terzo del XVIII. Secolo. Impiccolita. Dal R. Museo di Brusselles, secondo Overloop.

179

Tafel 180
Brüsseler Klöppelspitze. Letztes Drittel 18. Jahrhundert. Verkleinert. Aus dem South Kensington Museum in London, nach Alan S. Cole.

Plate 180
Brussels pillow lace. Last third of 18th Century. Reduced. From the South Kensington Museum, London, after Alan S. Cole.

Planche 180
Dentelle de Bruxelles aux fuseaux. Dernier tiers du XVIIIe siècle. Figure réduite. Collections du South Kensington Museum de Londres; d'après Alan S. Cole.

Tavola 180
Trina a fuselli di Brusselles. Ultimo terzo del XVIII. Secolo. Impiccolita. Dal South Kensington Museum di Londra, secondo Alan S. Cole.

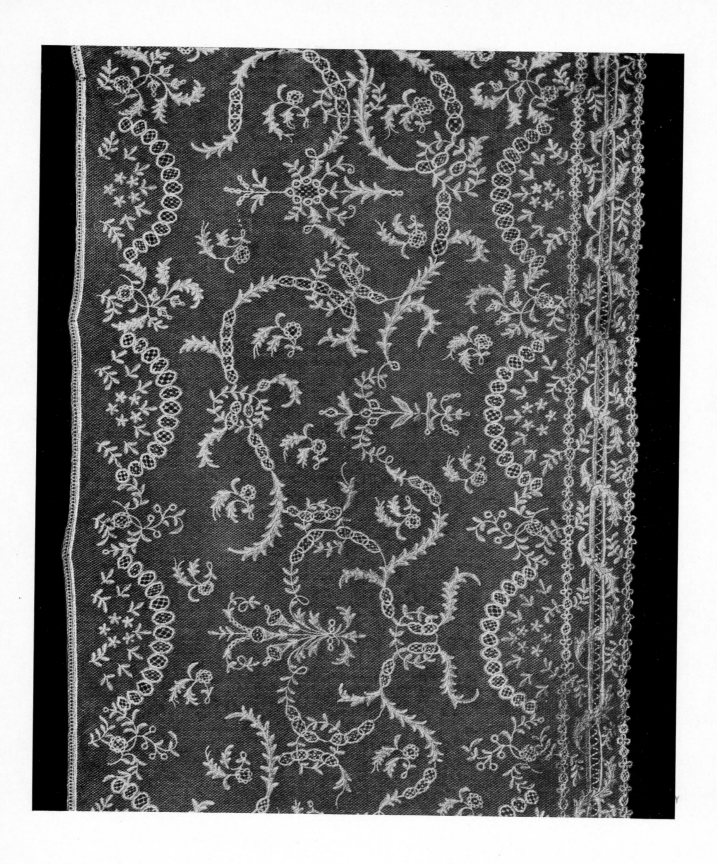

Tafel 181

Brüsseler Klöppelspitze. Anfang 19. Jahrhundert. Verkleinert. Originalgröße 92×145 cm. Aus der Samm‑
lung Alfred Lescure, nach Overloop.

Plate 181

Brussels pillow lace. Beginning of 19th Century. Reduced. Original size 92 × 145 cm. From the Alfred
Lescure Collection, after Overloop.

Planche 181

Dentelle de Bruxelles aux fuseaux. Commencement du XIXe siècle. Figure réduite. Dimensions de l'ori‑
ginal: 92×145 c/m. Collection Alfred Lescure; d'après van Overloop.

Tavola 181

Trina a fuselli di Brusselles. Inizio del XIX. Secolo. Impiccolita. Grandezza originale cm 92×145. Dalla
collezione di Alfred Lescure, secondo Overloop.

181

M